Adventurers
Against
Their Will

What people are saying about

Adventurers
Against
Their Will

and author Joanie Schirm...

"*Adventurers Against Their Will* is a brilliant and compelling account of men and women caught in the turbulence of war. Part insightful history and part family drama, the book leads readers on a journey into the past, answering many questions and posing new ones along the way. Joanie Schirm has made a fresh and vital contribution to our understanding of World War II's impact on the lives of people in Central Europe."

–MADELEINE ALBRIGHT, FORMER U.S. SECRETARY OF STATE

"I could say that this reads like a novel but I've read a lot of novels set during the Holocaust and most of them, no matter how carefully researched, fall flat; you can always tell precisely where the research stops and the plot begins. What makes *Adventurers* so compelling is that none of its characters are aware of the roles they're playing. It's heartbreaking to realize how forward-looking and hopeful they'd been—how excited to be a part of Masaryk's doomed democracy. Their warts-and-all humanity brings home the horror of what was lost so much more powerfully than the pathos of cheap storytelling ever could."

–ARTHUR GOLDWAG, AUTHOR OF *THE NEW HATE*

"In the dynamic world of publishing today, the value of a good story told by a passionate, well-suited author is more important than ever. I believe *Adventurers* has all the elements for success—adventure, mystery, tragedy, love, discovery and truth."

–ANN SONNTAG, FORMER PUBLISHER, *ORLANDO BUSINESS JOURNAL*, A PUBLICATION OF AMERICAN CITY BUSINESS JOURNALS, THE LARGEST PUBLISHER OF BUSINESS JOURNALS IN THE US

"I first came in contact with Joanie Schirm in 1991 when we worked together to bring the World Cup games to Orlando. It was no small feat. Quickly I knew she reflected perfectly what Walt Disney called the Four C's: curiosity, confidence, courage, and constancy. I had no idea she would later use all these "C's" so productively again to deliver the story of a lifetime— her father's—in the book *My Dear Boy: The Discovery of a Lifetime*, along with the companion book to *Adventurers Against Their Will*. I predict it will someday make a fine movie. As a 1992 recipient of the prestigious Walt Disney World Dreamers and Doers Award, I know this strawberry-blonde force of nature will turn the book into a bestseller."

–RICHARD NUNIS, FORMER CHAIRMAN, WALT DISNEY WORLD PARKS AND RESORTS

"Some writers have a great story but don't know how to tell it. Other writers tell it well but don't really have a great story. In *Adventurers Against Their Will*, Joanie Schirm not only has a great story but knows how to tell it."

–JAMES COFFIN, EXECUTIVE DIRECTOR, INTERFAITH COUNCIL OF CENTRAL FLORIDA

"Adventurers Against Their Will is a powerful wartime story revolving around true historical events. Based on scrupulous research, Joanie Schirm has dug deep into her own family history and beyond to recreate the lost world of Jewish culture in interwar Czechoslovakia and the horrors that followed during the Nazi occupation of Bohemia and Moravia. An emotionally powerful book for anyone interested in the vanished universe of early twentieth-century Central Europe and the war that destroyed it."

–ROBERT GERWARTH, AUTHOR OF
HITLER'S HANGMAN: THE LIFE AND DEATH OF HEYDRICH

"Adventurers Against Their Will is like reading a Ken Follett novel, except it's not fiction and every character has a personality and story that seems larger than life. The entire book is an emotional rollercoaster packed with despair, euphoria, triumphs and challenges."

–MIKE COONEY, CHIEF EXPLORER, COONEY WORLD ADVENTURES

Amazon review samples:

"...You'll get wrapped up in the stories. Joanie Schirm does a wonderful job of weaving her own life story in with that of her parents and their friends during the rise of the Nazis. You begin to think you know the characters and the writing transports you to the far-off places in which the scenes are set: a smoky cafe in Europe or a mission in China."

"...Joanie's writing style is stellar, the historical context woven throughout is fascinating, and the emotional wallop the stories pack is undeniable. A truly compelling read from a talented writer."

"...*Adventurers Against Their Will* is an amazing story about survival, loss, hope and the importance of carrying on the message of generations as they pass. It made me want to run to my parents and grandparents and capture their own life stories before it's too late."

"...These letters highlight their feelings not only about their personal situations and relationships, but also about the broader political events around them. I had trouble putting it down."

"...The question raised, ultimately by the letters, is, at what point, do any of us decide to risk all when leaders on our own soil choose to betray all that we believe in and stand for?"

"...The letters take you on a journey you will not forget. These letters may have the power to help change the world. Read it!"

Adventurers Against Their Will

Extraordinary World War II Stories of Survival, Escape, and Connection—Unlike Any Others

Joanie Holzer Schirm

Library of Congress Control Number: 2013930362

ISBN 978-0-9886781-2-5

Manufactured in the United States of America.

First Edition, March 2013; Revised January 2014

Jacket design and interior design by Kim Leonard, Bookcovers.com

Map credits: *"Partition of Czechoslovakia 1938-1939"* and *"Theresienstadt Ghetto in German Protectorate of Bohemia and Moravia (1941-45)"* from the United States Holocaust Memorial Museum; all photographs provided by *Adventurer* family members and Holzer Collection

Quote credit: Page 302 - Stephen Grellet, Quaker Missionary

ATTENTION SCHOOLS AND BUSINESSES: For special bulk purchase with discount for educational, business, or sales promotional use, contact joanie@joanieschirm.com

Dedication

For my beloved father who preserved the letters, for the correspondents who communicated their lives, for their descendants who shared their family stories and secrets so the significance could be understood, and with enduring appreciation for displaced people around the world who have the fortitude to keep going despite the obstacles.

Author's Note

*A*dventurers *Against Their Will* is a nonfiction book based primarily upon stories told to me by my late father, Oswald A. Holzer, MD, and information gathered from a large collection of WWII-era letters and documents. Much of the material cannot be independently confirmed or corroborated and I make no representation as to its veracity. With the assistance of experts, I have worked diligently to ensure historical facts are presented well. If someone wishes to correct misinformation, add additional detail, or share related stories, I welcome your contact at joanie@joanieschirm.com.

The people included in my story are mostly my father's Czech friends and relatives. For clarification, at the beginning of pertinent chapters I've included a chart listing the "Dramatis Personae." Sometimes used in a theatrical play, the phrase signifies the people who figure prominently in the performance—in this case, a true life drama.

A Timeline and Glossary appear at the end of the book. I encourage you to refer to them as they mix historical background with Adventurers' personal milestones. They help enforce that this is a story written by life itself, as the pages of history turned around the Adventurers.

When my father was in China during 1939, 1940, and 1941, the Wade-Giles system of transliteration was in use; thus his letters are filled with Chinese place names not seen today. The modern pinyin system expresses words closer to the native pronunciation of standard Chinese, for example "Beijing" rather than "Peking." In an attempt to stay true to my father's voice in both his taped interviews and his letters, I have stayed with the Wade-Giles system. For reader clarification, at the first use of the word I place the more modern pinyin version in parentheses.

An appraisal by Allan Stypeck, Jr., president of Second Story Books, Washington, DC, of the Holzer Collection of documents, letters, 8-mm film, clothing, personal artwork, and pictures is available for review. Many of these items were used to paint in words the story images. A few are reproduced in the book. Stypeck, a senior member of the American Society of Appraisers, has worked closely with major institutions, including the Library of Congress, Smithsonian Institution, and United States Holocaust Memorial Museum. After completion of a series of related books, the Holzer Collection will be donated to the United States Holocaust Memorial Museum in support of its mission to inspire citizens and leaders worldwide to confront hatred, prevent genocide, and promote human dignity.

Table of Contents

Foreword

In *Adventurers Against Their Will*, Joanie Holzer Schirm has reached deeply into the well of her family's past and the unfolding events in Europe at the very moment the world was erupting into the conflagration that history calls World War II. Meticulously researched by Schirm, the voices of seven correspondents echo from her Czech father, Valdik's, historic collection of over 400 letters by seventy-eight writers. Written between 1939-1946, the missives reveal the hopes, fears, desires, and all-too-late realizations of Jewish victims caught up in stasis, emigration, immigration, and most dastardly "resettlement"—that Nazi euphemism for transit to concentration, or death, camps. Since forty-four of Schirm's family members met this latter fate, Joanie Schirm's own retrospective, scholarly odyssey via the letters is poignant indeed.

The centerpiece of Schirm's *Adventurers'* story includes four friends and three cousins who communicated across four continents. The result is a real-time view of the world through a group of companions who supported one another, sharing their raw emotions and greatest fears during the worst times of their lives. Fortunately, most of the writers went on to recreate productive lives, a hopeful and timely message for generations now and those yet to come.

Schirm's research proved to be a true mystery in the unfolding; a genuine sleuthing search for the thread that bound European Jews together as they faced a myriad of choices. Valdik and his family, as well as their friends, often faced what Holocaust scholar and author Lawrence Langer calls "choiceless choices," that is, choices between the impossible—and the unacceptable.

Adventurers Against Their Will is a title that means exactly what those four words state. The story reveals the crucial moments when Nazi leadership successfully perpetrated the deprivation, degradation, desolation, destruction, and death during the Final Solution. Whether leading adventurous lives, as did Joanie's father, Oswald Alois "Valdik" Holzer, or being caught up in an adventure not of their own choosing, as were forty-four Holzer family members and dozens of their friends, all became adventurers in their own right.

"Against" means to be caught up in and around that genocide known as the Holocaust, in its unfolding.

"Their" refers to seventy-eight people on at least four continents who communicated personal hopes, fears, desires, and all-too-often fatal realizations, via 400 multi-paged letters exchanged between 1939 and 1946.

"Will" here is a double entendre, acknowledging the fact that Hitler and the German Reich set out to expand that nation in order to provide *Lebensraum* ("living space"), and, in the process, to destroy "undesirables" and non-Aryan peoples, targeting the Jews above all. As many of the letter writers reveal, however, the strongest human will of all is, poignantly and ultimately, the will to survive.

Indeed, *Adventurers Against Their Will* conveys a message not stressed, or too often overlooked, in Holocaust narratives about Jewish émigrés who tried to leave, who remained behind, or who were left behind. Those very choices shaped their lives. Schirm touches on more than sixty historical events that reveal just how perpetrators and collaborators carried out their evil designs. Serious students, particularly, need to understand the fragility of nation states, even democratic ones.

Recognizing she had to look backward to see forward, Schirm's relentless worldwide search for the letter writers or their descendants brings forth the promise of her story. By surviving and purposely rebuilding new lives, the adventurers outwit the Nazis, as the following generations live on. Built upon memory and new understanding, the story recognizes how deep the place is from which our lives flow. Most importantly, it reminds all of us of the individual role we must play to avoid the consequences of indifference when hate once again raises its ugly head.

Bill Younglove

Bill Younglove, a United States Holocaust Memorial Museum trained Museum Teacher Fellow, is a graduate of Yad Vashem Summer Seminars in Israel and Advanced Seminar in Poland and Lithuania. An Association of Holocaust Organizations member, he also serves on the Editorial Board of Yeshiva University's *PRISM: An Interdisciplinary Journal for Holocaust Educators*. An educator (Ed.D. from UCLA), he has taught language and history at secondary and university levels for over fifty years. His Holocaust-related articles appear in the *Encyclopaedia Judaica*, various journals, and books. He frequently presents at conferences on Holocaust-related issues.

And here the incidents both marvelous and interesting start, about which I would like to write to you briefly—so that you would know in that committee of yours what "our" emigrants do elsewhere, that not all of them are in Oxford but also not all at the front, that they became adventurers against their will.

—Oswald "Valdik" Holzer, March 3, 1940

Prologue

Paper can withstand anything.

—Czech proverb

The red Chinese boxes loomed just out of reach throughout my childhood. Those fanciful sword-fighting figures painted in luminous lacquer against a backdrop of lush trees and towering mountains beckoned, but my brother and sister and I paid no attention. The twin boxes were part of our familiar-to-the-point-of-being-invisible landscape, like that big tree outside your window with a botanical name you never learn.

It's just the big tree, and these were just the Chinese boxes.

One of us might have been tempted to climb the bookshelf to get to those boxes if they'd stood out as much as they might have in most American homes in the 1950s, but our house was packed with art objects from around the world. China was the dominant theme—Chinese paintings, Chinese calligraphy, Chinese sculpture, and books about China were everywhere. When I was small, I used to imagine the Yangtze River flowing past our house, not Florida's tranquil Indian River Lagoon. We even said a prayer in Chinese before meals.

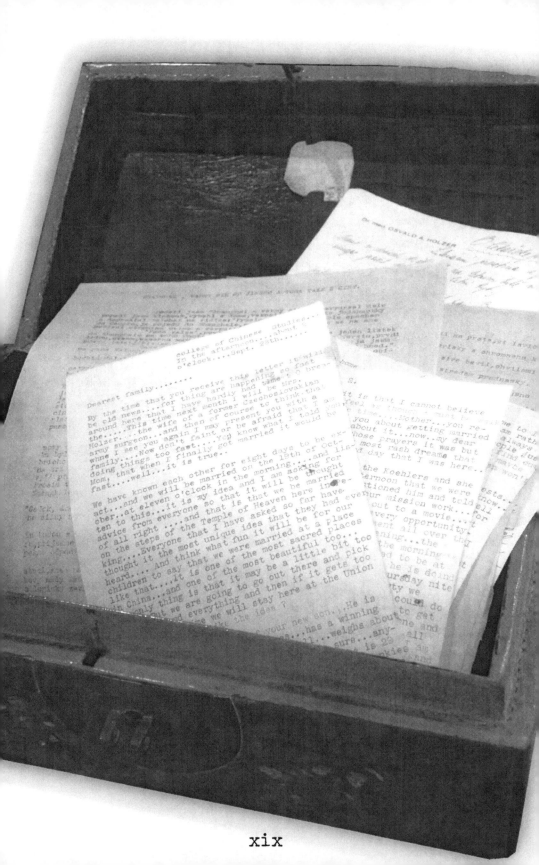

China was the leitmotif of our family life. It was where my parents—a young Czech doctor and the daughter of American missionaries—met in 1940, fell in love, and married before moving to America, where they died within two days of each other in January 2000. After their memorial service, my brother, sister, and I lovingly sorted through their possessions. Among the many treasures of travel and friends and family was a particular red lacquered Chinese box. Its contents transformed me.

For sixty years, my dad had kept four hundred letters inside that box as well as in other hiding places. They held the voices of seventy-eight writers from World War II who carried on a conversation with him that reached around the world—China, Czechoslovakia, Ecuador, America, France, England—documenting the horrors and hopes of a time and place that most of us can't even imagine.

I made it my mission to unravel the stories, the truths in the letters. With the fervor of an archeologist, I needed to satisfy my curiosity about my father's correspondents. For my investigation into their lives, I traveled the globe both virtually and physically. Many leads took me in the wrong direction, but I persisted. Revealing these histories and their meaning became my obsession.

Some of the letters were mundane, plenty were humorous, and several were profound. It took only a few accounts from within a forced labor or concentration camp for my journey to grow emotionally difficult as I encountered intimate descriptions of the pain, loss, and arbitrary cruelty of the Holocaust. But there was joy, too. These were real people living their lives as best they could in extraordinary circumstances. So in the midst of it all—outsmarting the Gestapo, crossing oceans laced with exploding mines, facing armed Japanese soldiers, or enduring disease and hunger—there was humor and love. I learned that the poetry of everyday life endures despite the circumstances.

I hope that you will find these adventurers against their will as interesting and important as I do. This book is a companion volume to *My Dear Boy: The Discovery of a Lifetime,* which chronicles my father's journey from Prague to China to America. *Adventurers Against Their Will* is based on the letters of my father's close friends and cousins: Karel and Franta Schoenbaum, Karel "Bála" Ballenberger, Hana Winternitz, Pavel Kraus, Rudla Fischer, and Vláďa Wagner. These people mattered. And their stories have universal relevance.

I am forever indebted to my father for the gift he left behind; he taught me that life is all about the messages you receive along the way and what you do with them.

Dr. med. OSVALD A. HOLZER

O lékařské praksi v Tsingtao.

Literární prvotina a příloha dopisem.

(Psáno v dobách dětinných na letním bytě v Tsingtao, Čína – je to chuťse jezdit do Číny na letní byt.)

"Chuuy," pravil pan Brown, vysoký, suchý Angličan s přihořalou tváří a postavil na stůl tři destičky ze slonové kosti, obě jsme pozměr mu však stáhl v tváři. Ma-jong, kláním a odkrývám řadu plokovek s čínskými charak... jak je skoum a přihlásí, ruku hustě při, v múdrosti je dusio k sealkums; starý Maceček Góm... studeného klu... klam máje opčienu o kroukovou pram, která... je zdravoji krazpo domu... Telefon, kolo u auta obvovje o noci Maceček sveda klam, měsíců okolo řeke – tery volá k aparáčn mne, na asi to bude smyl, vždy má... m nikdo nevná. U telefona se... hlas, on prý chysel, ze ti charov europejský doktor, ten mu... pomóže, da a přichodil ovšem čas na 14 Ynen Miny Road Gospodin Blackmann – oh jaká bolest, jaká bolest. Podle neu ve sluchátku gospodin bude asi rediť. Mr. Brown gospodin a gospoda kiškoví líbiji, ze mnusíme nechat Ma-jong, zítra bude ovšem zase psát, jak se bude hra? Kolančke. Bry volá míšsa ja tak jedu se svými pidláťky na 14 Ynen Min... když mi oslovela asi toři léta paní Asij... ...nul jsem u dač s nekkým, anglicky Aron Blackmann – Russian Fur ... lá pan v kimone s velikým čopceu ...krasohujte a vstupaji do ... ...ím, zápachem nezďamého jou vodu ...mann, ktery zesiluje moji jou lannou ...lkoast a vstupuju k nemocné mne ...lusty taječne vypadaji ...ces ...a pravou paři, na kterou na... ...i naukasi. Požádal jsem jej, ...začal jsem omínat mokre ... ...anou spadla hlava spět a z n... ...ady, nyní jsn oja, kaučeně je po...

Chapter 1:

Voices from the Past

Dramatis Personae

<u>Joanie Holzer Schirm</u>

(Author; Valdik's daughter)

Paternal great- grandparents: Alois and Marie (née Porges) Holzer

Paternal grandparents: Arnošt and Olga (née Orlík) Holzer

Maternal grandparents: Horace and Emma (née Kroeger) Lequear

Parents: Oswald "Valdik" Holzer, MD,
and Ruth Alice "Chick" (née Lequear) Holzer

Siblings: Thomas "Tom" Holzer and Patricia "Pat" Holm

Husband: Roger Neiswender

Daughters: Kelly (née Schirm) Lafferman
Susan (née Neiswender) Black

Son: Frank F. "Derick" Schirm IV

Grandchildren: Ty and Ava Lafferman, Michael Leubscher

Paternal granduncles: Leo "Lenda" Holzer, Rudolf Winternitz,
Jaroslav "Sláva" Mařík, Leopold Fischer

Paternal grandaunts: Karolina (née Orlík) Fischer, Olga (née Holzer)
Winternitz, Valerie "Valda" (née Holzer) Mařík

Paternal cousins: Thomas (Fischer) Weiss, Pavel Mařík, Jirka Mařík,
Tomáš Mařík, Hanuš Holzer

I myself am living an adventurous life against my will. It would actually be quite nice if I did not have great responsibility at home.

—Oswald "Valdik" Holzer, August 10, 1940

*M*y father was eighty-eight and my mother was eighty-three when they died. I didn't think they would have many friends left. I was mistaken. Hundreds of people crowded the Eastminster Presbyterian Church in Indialantic-by-the-Sea, Florida, where my mother had dutifully engaged herself and her children every Sunday in the worship and work of the Lord while my father, an avowed agnostic, supported my mother's spiritual side. Condolence letters arrived from all over the world—Basel, Prague, London, Toronto. The memorial service was a huge affair. It was as if a dam had broken and there was no stopping the flood of people who wanted to pay their final respects and share stories.

The celebration of my parents' well-lived lives—or at least, the parts I knew about—was perfect. Mom was the founder of the Youth Choir, and the children in white robes sang their hearts out. I even played my father's audiotape account of falling in love with my mother in Peking, (Beijing) delivered like a voice from heaven through the church speakers. The service ended with my husband, Roger, daughter Kelly, son Derick, and me joining many relatives at the front of the church, holding hands, and repeating from our hearts the grace my parents had learned in China, which we'd said every evening at our family dinner table: *Gǎnxiè nǐ gǎnxiè qīn>ài de tiān fù, nǐ zhè zhǒng shípǐn.* Thank you, thank you, dear Heavenly Father, for this food. Amen.

After the memorial, my sister Pat, brother Tom, and I sent our families back to their routines so we could make the hard choices about which family possessions to keep. When we walked into my parents' condominium, it looked as if they had just stepped out the door to visit friends—water glasses half full in the sink, bills in the mailbox, and the refrigerator filled with my father's collection of specialty mustards and some stinky prime aged cheese.

Despite the evidence of two lives ended mid-gesture, the house was neat and orderly...except for my father's study. That room had remained an extraordinary mess for years, a rare sore spot between my parents. It was crammed with collections likely untouched for the two decades Valdik and Ruth Holzer had lived in the condominium: canes, wooden pipes, magazines, coins, stamps. The wood-paneled walls were lined with shelves full of books mirroring Dad's diverse interests: medicine, music, religion, history, travel, plants, pottery, masks, the Olympics, and, of course, China. He had a tendency to hoard papers, a trait I inherited. My siblings and I decided to save that room for last.

We gathered at the dining room table, clearing space amid stacks of unread mail to put down our glasses of iced tea. So many memories were made here—Thanksgiving and Christmas dinners, birthday parties. It felt strange to sit at the table without our parents present, but I could swear the scent of my mother's Chanel No. 5 still lingered.

We reminisced about the memorial service, agreeing that the ceremony had exceeded our expectations. Mom and Dad would have approved. Then we all fell silent until Pat brought us back to the task at hand. "Where do we start?"

"With the Chinese red lacquered boxes, of course," Tom said.

We all laughed. Those wooden boxes had moved along with our family all our lives, from the cottage in rural Chattahoochee to the big house on the river to the condominium where our folks lived out their retirement, but none of us had ever peeked inside them. Climbing onto a footstool, Tom retrieved the first box from a bookcase in the living room. He carried it gently to the dining table as if it were the Ark of the Covenant.

Tom opened the traditional Chinese latch, and we gasped in unison. There, slightly curved to fit the container, were dozens of old letters. Some were written on yellowed onionskin, others on heavy linen paper. All appeared ready to crumble. Tom tenderly lifted the bundle and placed it on the table. The first letter was typewritten in English on four five-by-seven-inch pages, in Courier font, using a ribbon that allowed for both black and red ink. In the old days, a writer usually switched to red type to mark words of particular significance. The red was mesmerizing.

Tom handed the letter to me. It was from my mother in China to her missionary parents, Horace and Emma Lequear, in Pennsylvania. As if intentionally placed there for us to discover precisely at that moment, it was the unabridged version of our parents' "meeting story" in Peking in 1940.

College of Chinese Studies…in the afternoon… about 2 o'clock…Sept. 28th…

Dearest family…

By the time that you receive this letter it will be old news…This time next month I will be Mrs. Holzer…the wife of a former Czechoslovakian army surgeon…

We have known each other for eight days to be exact…and we will be married on the 19th of October…on the steps of the Temple of Heaven… He is dark…black hair and grey eyes…has a winning personality...five feet eleven tall...weighs about 186 pounds...or maybe less. He isn't sure... anyway it is distributed well...he is 29 years old... and more fun than a barrel of monkeys.

Doc has one fine dream of opening a fine charity hospital here in Peking but that could not be now and probably [not] for a long time...I simply cannot understand how it all happened unless some higher power was saving us for each other... we fit like old shoes...and when he is with me I don't give a hang what the rest of the world might be doing...I only wish that you could see him and know him...I know that you would take him right into your hearts...everyone likes him...

My brother, sister, and I sat stunned, motionless. Here we were, raw with grief, the children of the letter writer, transported back to the moment our lively young mother first shared her story with our grandparents about falling in love. Tears streamed down our faces. We knew from old photos and flickering home movies what Mom and Dad looked like in their youths: she was a freckle-faced, blue-eyed, strawberry blonde with the agility of an athlete and the poise of a princess; he was a tall, olive-skinned, square-jawed pipe-smoker with black, curly hair and powerful sculptor's hands. But these might as well have been images sketched from shadows. You don't think of parents as having actually existed, much less loved, before you were born. Here we faced our mother's feelings and our parents' dreams spelled out in black and red ink, stored for six decades in a Chinese lacquered box.

Along with that letter, the box contained about fifty more. All were dated between 1939 and 1943 and mostly written by hand in Czech. We were intrigued, but we had other work to do—we turned our attention to our father's study and its cabinets full of papers, books, records, and slide albums. By the time Tom, Pat, and I finished going through every room in the condo, we had found scores of documents, dating back to the 1800s, along with wartime film reels and hundreds of photographs depicting places all over the world.

While sorting through a batch of papers, I unearthed an old Czech menu blanketed with a layer of fine dust. On its cover was the picturesque Prague Castle, the place from which kings and leaders presided over my father's native land for over a thousand years. I smiled in wonder at how the menu came to rest on the shelf of a house in Florida. Then I opened it.

Inside were several official documents with elaborate Gothic lettering. One of the papers had the heading "Oddací list," followed by the names and birthdates of my Czech grandparents, Arnošt and Olga Holzer. It was dated June 27, 1909. From the year, I guessed it could be my grandparents' marriage certificate. The two other records had "Rodný list" printed at the top. Those looked like birth certificates.

The next two pages contained typed information related to Arnošt and Olga. I stared at the words, wishing I could read Czech. I noticed another date: 1946. Perhaps these were official death notices, issued after the war? Why were they tucked away in a Czech restaurant menu? Did my father receive them while having dinner? I felt an inexplicable emotional connection to these pieces of paper and decided to keep them.

So it was with the letters, which continued to reveal themselves as we pried open the second Chinese box and later discovered a half-dozen more hiding places. We unearthed nearly four hundred letters that day, all dated from 1939 to 1946. It was as though we'd received a massive mail delivery from Europe, China, and South America, delayed by more than half a century. As my brother and sister sorted through paintings and bills and clutter, I sifted ever so gently through the letters. The papers in my hands were fragile, yellowed with time. Some of the pages had turned gray but a few that had faded on the outside still held their original blue backgrounds like the outside of a Tiffany box. Depending on the ink used, I could easily decipher the contents or had to struggle to make out the words. Even when I could read them, I couldn't understand them—but I knew instinctively that they held voices waiting to be heard by a new generation.

Somehow, I felt they were already speaking directly to me.

Eight years after my parents' deaths, in January 2008, I retired from thirty-five years in the business of engineering. With the loving support of my husband, Roger Neiswender, I began in earnest to study the letters my father had hidden away, although I still couldn't decipher their Czech and German sentences. I counted the signatures and found seventy-eight different writers. The tops of many pages were frayed, sometimes making it hard to determine the dates. I printed a list of calendar months translated into Czech so I could group the letters by date. There were no saved letters from before my father left Prague. He must have assumed he would return home one day and his possessions would be safe where he had left them.

As I organized the material, it became evident that my father had sorted the letters by correspondent and interwoven incoming mail with copies of his responses in chronological order, creating a record of a dialogue. The most exciting discoveries in the trove were eighty of my father's own letters. Most had been duplicated using a thin sheet of carbon paper placed between delicate and now yellowed onionskin sheets. I imagined Dad's hands covered with black carbon as he slipped the onionskin into envelopes, ready to wing their way around the world. Sometimes, to save his scarce paper, my father typed another page on the reverse side, making the text hard to decipher.

Some ink was faded after sixty years stored in closets, mostly in humid Florida. I knew these words could be enhanced with modern scanning technology. The letters were fastened together with rusty paper clips that often fused the top corners of the papers. Once removed, they left an indelible dark mark. I tried my best to gently remove the clips and separate the pages without damage. For those I couldn't preserve, I sat for a moment mourning the wound.

Holding these delicate fragments of history in my hands, I felt more than curiosity. I *had* to know what they said, even if they were only keepsakes from my father's early life—but I sensed they were more than that. A few inquiries to experts at the United States Holocaust Memorial Museum and elsewhere confirmed my suspicion: in saving those letters, my father had gathered and preserved something of historical value. While individual memoirs existed, a record of extended correspondence among a community of friends and relatives caught up in the tumult of the Second World War and the Holocaust was rare.

I knew then that these letters had to be shared as well as preserved, and the obligation had fallen to me. The first challenge was clear, since most of the letters were written in Czech, a language I can't read or speak. Translating the letters took several professionals two years and put a big dent in my retirement funds.

I began reading the moment the first English translations arrived. And as I did, the personalities of the writers immediately began to take shape. Their words transported me halfway across the world to a time over half a century ago when my father was still in his twenties. I met his friends and cousins, and perhaps most important, his parents—my grandparents—for the very first time. I uncovered the details of their fates at the hands of the Nazis and sobbed for these gentle-souled people and their unforeseen arrival in my life and heart when I was sixty.

As my Czech grandparents came alive for me, I grew to know my father as a young man. Valdík escaped the Nazis in Prague with his medical bag, his camera, and perhaps a few aerograms, and traveled to China. There he worked as a doctor and chronicled his adventures, culminating in Peking, where he fell madly and immediately in love with my mother. Ruth Alice Lequear was the daughter of American Protestant missionaries, on her way to teach children in the same Hunan Province mission where she had been born. She never made it. Instead, she married a handsome Czech doctor on a crisp fall day just a month after she had met him. Their love story spanned over sixty years and led them from the exotic coast of China to its interior, through ruthless civil war and Japanese occupation. They traveled around the world and finally settled in America in 1947. And all the while, my father wrote, received, and saved letters.

I didn't always know whose secrets I was trying to ferret out. I recognized some of the signatures and names mentioned from a list my father had compiled of forty-four relatives who had perished in concentration camps. The rest of the letter writers were a mystery I pondered during the hours I spent slipping the fragile pages into plastic sleeves. I assumed some were friends from medical school; others were likely Czechs who, like my father, had emigrated to escape the Nazi terror, or people he became acquainted with in China.

Most of the letters began with *Milý,* meaning "dear." This was followed by a multitude of Czech diminutive endearments and nicknames: Valdik, Valdík, Valdi, Valdo, Valdemar, Valdíku, or *příteli* (friend). Often the letters were written by more than one person. There were instances when two or three friends escaped Czechoslovakia together and jointly wrote from Palestine, France, or England. My father's address changed numerous times but somehow letters still reached him. Tom Weiss, the son of my father's cousin

Chapter 1: Voices from the Past

Rudla Fischer, sent me copies of pages from his mother's address book. She listed eight different addresses for my father in China as well as multiple addresses in the United States and South America.

Several people wrote to my father saying they had mailed him letters and then learned he had moved. I could feel their apprehension and sometimes disappointment. Stickers were pasted on the envelopes' edges: *Opened by Examiner 6112* (or whatever the intrusive censor's number was) followed by a stamped swastika. With stickers printed in English, I assumed some English-speaking government beyond the German-occupied countries added its mark to the letters as they made their way around the world. I imagined a sharp letter opener, held in the stern hand of a Nazi-uniformed censor, slicing open these tender missives.

Due to the complicated routes that the letters traveled from Prague to China, my grandfather, Arnošt, took to numbering the envelopes he sent. I believe he did this so my father would be able to keep track of which ones reached their destination and when. I do not have copies of correspondence from my father to his parents, so I will never know how well Arnošt's system worked. When he wrote from Prague in early 1941, thinking my father was still in China, his letters went first to Vienna for censorship, then traveled "via Siberia-Tokio-Pacific," as was stamped on one of the saved envelopes in my father's stamp-collection books.

I ached when there was a gap in the chronology—letters that likely became lost as they crossed oceans or traveled over Siberia to reach my father in far-flung places deep in the interior of China, the United States, and Ecuador. The ones that made it divulged left-behind dreams, hopes for the future and secrets shared — first with my father and now with me. I learned to appreciate the writers' sarcastic Czech humor. As I grew acquainted with the correspondents and discovered their relationships to Dad, I encountered someone different from the adult father I knew. I realized I was meeting the young man my mother fell madly in love with.

Names previously unknown to me started to feel familiar as I became acquainted with everyday details of people's lives. Some stayed in the Nazi-occupied Czech Lands of Bohemia and Moravia. Some fled, seeking refuge around the world. With the benefit of hindsight, I read their words with an awareness of the coming dangers. I became distressed when they misjudged the immense danger they were in, not escaping the Nazis or lingering in France until it was too late.

It was sometimes difficult to tell how much they knew about the peril all around them. Everyone who remained behind German lines understood that expressing any views against the occupying power or disclosing details of value to the German war effort was a serious offense. Even telling a joke about Hitler was considered a transgression.

The most revealing information in the letters was the litany of rights lost through various Nazi decrees as the war progressed—the right to sing in a pub, go to a cinema or theater, eat at a restaurant, visit a museum or an exhibit, read a newspaper, own a radio, keep a driver's license, live in one's home, practice a profession, maintain one's possessions, or walk on the banks of the Vltava River.

Foreign newspapers were unavailable to Jews and soon even Germans ones, which were filled with propaganda, became forbidden. Most of the information they attained was through hearsay and gossip. In late 1941, Jews were ordered to surrender their typewriters to the Nazis, which explained why Arnošt began to write his letters by hand.

Over time, as more and more of the letters were translated, I began to understand the use of code words, such as "spa" for concentration camp, and I recognized my grandparents' attempt to create the illusion that "all is fine" for their adored son, just as my father did in his letters to them. They shared false optimism with one another as they lost their home and homeland, their positions, property and belongings, and any real control over their futures.

After Germany declared war on the United States in December 1941, mail communication became extremely difficult between enemy territories except through very short and even-more-highly censored forms provided by the International Red Cross in Geneva. The Red Cross Postal Message Scheme allowed civilians cut off by the war to communicate with one another, but only in messages of twenty-five words or less. The German Red Cross looked over the messages and sometimes censored them before sending them to Geneva to be mailed. The International Red Cross was overwhelmed by these messages over thirty million were received by the war's end. Following the December 7, 1941, attack on Pearl Harbor and America's declaration of war on Japan and Germany, the number of letters from Czechoslovakia diminished.

The letters made clear how painful this period of my father's life was for him—leaving his family and friends and shipping out to a distant and, by European standards at the time, primitive country, where he knew no one and didn't speak the language. He couldn't pick up a phone (or send electronic mail as we might today); he could rarely even send or receive a telegram. Most important, he must have lived in relentless uncertainty and fear for those he'd left behind. As I sifted through the piles of paper, I began to understand why my father had stored away the letters and not shared them with us as souvenirs of his youth.

As the picture of Dad's life became more vivid, it also became more complicated.

One of the greatest surprises revealed by his cache of letters was how much he never told me. This was especially strange because he had always been a champion storyteller—my favorite life poet. Throughout my childhood his stream of narratives taught me, soothed me, and carried me to exotic worlds. His favorite destination was the terra firma of his birth, Bohemia, a word that adorned every one of his personalized license plates. It conveyed an identity as powerful as the Alfa Romeos and Porsches he drove so skillfully along the narrow island roads, but also as complex and turbulent as the history of that old region wedged precariously between Germany to the north and Austria to the south.

For me, Dad's storytelling was as essential as oxygen. The images he painted with words were so tangible; I could almost taste Czech roast pork with dumplings and sauerkraut. He expressed his *joie de vivre*, filled with adventure, a passion for justice, and sincere affection for family and friends. I could never get enough of the eloquent memories of his escapades, the people he met, or the places he traveled.

My father's rugged, exciting Bohemian youth was a world apart from my idyllic childhood of sunny days and warm, rolling surf on a barrier island in Florida. I loved the mystery he created as he trailed off midstream, as if floating into some sort of trance. His deep, slightly accented voice would eventually resume near where he had left off and flow into another story, creating a tangle of tales like the wavy black curls on his head.

It was many years before I came to understand that those tantalizing drifts and pauses weren't merely for dramatic effect—my father was editing his life.

He did this so skillfully that I grew up believing I knew far more about him than I actually did. I knew he was Jewish in a time and place where that could have had tragic consequences. I knew his parents suffered those consequences when they perished in the Holocaust. I knew he escaped the same fate by fleeing to China, where he found my mother and happiness, only to flee once again as World War II closed in around them. I knew about my parents' lives in Florida, and my father's career as a compassionate doctor. Most of all, I knew we were different, and I loved that. Who else had a dad who fled the Nazis, or a mother who spoke Chinese?

But he'd never told me the whole story. I knew my father had been serving in the Czechoslovakian Army when the Germans invaded in March 1939. Overwhelmed, his country surrendered. My father slipped away from his unit and boarded a train for Prague. He made plans to emigrate, and his medical degree became his passport to a brighter future. He'd worked for the Bata Shoe Company's medical department three summers before and was able to use his connections there to arrange for a document stating he was taking a new job in the company's branch in China. The Germans were quick to clamp down on Czech flight, so the Bata employment papers were important for Gestapo clearance. In my father's telling, this was a stroke of good fortune that would allow him to establish himself in China and eventually send for his parents if they decided to join him.

But after reading a letter my father wrote on February 7, 1940, to a Czech neighbor, Dr. Veselý, I realized Dad had never intended to go to China.

> …As you know I left Prague in May and got to Marseilles, where I boarded a ship for China. I totally did not intend to reach the destination, I wanted to stay somewhere along the journey. Disregarding the fact I had no visa, money, etc. It was damn difficult as I did not even know well any world language, except for German.

What started out as a destination to satisfy the Nazi bureaucracy became the best and probably only choice, so he embraced it—

motivated by his spirit of adventure and his youthful sense of fun, despite all the sorrows that were unfolding in his world. The more I understood, the more I tried to piece together. I matched details from one letter to another and then cross-checked them with other sources. The effect was overwhelming. The letters were full of beauty, adventure, and joy, but also loneliness, confusion, and grief. It was a rugged world for me to live in day after day, and I began to fear that the project of organizing, translating, and preserving the letters was more than I could handle. But I was propelled forward by a powerful sense of obligation to my father, who surely knew I would find the letters, as well as to the people whose lives and struggles they detailed. I realized this was a larger, more powerful story than I'd anticipated. I also realized these letter writers were only telling incomplete tales and there was much more to uncover.

My father never told me about the close friends he lost to the horrors of war, or the others who suffered gravely in concentration or forced labor camps, or simply from the effects of the ruthless Nazi rule of their homeland. Forty-four relatives perished in the Holocaust. Displaced by the Nazis, Dad and his friends who survived suffered from guilt for the rest of their lives, either because they escaped and others didn't or from a sense that they could have done more. Some buried their guilt deeper than others, yet in the end, most displayed the indefatigable Czech resilience. They went on to rebuild lives, bringing a haunted peace and fulfillment to themselves and those they loved.

Through the letters and my research, I became a part of these friendships, many begun at the Mánes Café in Prague during the First Republic of Czechoslovakia's glory days after the Austro-Hungarian Empire's collapse and before the arrival of the Nazis in 1939. Most of us remember gathering places from our own pasts that represent the brave and hopeful moments of youth and future, and Mánes was that place for Prague's creative young people before the war. It was such an important and profoundly influential part of the lives of my father and his friends that it became essential to understanding who they were and who they became.

Chapter 2:

Mánes Café

Dramatis Personae

Mánes Café (Kavárna Mánes)

Functionalist-style designed café,
garden restaurant, and artist exhibition hall

located on the banks of Prague's Vltava River.

1930s

My father:	Oswald "Valdik" Holzer
His friends:	Karel "Bála" and Milena Ballenberger
	Karel and Katka Schoenbaum
	Franta and Andula Schoenbaum
	Vláďa Wagner
His cousins:	Hana Winternitz
	Pavel Kraus
	Rudla and Erna Fischer

We talked about everything from involvement with girls, to camping, to life after the university and matters of life and death (and of course about the gathering clouds on the international horizon and about the future).

—Vladimír "Vláďa" Wagner, MD, 1987

*E*very box has a key! And the red Chinese box was no exception. I found its metaphorical key among the letters: a twenty-five-page collaboration between my father and his close friend and fellow doctor, Vladimír "Vláďa" Wagner. *A Memorial to Friends, or How I Met Jews* (titled, I assume, by Vláďa, a non-Jew) was written in Czech in 1987, and offered a scrambled but vivid collection of vignettes of some of the denizens of Mánes Café—the adventurers against their will—before, during, and after World War II.

The rambling text appears to have ping-ponged between my dad and Vláďa—one in Florida, the other in Prague—as it was expanded and edited. Although I don't know its original purpose, it was a gift of inestimable value at a time when I needed an understanding of the prewar setting that bound the friendships of the people whose mail I was reading.

My tour guide on this journey was as important as the newly discovered text. Margit Meissner, volunteer translator at the United States Holocaust Memorial Museum, understood the Holocaust as well as the words of these two strangers. Born in Austria to a wealthy Jewish family, Margit was raised in Prague. Just sixteen when Hitler annexed Austria in 1938, she was sent to Paris for a practical education. When France fell in the summer of 1940, she escaped on a bicycle. Eventually Margit and her mother made it to the United States.

specific restaurants, bars, and cafés—one of the most famous of these being Mánes—became known in the 1930s for their anti-fascist attitude. But it was not as much for its attitude as its location near Charles University that my father and his friends first visited Mánes.

Construction of the gleaming, streamlined building had begun in 1928 on the site of the Šítkovský mlýn (Šitkovský Mill), alongside a fifteenth-century water tower. It was finished in 1930, two years before my father entered the university. Mint-green window trim and Kelly green fluorescent signs contrasted sharply with the white exterior walls. The building was a product of the Mánes Association of Fine Arts, a renowned artists' alliance and exhibition society, and designed to house collections of avant-garde art. The association sought to promote and showcase all kinds of artists, including rising Czech stars and international talents like Picasso.

For Valdik, a young medical student with well-developed aesthetic sensibilities, the creative environment of Mánes was the perfect home away from home. He relished the company of some of the finest sculptors, architects, graphic artists, animators, and painters of the day. Throughout his university tenure, from 1932 through 1937, he drew caricatures of his medical school professors, which he shared with the Mánes art circle, including artist, writer, and lawyer Adolf Hoffmeister.

In addition to the large exhibition hall with its filtered natural light, the Mánes complex featured a French restaurant on its lower level, with a wall painting by Czech artist Emil Filla, an important Mánes member. Filled with wooden tables covered with pristine white tablecloths set against blue walls, its large windows overlooked the mute white swans on the Vltava River.

Below the French restaurant was the smoky basement café and bar; Valdik introduced fellow medical student Vláďa Wagner to this perfect place to discuss their youthful ideas.

…As a matter of fact, that bar was an artistic delight in itself. The walls were painted with beautiful and sometimes risqué (today that would not appear any more) nudes of girls. It was rumored that the painter, Štika, who created them so beautifully, did it for payment with the perfume of the heavenly Jamaican rum (but that could also be just a rumor).

The rest of the unadorned walls were covered with a smoky patina produced by the blue haze made by the smoking students who filled the windowless space.

…the period of the turning point of 1932 and 1933 was when our private sky, created for us by the welcoming milieu of the Mánes, seemed painted primarily with cigarette smoke. I can't remember that any one of us was a non-smoker; there were only some who didn't like the taste.

This became the hub of my father's daily student life in a time of burning idealism and young adulthood. Dad and his friends gathered there to listen to music, smoke cigarettes or pipes, and drink strong *turek* (coffee) or *pivo* (beer) while discussing politics and sports.

In a city brimming with young intellectuals, the Mánes group stood out. They embodied the bright promise of their young country's future. Predominantly from upper-middle-class and wealthy families, they seemed destined for success.

My hard-charging father occupied the bottom of the economic strata of his peers. The only child of a middle-class businessman and his wife, he achieved his life's aspiration of becoming a physician through his parents' loving sacrifice. When Valdik graduated from gymnasium (the equivalent of US high school) in 1932, his father closed his wholesale grocery business in the small town of Benešov. Arnošt, Olga, and Valdik moved twenty-three miles to a cozy apartment in the Vinohrady neighborhood of cosmopolitan

Prague, and Arnošt went into business with another man selling plastic buttons and other notions. From that apartment, Valdik could easily catch a tram to his university classes and Mánes Café.

As the 1930s progressed, my father and his friends settled into the cultural circle of artists, writers, actors, and filmmakers in interwar Prague. What united them most were their feelings about the monstrosity of Hitlerian fascism and the geographical proximity that forced them to take a position against it. The National Socialist German Workers' Party, known as the Nazi Party, was not only a right-wing nationalist group but adamantly anti-Semitic. These Germans internalized the words of the Reich Chancellor Hitler and his intent to restore Germany to its former powerful status. One of their strategies was to read nationality back into history, taking primary sources out of context to reinforce ethnic divisions and stake their claims for political power. By the end of 1932, the Mánes friends knew danger was encroaching.

The crowds would ebb and flow, sometimes with over thirty people filling the café—among them banker Rudla Fischer, and young lawyers Karel "Bála" Ballenberger and Karel and Franta Schoenbaum, all of whom were pipe smokers. Less frequently in attendance because of their age were my father's younger cousins— Hana Winternitz and Pavel Kraus. But no matter who was there, it was always the same—passionate discussions of current events and culture in a fragrant tobacco haze.

When they weren't debating, they challenged one another to chess and other board games, and listened to music by an array of artists, especially the popular jazz and classical composer, Jaroslav Ježek. While the men laughed, talked, and smoked, they cemented friendships they thought would last forever. Some might say they shared a kind of arrogance from lives that had come easily, but what they really shared was a youthful confidence in their future.

The young women who sometimes joined them, such as wives Milena Ballenberger, Katka Schoenbaum, and Erna Fischer, all dressed in the latest fashions and pinned and curled their hair like the leading Czech actresses of the time. Incorporating shoulder pads, their stylish dresses—snug at the waist and then slightly bowed out, with hems between knees and shin—were designed to show off their most feminine features, as were their smartly heeled shoes. The men looked like real gentlemen, suited each day for the occasion, a favorite hat in hand.

Much like the contemporary gilded youth of the same class elsewhere in Europe and North America, the denizens of Mánes were sophisticated, elite, well-educated, and comparatively well-off. Not one of them came from a working-class family. Like many students of the times, some veered to the left in their political philosophy. The rest made fun of these emerging leftists, calling them "Salon Communists."

Because this close-knit group of friends did not dwell on religion, no separation was made between Christians and Jews. Most Christians who frequented Mánes were not actively engaged in their inherited faith at this point in their lives. Occasionally, Jewish students declared no religious affiliation in their university registration papers, envisioning themselves as assimilated in the young Czechoslovak secular democracy of the interwar period. Valdik and his friends believed that they belonged to the Czech people, regardless of their heritage or the language they spoke (Czech or German). Some felt their individual religions were unimportant or a personal matter, as Vláďa described:

> …To some extent the economic crisis of the 1930s also influenced us and in particular our moral compass. Our anti-Nazi thinking also contributed to this. You could say there were opposing moods

that led to the admiration of fascism and to changes in everyday life. In the beginning it did not occur to any of us that we would arrive at completely circumscribed and clearly formulated political opinions. We only wanted to fully seize our youth and utilize our hunger for knowledge and to participate fully in all aspects of life. And why should I want to deny that we wanted to have fun, fall in love, engage in sports, study, drink a little, go to the theater; in short, fill our life with everything that could be offered to us.

Eventually, the fun at Mánes began to be disrupted by the reality of the times. In 1933, Germany's parliament building—the Reichstag—was set ablaze by arsonists. Nazis cited this fire as proof that the Communists were conspiring against the elected government and initiated a wave of violence throughout Germany against those they viewed as political opposition: Communists, Social Democrats, and Liberals. Civil liberties were suspended under the Reichstag Fire Decree. This led to a police state. Soon the Nazis issued a decree ordering compulsory retirement of non-Aryans from civil service and a boycott against Jewish businesses. The Nazis regarded non-Jewish white Europeans as Aryans, which they considered a racial category, whereas Jews were Semites and the main target of their persecution. Outbursts of violence both by and among the Nazis made clear what brutality they were capable of. The Jewish population was in grave danger.

At the end of 1935, the elderly founding President of the First Czechoslovak Republic, Tomáš Masaryk, resigned and an experienced diplomat, Edvard Beneš, succeeded him. Germany's new Nuremberg Laws deprived Jews of civil rights and prohibited marriage to non-Jews, something that had been commonplace in Czechoslovakia and Germany. Jews were legally defined not by their religion but by their ancestry. The Nazis had begun to formalize their racial persecution.

More and more refugees streamed over the German border into Czechoslovakia, the majority of them Jews and leftists. In Prague, the situation inflamed many people who were already leery of the full assimilation of the Jewish population begun under the leadership of Masaryk.

In 1936, Valdik's classmate, Pavel Körper, traveled to Germany for a vacation. When he returned to Mánes Café, he spoke of seeing huge outdoor rallies. Körper, fluent in German, was a Jew with blond hair from his mixed heritage. Just like my father, Körper listed himself as "without religion" on his Charles University papers.

With shoulders hunched, Körper sat at the white-clothed table with the crowd hanging on his words as he told the anxious group of Jews and non-Jews of Hitler's fanaticism for racial superiority. The intensity of the German crowd had frightened him. Körper had seen a man reach out in a frenzy, desperate to touch Hitler. When the Führer approached him, the man broke into tears and sobbed that he could die now that he had seen the Führer's face. Körper said he felt sick to his stomach.

Here is how Vláďa described it:

> ...Then one began to hear from those who returned from Germany. They spoke of huge rallies where a certain "Hitler" spoke. They described the marchers, very organized rows of men all dressed in brown uniforms. It was rumored that the Nazis had bought unsalable bolts of brown cloth and created a central European fashion. Then, came news of skirmishes with Social Democrats or Communists who were not able to agree on a way to oppose Hitler. It all created interest but not concern...for the time being. It is that damned

ability of people to remain unconcerned since it is only the neighbor's house that is on fire.

Our calm, as well as that of a lot of other people, was shattered with the elections that brought Hitler to power. For a while the most naïve ones believed that his power was limited by a government of laws. That lasted until the moment when an awkwardly organized but highly effective event occurred. That was the fire of the Reichstag. That permitted the Nazis to start a wave of violence, the likes of which the world had never previously known.

After Körper's account, the listeners recalled that it was as if the air had been removed from the room. They couldn't process what they were hearing. Who were these people that worshipped someone who spoke with such hatred based on his Aryan racial doctrine? For a while, not a word was uttered; each man was filled with anxiety about his own looming compulsory service with the Czechoslovak Army. Valdik knew that upon his graduation in spring 1937, he would become a soldier.

Finally Körper broke the quiet, trying to allay everyone's fears: "Our country is building massive fortifications along the border with Germany and surely it will protect us all." The optimism of their youth made it hard for them—whether Jew or non-Jew—to realize the immensity of the growing threat that would forever change their lives, and so they returned to their beverages.

While they consumed their *turek* and rum and the jazz played on, the critical factors that would contribute to the outbreak of World War II unfolded. Thirty-five thousand Soviet officers were "dealt with" by the Soviet leader, Joseph Stalin, as he purged his party with ruthless mass executions of those he deemed disloyal. Fascist General Francisco Franco continued Spain's bloody civil war, aided by a soldier horde of thousands from Nazi Germany and Fascist Italy. To aid their efforts, Adolf Hitler, who had denounced the earlier Treaty of Versailles clause providing for German disarmament after WWI, rebuilt Germany's capacity for aerial warfare headed by Reichstag President and Gestapo founder Hermann Göring.

In the Spanish Civil War, the Popular Front's Republican Army with its Socialist and Communist international brigades reflected wider issues of international relations at the time. Russians, Brits, Americans, Czechoslovaks (many Jews among them), and other Europeans helped the Popular Front, even inspiring Ernest Hemingway's stories. As Vláďa wrote:

> …Soon that became, and rightfully so, the burning topic of our debates. The danger clearly increased, but at that time we still believed that we could somehow influence the outcome with our attitudes. At that point it was still far from clear that in the end decisions would depend on the number and quality of tanks and airplanes. Until the very fateful days at the end of August 1938, we had faith that we could somehow stop it.

All of this was taking place near Prague's doorstep, while in the distant east, the Japanese were poised to escalate their invasion of China, another raging struggle affecting the globe and the gilded future of the young men and women who frequented the remarkable Mánes Café. These lines written in my father and Vláďa's collaborative memoir continue the story:

> …I believe now the time has come to present the actors of this story that started with completely innocent coffeehouse meetings, and eventually turned into tragedies with so many corpses that it contradicts the good taste of a properly positioned drama. Of course to speak about good taste

35

when it comes to the acts of Adolf Hitler and his minions would at that time have been considered a good joke...not suspecting that the whirlwind of the occupation would harden our faces for six years and that for many of us it would become our obituary.

Valdik's Family

(Referenced in Adventurers Against Their Will)

Oswald "Valdik" Holzer

Wife: Ruth Alice "Chick" (née Lequear)

Children: Tom, Pat, and Joanie

Grandparents: Alois and Marie (née Porges) Holzer

(Father)	*(Mother)*
Arnošt Holzer	Olga (née Orlík) Holzer

Siblings mentioned:	*Siblings mentioned:*
Valerie (Jiří and Pavel's mother)	**Karolína** (Rudla's mother)
Olga (Hana's mother, Pavel Kraus's aunt)	**Ernestine "Erna"**
Leo (Hanuš's father)	

The *Adventurers*...Valdik's friends and cousins

(Featured in the book)

Friend	*Friend*	*Cousin*	*Cousin**	*Cousin*	*Friend*
Schoenbaum	Ballenberger	Winternitz	Kraus	Fischer	Wagner
Karel	Karel "Bala"	Hana	Pavel	Rudolf "Rudla"	Vladimír "Vláďa"
Franta					

*by marriage

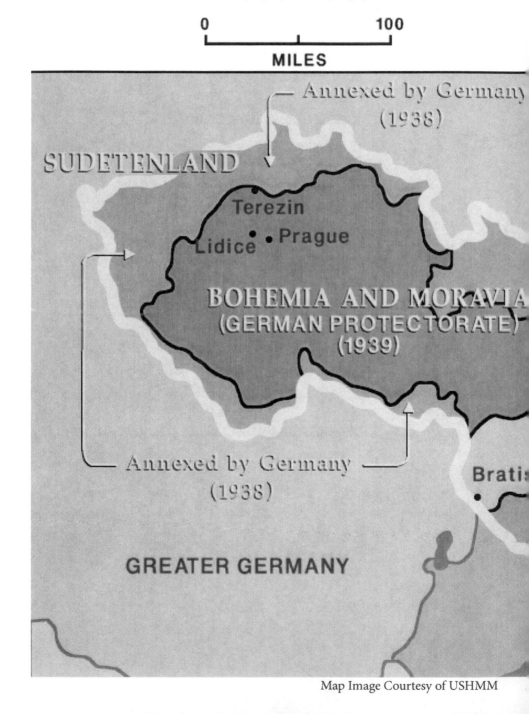

PARTITION OF CZECHOSLOVAK
1938–1939

0   100

MILES

Annexed by Germany
(1938)

SUDETENLAND

Terezin

Lidice   Prague

BOHEMIA AND MORAVIA
(GERMAN PROTECTORATE)
(1939)

Annexed by Germany
(1938)

Bratis

GREATER GERMANY

POLAND

N

CZECHOSLOVAKIA
1933 BOUNDARY

SLOVAKIA
(1939)
• Banska
Bystrica   • Kosice   • Uzhgorod
                        • Munkacs

—— Annexed by Hungary ——
(1938-1939)

HUNGARY

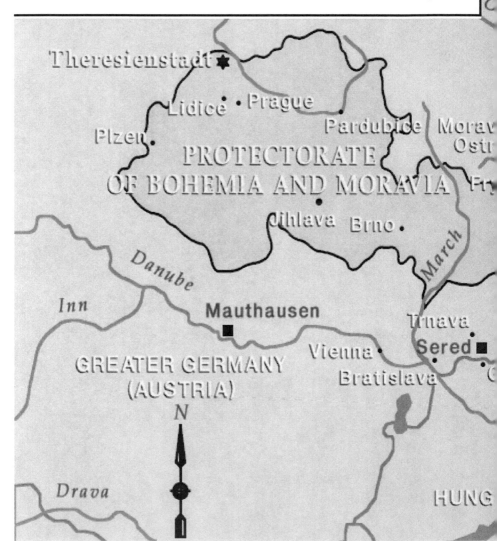

THERESIENSTADT GHETTO IN GERMAN PROTECTORATE OF BOHEMIA AND MORAVIA 1941–1945

- Cities
- ★ Ghettos
- ■ Concentration Camps
- ▣ Extermination Camps

Theresienstadt ★

Lidice · Prague

Plzen ·

Pardubice Morav
Ostr

PROTECTORATE
OF BOHEMIA AND MORAVIA

Jihlava Brno ·

Danube

March

Inn

Mauthausen ■

Trnava

Vienna · Sered ■
Bratislava

GREATER GERMANY
(AUSTRIA)

N

Drava

HUNG

Dr. Karel Chr. Schoenbaum.

NEW COLLEGE,

OXFORD.

31. III. 1940.

Dr.O.A.Holzer, Esq.
P.O.Box 1591,
SHANGHAI.

Drahý Valdíku,

i "obratem pošty" korespondence mezi námi teď
trvá hezky dlouho, že! Jsi někde daleko v kraji, který ani
pojmenovat neumím. Doprava trvá dlouho, ale ke všemu jsem
ještě tentokráte nemohl hned odepsati. Katka i já jsme měl
postupně řadu sezonních chorob, i jakési spalničky, které
tu řádily, German measles se to jmenuje, a většinou to je
docela lehké. Asi to co nyní skutečný "primář" budeš znát.
Ostatne hned k tomuto úspěchu přijmi naše velmi radostné a
upřimné blahopřání!- Také jsme měli klimatické chřipky atd.
ale jsme již zase zcela v pořádku. Jinak jsem měl nesmírně
mnoho práce. Věř mi, že se Škodovkouse to nedá srovnávati.
Tam mi sice docela slušně za to platili, ale přes to mne to
zde nějak více těší. Mnoho práce jsem měls přípravami 7.
března, kdy jsme tu měli dvě přednášky, či vlastně 3, presi-
denta Beneše, jenž také dostal čestný doktorát oxfordské
university. Asi jsi o tom již slyšel nebo četl, byla to vel
ká věc, jejíž význam hodně přesahuje rámec Oxfordu. My jsme
ve vypůjčeném fraku dělali honoraci při večeři na počest,
na čaji se samými potentáty atd. Ale na to si tu člověk už
nějak zvyknul. Druhý den také Dr. Beneš mluvil česky v na-
šem kroužku, jehož mám čest být předsedou. Sjelo se skoro
90 Čechoslováků a bylo to moc krásné, zase člověk načerpá
dův ery atd.   e by to Tobě bylo také udělalo moc

            e chápu Tvé rozhodnutí zůstat již v
            mů se dívat. Také dovedu nějak po-
            bude chtíti z Dálného Východu. Bez-
            k s několika velmi zajímavými Číňa-
            ktuálové to jsou-, a jednak s něko-
            m dlouho žili. Musí to býtô velkole
            užil se tam podívati. Tbe při tom
            že tam konáš velkou a užitečnou
            poměrně dost krátkou dobu jsi už
            upřimně, že to nové místo v nemoc
            obré, jak si jen sám můžeš přát.
            iresu, tak Ti ještě píšu do Shai.
            "Imrhýn". Také ten PUMC bychom Ti
            kou palce!

Chapter 3:

Karel Schoenbaum/

K. Charles Sheldon, JUDr.

Dramatis Personae

Karel Schoenbaum/K. Charles Sheldon, JUDr.

(Valdik's friend)

Paternal grandfather:	Mořic Schoenbaum
Parents:	Rudolf and Hedvička Schoenbaum
Uncles:	Karel Schoenbaum, Emil Schoenbaum
Brothers:	František "Franta" Schoenbaum (married to Andula) Honza Schoenbaum (married to Míša)
Sister:	Anka Neuman (née Schoenbaum)
Nieces:	Věra Neuman, Jarmila "Jerry" Held-Kovell (née Neuman)
Brother-in-law:	Kamil Neuman (originally Neumann)
Wife:	Kateřina "Katka" Schoenbaum (née Graber; later Mrs. George A. Pughe)
In-laws:	Eugene and Margaret "Mitzi" Graber
Daughter:	Carol Sheldon Hylton
Grandson:	Kevin Hylton

The sense of a true home has probably ceased to exist for our generation.

—Karel Schoenbaum, May 23, 1941

A mong the many kind gestures and sympathetic words that we received when my parents died was a note from Carol Sheldon Hylton.

> …I remember your parents and their importance
> to both my parents and me…Your father and mine
> had been friends from Czechoslovakia. His voice
> and laugh still ring in my ears. He shared jokes that
> I recall forty years later. Actually, as Mother and I
> talked about how many ways your parents and mine
> were connected, we spoke of your grandparents as
> well and our memories of them.

Carol's name brought back distant memories of her family's visit to our home when I was about nine years old. Her kind gesture was followed a week or so later by a note from her mother.

> …I would very much like to talk to you and share
> my memories. Your parents were such constructive,
> caring, and positive people. They will be greatly
> missed…I would like to embrace each of you and
> let you know that your parents' children will always
> be close to my heart.

I was touched, and eager to renew my connection to Carol and her mother. But I was also overwhelmed by the deaths of my parents within days of each other, and by all the obligations and duties that followed. I resolved to reach out to these kind and wonderful people as soon as the crush of events eased. Predictably, my busy life intervened. It was eight years before I shared Carol's laughter and felt the warmth of her mother's embrace. The catalyst for the long-delayed fulfillment of my resolution was a clue contained in the last of the eleven letters exchanged between my father and Karel Schoenbaum.

Karel was a superb writer. As I followed the emotional and evocative dialogue between these two old friends, I felt powerfully drawn to Karel as well as to Katka, the wife he never hesitated to admit he loved madly. Somehow, I felt like they were more to me than strangers who knew my father in another time, another world. And, as it turned out, I was right.

What I knew from the translated letters in my father's cache was that he and Karel were friends from childhood. I later learned that Karel's Jewish roots ran deep in my father's hometown of Benešov, where Karel's father, Rudolf, was a friend of Valdik's father, Arnošt. Rudolf operated a steel mill. Karel's grandfather Mořic, owner of a hardware store, was a friend of Valdik's grandfather Alois, the grocer.

Karel went to work as a young lawyer at the Škoda Company, a vast industrial enterprise that manufactured everything from automobiles to armaments. The Latin abbreviation from Juris Utrisque Doctor, JUDr, following his name denoted his law degree. Five years older than my father, Karel was thirty-one and still single when he reluctantly accepted an invitation from his parents to join them for dinner with fellow steel distributor Max Graber. Karel's hesitation melted when he met Graber's charming daughter, Kateřina, nicknamed Katka. Eleven years younger than Karel, Katka was a student at Charles University's law school. She had been born in Budapest, Hungary, but raised in Slovakia. Karel and Katka were married in Prague on October 24, 1938, first by a City Hall official (somewhat comparable to a Justice of the Peace) and then by a Roman Catholic priest.

Katka was about to take her final law school exams in March 1939 when Karel came home and said he'd received information at work that the German Army was about to invade Czechoslovakia. They needed to leave the country immediately. Without questioning, Katka helped him gather what they could. They wired money to London and left on a train from Prague's Wilson Station. The correspondence with my father started a few months later, after Karel secured a place at Oxford University and began work on his second doctorate. The first letter in the chronology, sent to my father in China from Karel in London on June 6, 1939, introduced an oft-reprised theme—Karel's disenchantment with their mutual friend, Bála.

> …These are strange times. Everyone is in a different part of the world. Who would have thought last year that we would live in a not exactly pretty, small room in a dirty section of London and write to you in some place far away in Asia? Maybe we'll meet there sometime soon or in the trenches.
>
> I read your letter to Bála. He will no doubt answer all your concrete questions, especially since you sent him a dollar for postage. I hope you will soon find yourself a job. I wish it for you. If I were to write to you about our life here, it is mainly that we are waiting. I run about the interminable streets of London and constantly try to find a way to get friends and relatives out of our homeland to which, God willing, we might return some day. In particular, I am trying to rescue my brothers, Honza and Franta, and my cousin Jirka, and my cousin Sušička. I would like to get them out and, of course, also friends, such as Jiří Glas, etc.
>
> As for me, I am fairly well when I don't think of the family. Katka is really a very good and efficient girl; not only does she do all the housework, but she makes a few extra shillings by taking care of two

47

children, and she learned how all by herself to press my suits, with a small electric iron. I must admit that the suit looks better than when done by the tailor. The English are very kind to us, especially when we don't want anything from them. They frequently invite us on the weekend for tea, etc., but as for a future, there isn't any, of course.

Katka followed on August 15, 1939, with her own note.

> ...I remember the clear day when you came to our [Prague] apartment, and you used the phone— and I was very upset that you talked so openly over the telephone. You and we are now outside; we are grateful for that, but what the future will bring, who knows? We hope for the best.

My father, meanwhile, had arrived in China in May. He made his way to Shanghai by way of Hong Kong. Shanghai was overrun with eastern European emigrants and after two months without any livelihood, Valdik found a temporary job in Tsingtao (Qingdao), nursing an elderly ill man back to health. As he was returning to Shanghai in September, war broke out in Europe. He wrote to Karel from Shanghai on September 14, 1939, sharing his national pride and uncertain circumstances.

> ...Naturally I immediately signed all the declarations and applications for the Czechoslovak Army in Shanghai, which put itself at the disposal of allied offices. I would prefer to leave for Europe immediately, but for now they don't want us there. I beg you, should you have any other information, convey it to me. We are looking forward to the Czechoslovak resistance also being successful; we believe in a beautiful future, and we are embittered about the conditions in our homeland. Daily we

sit at the Czechoslovak club, listen to the news from the whole world and debate passionately. The distance does not diminish our interest. We envy your being close to the source.

I got a position as the chief of an ambulatory hospital, which provides me with a decent living. I was just thinking about opening my own practice but now I have naturally postponed that. I don't know how much longer I will stay here but even after the end of the war I would probably return here.

In his reply from Oxford on November 15, 1939, Karel promised to pass along whatever he learned.

...I got a free place at Oxford University where I am preparing for my PhD studies. I am at the New College, which is not new but very old and very prestigious. Everybody is really nice and pleasant and apparently they like us, especially my wife, Kateřina. That won't surprise you! There are approximately thirty Czechoslovakians here and we have organized a small discussion group of which I was chosen the leader, and we do what we can. From home we have little news, nothing direct, of course.

But that which we know is in no way reassuring. About my parents I only know that they had to leave the villa in Bubeneč and they are either with the Nejedlýs {Andula's relatives} in Mezimostí or in our little house in Jevany [a village east of Prague]. Uncle Karel, whom I like so much, was arrested. My uncle Emil got out and will be a government consultant in Ecuador. My old friend Emil Sobička was apparently dragged to a concentration camp; Zdeněk Thon also taken, if he is alive. The Matuška family is relatively well off. The Slovaks are better off than those in the so-called Protectorate...

Germans used the term 'Protectorate' to signify that Bohemia and Moravia, as a result of Germany's 1939 military occupation, were shielded from independence and threat of other interventions. The Protectorate was established to create an illusion that the remaining government had some level of internal control.

Karel continued:

> ...We are already looking forward to the first sausages. Are you too? But what will they look like after all that?!

> It is interesting that you plan to return to the Far East after the war. We, too, wonder whether we should settle in some Anglo-Saxon country and then go home only for visits. But why should we wonder now when we really don't have any choices?

> As far as Bála and the other geniuses are concerned, they are in London "still busy" in the immigration office—or, more properly, immigration offices—where different contingencies never stop butting heads. We are glad to be out of that disgrace. When these people finally are in charge, we will see who is who and the fights and personal grievances will stop as well. It is sad, though, that the men of the Moscow religion have not acquitted themselves.

Four months later, Karel wrote from London on March 31, 1940, and excitedly relayed news that Oxford had presented an honorary doctorate to the Republic's second president, Edvard Beneš, who went on to lead the Czechoslovak government in exile in London.

> ...You have probably heard or read something about it; it was a big deal, the importance of which greatly

exceeds the framework of Oxford. We, in borrowed tuxedos, posed as notables during the dinner in his honor, at a tea party with all kinds of big shots, etc. But one has somehow gotten used to that here.

The next day Dr. Beneš also spoke in Czech to our club, of which I have the honor to be the chairman. Almost ninety Czechoslovaks came by, and it was really beautiful, as such a thing allows one to have some faith again. It seems you could do with some yourself as well…

About our folks I have no direct news; only thanks to the help of Anka and Kamil [his sister and brother-in-law in New York], but it takes a long time, and they always mention them quite opaquely. Kamil took additional medical exams in NYC, but he does not yet know the results so he has to keep on studying, just in case. Stupid world.

Karel noted his efforts to obtain permission for his brothers to leave Czechoslovakia.

…Now the question is, though, whether those scums will let them out. I am somewhat afraid, according to the last news, that it will not happen. About the conditions at home I have very precise and regular news, also thanks to listening to broadcasts from Prague. It is not cheerful, believe me, Valdik! Those of us who luckily got out early cannot even imagine. I remember how we were hunting for those documents and tickets together; it has just been a year! How the time flies.

The letter that you mention, the one that was supposed to be passed on to me by Bála, I never received. But we aren't in touch at all now. He is the only person with whom I had to, here in emigration, part in bad blood. He did not behave properly to Katka or me, and, mainly, he couldn't take the fact that I got this position here in Oxford.

I can understand his situation, with Milena and the children being in Prague, and I continue to have a lot of sympathy for him, particularly vis-à-vis this aspect. Though he bears a lot of guilt that Milena did not get here, he kept hesitating and fearing that life in exile would not be sufficiently comfortable, etc.

Above all, he doesn't allow himself to go without much. He is a person constantly driven by inner restlessness, incapable of staying in one place and without company for one second. In reality, I really pity him—after all, we were friends for a long time. He acted in a strange way, however, so what. Please send your letters directly, then.

Karel's mysterious, disintegrating relationship with Bála made me feel remorse over the struggle obviously overtaking these old friends in the stressful circumstances of war. Sadness poured over me as I read my father express his feelings about what was happening to his peers and himself, what he termed the "emigrant psychosis" in his letter to Karel from Ping Ting Hsien (Pingding County), Shansi (Shanxi) Province, written on May 18, 1940.

...It has been five months since I wrote my last letter to you; I consider this to be the endmost deadline to keep in regular touch. Since I just received your letter, it propelled me a little to make myself heard again. As I can see from it, you are thoroughly busy with your studies and social obligations. The only thing in your letter that vexes me is your relationship with Bála. Believe me, it is this emigrant psychosis that causes one, for a trifle, to part even with people with whom one has been friends for years.

The whole emmie milieu has a malign effect and I am happy I managed to totally extricate myself from it; in Shanghai I would have probably turned the whole Czech community into my enemies. I was rebuked for all kinds of things: for having too many foreign friends…lukewarm patriotism and who knows what else. Now, when I am far away from this witch hunt, I am a decent member of the National Club, who pays his membership fees regularly.

But it was my father's analysis of the Czechoslovak experiment with Jewish assimilation that caused my greatest pain, knowing how lonely my father was as he thought about his young life and his acceptance in the world.

…I think you did not correctly understand my decision to stay abroad, or better said, my reasons for it. It is not for the love or liking of the Far East. You can believe me that I feel at home in Bohemia. But lately, especially lately, I have been thinking much about all that I have lived through and then I came to the realization that I was always considered a second-degree citizen, that I never had full rights in my homeland and that it was really implied to me everywhere that I was only being tolerated.

Do you think that all this will change; do you really think that this present equality of sorts will last even after an eventual return to our homeland? Do you think that the various elements set against each other will again be able to unite toward some positive work?

You know in these matters I am a great pessimist. This is the main reason why I don't want to return and then, this so-called Czech feeling of mine was hurt too deeply. I never felt like and I don't feel like a Jew. That's the tragedy, yet now I see that the non-Jewish Czechs never really embraced me. I think it is the tragedy of all of us assimilated ones, of the second and third generations.

Possibly it is a mistake to try to adjust again in yet another country, but I am determined not to return to live this way. Maybe you discussed this issue in your Club, and I would surely be most interested in your opinion about our future in the eventual Third Republic. This is where I am turning to you for help, and I beg you to write to me according to your best knowledge and conscience.

My father's poignant disaffection as an assimilated Jew in Central Europe's most democratic country made me wonder about the effect of centuries of religious, ethnic, national, class, and linguistic conflict and persecution on its society. I realized that at that moment in his life, my father had decided an important piece of my own future.

Although at the time he was obviously not deeply connected to his Jewish heritage, his contemplation on how to move forward meant his future children would lead another kind of life. From information I gleaned many years after he wrote this letter, I realized that he was not alone in his analysis of Czech history in terms of a centuries-long ethnic and religious conflict. In 2001, a year after my father's death, Czech Republic census information showed that a remarkable 59 percent of the population identified themselves as belonging to no religion. For Jewish residents of Czechoslovakia, modern-day forces were constantly working against them, including WWII atrocities followed by an oppressive Communist regime. What remains is one of the smallest Jewish communities in Europe.

The next letter, written by Karel from Oxford on July 19, 1940, boosted my spirits when I learned of Karel and Katka's relationship and their determination to trudge forward through the morass of disaster.

> ...It would be wonderful to meet again and exchange experiences. You will probably have more of them than all of us! Maybe we will, in spite of everything, find each other sometime somewhere again, but we will have changed much, most of all those unfortunates who had to remain there. It was greatly interesting for me to read your thoughts about the possibility of return and the tragedy of assimilation. You are very often correct—in the days of your solitude you must have thought about it much, am I correct? We who are here have slightly different opinions, maybe wrong, and possibly only the result of "wishful thinking"?

> But then, we often notice all kinds of things even here; I mean, among fellow countrymen. I am not immodest but I think few have done so much successful publicity for our cause in England as I. Particularly for the Oxford Masaryk Society, to which I attracted a large number of members; to their board, the most notable personalities, etc. These English friends are now considered old collaborators working for our cause...

> I pity everyone who has to endure emigration alone—therefore I can also understand, though not excuse, Bála's dirty actions. At the same time, it is their own fault that he and Milena are not

together, since they were afraid that they would have to live in penury here; and he got a bit used to "freedom" again, so he did not exhaust every possibility to bring his family here. Otherwise I don't know anything about Bála, except for his occasional "shows," and I do not wish to know.

Do believe me, Valdik; I do not have any emigrant psychosis, as you call it. On the contrary, I have much more, and certainly much more interesting, work than I ever had at home. We also do not suffer from less human contact and you know my wish was always to work in science and not in the Škoda factory. However, worries for our folks are bad and, all in all, there aren't many reasons for happiness. But one has to go on and has to try to lead a decent human life, without compromising on one's moral tenets, if one has any.

The current times also do not help to calm the nerves during periods of convalescence. My logical thought is that the reasons for this "setback" stems from the hardships and worries of the past two years, with which Katka always put up, with remarkable courage but which were accumulating and only came to the fore now, when her body was weakened by the surgery. Starting with the tragic death of her father, the escape from Prague, etc., to the current gnawing anxiety that our military will send me to crumbling France—all that influenced her condition.

In the same letter, Karel also shared a possible major change in the course of their lives, resulting from a telegram from Karel's sister.

...They are securing visas for us to get to Uncle Emil...to Ecuador. He also urges us to go there.

But currently this is impossible—if for nothing else but lack of boat tickets. But otherwise it might not be bad.

In this same letter, two months before my father fell head over heels for the woman he would love for sixty years, Karel remarked about something my father had written earlier.

> ...Your life in Peking must have really been beautiful, but as you say, "Nothing lasts forever, not even love for one miss." As far as this sentence is concerned, I have objections to it, since if such a miss grows into such a wonderful woman as Katka, then it is something completely different!

Katka appended a note:

> Karel praises me much in the letter—should I start writing about him, the sheet of paper would not suffice. And so I will leave it to the occasion when we will tell each other personally.

By his next letter to Karel, written from Peking in September 1940, the shifting fortunes of war had forced my father to move again, once more disrupting his already irregular flow of news from home.

> ...I haven't had any news from any of our acquaintances for quite some time now. They are probably writing to me directly to Shansi Province, from which I strategically escaped the Red [Chinese Communist] occupation a few days ago. All my correspondence that is addressed there has been hanging in limbo somewhere on the road for four weeks already and so I don't even have news from home. I have to hope that all is well there.
>
> As I have already said, I left the hospital in the interior. On August 16, I had to leave for Peking in

order to shop [for Brethren Hospital supplies]. We constantly had some troubles, to which I attached little importance. During my absence, however, these escalated to the point that a few days after my departure it was no longer possible to return to the place, since in the meantime the government changed. All communications were disrupted; I hope only temporarily and that soon all will be fine again.

Nevertheless, I do not have the intention to go back, and I am looking for a job in Peking or Tientsin [Tianjin]. I am, however, still an employee of the mission and I still receive my pay; therefore I am living like I were on a holiday. I now work in the PUMC [Peking Union Medical College] hospital, which is one of the most modern institutions in the world. It is quite possible that I will have to stay, which would be splendid.

He noted that propaganda praising Hitler (whom he referred to by the disparaging diminutive "Adík") and exhorting Asians to rise up against the British was being broadcast on a Nazi radio station in Shanghai.

…Despite all that misery I am still a great optimist. Unfortunately, I fear that all this idiocy will take terribly long and cost much blood and many cultural values will be destroyed by this barbarian invasion. Sometimes I tend to compare all of this with the Chinese fatalism I observe. You wouldn't even believe how sensible those old Chinese seem to me now, with all their antiquated proverbs and remedies…

It would really be great fun if we met once again at home; surely we would all have plenty of things to report. I am a bit afraid though that it will never happen. Many of us, who will somehow manage to get a hold abroad, won't yearn for return, except maybe only just to show their son where Daddy was born.

I was struck by my father's prophetic words. I instantly recalled how in 1983 he took my brother Tom, the oldest of his three children, to Benešov to show Tom his birthplace.

By the time the next letter was written, it was Karel and Katka who were on the move. This time, they wrote from "on board R.M.S. *Orduna*...Somewhere between Cuba and Cristóbal," on September 3, 1940.

> ...You might be a bit surprised to see where we are writing to you from this time, but things are happening really fast nowadays and fates change overnight or even faster!

> Last time we mentioned to you an opportunity of possibly joining Uncle Emil in Ecuador, and we have now been on the ship for almost four weeks already. Anka and Kamil and Uncle Emil got us visas, but we did not believe we would be able to secure a departure permit and tickets for the boat. Then both suddenly arrived, and we only had a few days to do everything: packing, closing down our little household, which we loved so much, a few most essential purchases, etc. There was no time left to part with many and many good friends, except for a handful of the closest ones, both locally and figuratively. Then, after a few feverish days and nights, we set out for the port and felicitously got all the way here.

> We nonetheless experienced a few adventures and maybe we will one day tell them to you. They will

make for interesting stories, but so far it is too hot for that. In your last letter you wrote that you have to finish, since your thoughts were starting to fry on account of the heat. Well, now we can imagine it precisely—though I think mine have all evaporated already.

The sea lies all around without movement; the flying fish can't stand the warm water and jump out, but the air is even warmer and so, frustrated, they return to it again. We are suffering here from the heat quite a bit, particularly at night when the windows on the whole ship have to be shut and blacked out. But nothing doing; we have to be grateful to God and the Navy that they have taken us so far so securely, and we hope that the rest of the journey will pass safe; you as well, too.

On the ship there is a collection of all possible, and also impossible, people, and it would be an interesting opportunity for a study, if one did not have so many other worries. We are also learning Spanish. It's going quite hard and slow, particularly in this heat. But in Havana I spoke a little and could make myself understood, though one little black boy—to whom I explained in fluent Spanish that he was not going to get another penny—told me that he did not understand English. So I don't know.

Soon I was immersed in the news of Karel and Katka's life in Quito, Ecuador, and their congratulations to my father on his surprise marriage to my mother. In September 1940, Karel wrote:

Dear Valdík and dear Mrs. Holzer!

Both of your letters—the first one from September 11, and the second one from October 24—arrived here almost simultaneously. The first one was still addressed to Oxford and was forwarded to us here. From the second one we learned only little, except for the happy news of your marriage and of clearly making a lucky choice. As soon as we opened the letter and the picture fell out of it—by the way, a very nice one!—we told ourselves: "Valdík married well." Mrs. "Chick" [Ruth Lequear Holzer's nickname] reminds us unbelievably of one of our best friends, Mrs. Roddy Lobel, MA, etc., from Oxford, really a dear person and in every sense lovable. Just for that we immediately took a liking to her and if she is a wife of our old friend on top of it, there is nothing more to add. We therefore ask you to accept our sincere congratulations not only on your marriage, but also for Christmas and besides that, wishes of much happiness and good in the New Year 1941! We wish you that all your wishes come true and that the New Year brings us all a bit of calm, finally, and particularly better fortune to our dear ones at home!

We are also pleased by your news about the strides you have made as far as your knowledge of the Chinese language is concerned. Such knowledge can do no harm to us, though now more and more people have to assimilate knowledge of quite distant lands and tongues.

Katka goes daily to sew ladies' dresses, to one acquaintance of hers from Prague who opened up a "salon" here. I am in the meantime chasing after some earnings; I was promised a position as a "professor" but they keep on delaying it. You probably know that in these territories one magic word rules and that is "mañana"—i.e., "tomorrow."

They themselves sometimes add "mañana nunca viena"—"tomorrow will not come."

And so I keep waiting while our little capital is dwindling, but somehow we managed before and somehow we will manage in the future. That's the philosophy of today, isn't it? We nevertheless hope that one day our turn will come and we will depart for a country that, probably mistakenly, all people in our situation consider the Promised Land—USA...

Here in the Czechoslovak colony, squabbles and intrigues rule. As soon as we arrived, we were informed we were not to talk to this one and that one and that the only decent, politically reliable, and credible person is our very informant...

Maybe the English setting was less favorable to intrigue or maybe our people were more political and less personal and grudging—with some very bad exceptions, naturally—or maybe we didn't notice it that much, living in the beautiful, cultural Oxford milieu and more among the English. Whichever is correct, it is not too cheerful here.

Here we arrived well; we found the country better than the horrific stories that had been circulating about Ecuador on our ship, however only among émigrés. We were told that soap or toothbrushes could not be bought there and one had to supply oneself with such things beforehand, that there were a hundred churches per one bathroom, etc. We have a beautiful, white-tiled bathroom, almost better than we had in Bubeneč—of course it is a modern villa in the modern quarter, which we inhabit together with Aunt and Uncle, paying our share. It is not inexpensive here, though. And that bathroom has the disadvantage that during the dry season, when there is no rain for several days, there is no water, since we are up on a hill. But one could live here quite nicely, if one had some earnings.

In terms of landscape, it is one of the most beautiful countries in the world. The climate here in Quito is healthy and agreeable, since we are about 2.800 meters above the sea level and so one can sometimes hardly believe we are only twenty miles from the equator. Nights are often cool and it is never too hot. One disadvantage, however, is the thin air lacking oxygen. Breathing and sleeping are thus sometimes difficult.

There is much filth and one has to protect oneself against infections, particularly intestinal ones. I already went through one. At first, it looked like paratyphoid, but it was nothing serious. One advantage is there is no malaria here, up at this altitude.

People are mostly mixed—Indian, black, Spanish immigrants, and whatever else. Up here, maybe because of the climate, they are mostly of a peaceful nature, lazy and good-hearted, it seems. There is, however, much theft. Well, I think I have written to you, dear Valdík, almost too much.

I worried constantly about Karel's two younger brothers, Franta and Honza, and Franta's wife, Andula, left behind under Nazi domination. What became of them? Over time I would learn of immigration opportunities and failed attempts to get them to places like Bolivia, China, and Ecuador, like this mention by Karel from Ecuador in December 1940.

...We are at least trying to get our Franta with Andula and the boy here, and [my younger brother] Honza; my parents might be too old for this trouble. It is one of our main reasons for being here, so that we could do something for the less fortunate back home who have been suffering. We already have certain assurance about visas, I also sent some forms home to be filled out, and I hope that regardless of the unreliability of the local people, who rarely keep their promises, we will be able to achieve our goal. Money cannot play a role in this situation; we hired a famous attorney, so he can take care of the important stuff for us. Franta wrote that he may be forced to leave to go to Shanghai, but it seems the danger of that has passed. What news do you have? I hope it's good, if that is possible!

And then once again Karel and Katka's life changed, as they set off to the "Promised Land," the United States—a place where freedom and political liberty was guaranteed to all citizens; a country whose U.S. Constitution inspired Czechoslovakia's First Republic founding president Tomáš Garrigue Masaryk as he led formation of their own government in 1918. Karel wrote to my father from Ecuador on May 23, 1941.

...We will leave on June 12 from Guayaquil by the Chilean ship *Aconcagua*, which should arrive in New York on June 23...But write to us, just in case, at the address of [my in-laws] Anka and Kamil—just to be sure I am repeating it here: 1264 Crane Street, Schenectady, NY. I hope that your news will be waiting for us there. Here we fared very well, recently. I even got a house, so that we can return here should we want to; already tomorrow

I should receive definitive visas for my parents and brother [Franta]. The cable should have already been sent to the Consulate, so you know this has raised our spirits a bit, even though, otherwise, the news is not positive...

We are both, thank God, healthy; we are looking forward to the States, though we know there aren't only pleasant things awaiting us, but that's how it is. Here we are again, leaving a few good friends, and so it always is. The sense of a true home probably ceased to exist for our generation. Maybe it is for the better...

Thank you for the letter from Franta. We can happily see that he is as vulgar in his language and thinking as always. His humor is a little mischievous, but we hope their [Franta and Andula's] spirits will be lifted when he receives the actual visa, not just promises.

It saddened me that Karel would mention that a "sense of a true home" ceased to exist for his generation in a context that included "maybe it is for the better." I knew what loyal young Czechs they had been during the First Republic. But it was good to know that his sister, Anka, and her husband, Kamil Neuman, were finding their way around in America. From this news, I thought Karel's parents must have escaped the Holocaust, but Franta's visa quest still seemed uncertain. And then, as I read Karel's handwritten note of June 28, 1941, the last letter of his my father had saved, I was filled with joy as he wrote of their arrival.

...We arrived on Sunday last in New York and are really happy to be here in this country. We received a very enthusiastic reception from my sister Anka, her old friend Jeníček and his daughter Mima

Lowenbach, Jiřina Edwards, and last but not least, by Columbia University Professor J.P. Chamberlain [Karel's friend from Oxford], who took us to his beautiful house.

It was near the end of this final letter that Karel left a vital clue for me to find so many decades after he had written it.

...In our first entry papers application we changed our name to Sheldon—there are no difficulties or fees for this and we thought it wise to do. Do you like it?

I loved it! Like a brilliant spark arcing across the decades, the name Sheldon instantly linked Karel to Carol Sheldon Hylton. She was his daughter! This was the woman who had reached out to me in 2000 when my parents died—and now all I had to do was connect the dots. I realized I'd had my own link all along to these people whose letters had drawn me so close. I had re-read Carol's note not long before, as I began the daunting task of cross-checking all my father's correspondence against every possible source of family lore. The pack rat instinct I inherited from Dad served me well as I retrieved the box of sympathy cards from the back of a closet. I located Carol in Washington, DC, by telephone and on August 10, 2008, the relationship that began when we were little girls was reestablished.

After recovering from the surprise of my call, Carol went on to tell a story involving my father and his fancy red Alfa Romeo convertible. It was 1957 and they had gone for a ride on a cloudy Florida day, when it began to rain. My father, wearing his favorite plaid sports car riding hat, listened as Carol inquired about the need to put the convertible top up. She laughed, remembering his twinkling eyes as he replied, "Don't worry. I don't need to put the top up. I can drive faster than the raindrops."

And without missing a beat, Carol and I said aloud the Chinese grace my missionary mother had taught us both and started giggling.

Carol, divorced and a few years older than I, worked as an instructional specialist in Maryland's Montgomery County School District. She also held a full-time caretaker job, as she lived with her ninety-one-year-old mother. First widowed in 1958 after Karel's death, Katka was widowed for a second time after a long and loving marriage to George A. Pughe, Jr., a native of Colorado. I could feel the pressure Carol lived under when she said she wasn't able to "visit my family history since work and home swallow me."

At last, in November 2008, I flew to Washington for a week of research at the United States Holocaust Memorial Museum. I pored over primary sources for information on my forty-four relatives who perished in the Holocaust. I also sought records for several names from the letters, including the Schoenbaum family of Benešov and Prague. I learned that Karel's mother and father likely died in Auschwitz. After a long and exhausting day, I took a taxi to a comfortable home on Chain Bridge Road to get the answers to my long list of questions. I immediately felt the warm welcome of old friends in a home filled to the brim with personal treasures. Memories were everywhere. Nicely dressed for my visit, both women led me to the dining room where Carol had prepared a sumptuous meal.

Katka was still the tender woman I had met in the letters. Petite, with short hair, polished-looking like I imagined the ladies at Mánes, she was soft-spoken but had a strong spirit emanating from within. She was anxious to visit her past in conversation. Her daughter Carol, dark-haired and outgoing, exhibited a quick humor and a loving, protective manner toward her frail aging mother as she helped her make her way to the table.

As we began to banter about names and places, I found Katka's memory a little faded but still able to provide details about the

Slowly Valdik rose, chest puffed as he strode up the aisle. When he reached the lobby door, laughter broke out, followed by wild applause, as Valdik's many friends realized he had staged his moment. There was an electric feeling in the gilded hall as Valdik, holding his noble chin high, pumped his hands in the air and acknowledged his standing ovation. The usher, paid by Valdik before anyone arrived, had ensured everyone in the theater learned that the twenty-five-year-old Valdik had just achieved his lifelong goal of becoming a physician. I would hear the same story again a year later from my father's cousin, Pavel Mařík.

Katka recalled Mánes Café but could not describe how it looked; only that before the Nazi occupation, it was a place where all her friends gathered in the evening to have fun. Katka would start an anecdote but sometimes her mind grew fuzzy in the middle of the tale. Pushing back in her chair, sitting up straight, Carol would then pick up where Katka left off, obviously repeating familiar stories with great pride.

When Katka reflected on her dual wedding ceremonies, I asked why one took place in a Catholic Church, as both she and Karel were Jewish. I knew from my research that, at that time, many European Jews married as Catholics, hoping it might shield them from persecution. It rarely worked. Katka seemed puzzled by my question. She said her family hadn't practiced the Jewish faith, and her mother had been a Lutheran. This prompted Carol to tell me she was Episcopalian. Although her son Kevin had been raised in the Episcopal Church, he converted to Judaism and identified himself as Modern Orthodox.

I was reminded once again how complicated religious affiliation, particularly Judaism, and its links to ethnicity had become for Czechs during the interwar period. Raised in America as a non-Jew and without much discussion with my father about the setting

70

in which he grew up, I may never fully understand how Dad, or for that matter Katka and all their friends, really felt about these thorny matters. After all, the Czechoslovak government recognized Jews as a nationality until 1939. When the Nazis arrived in March 1939, they didn't consider Jews Czechoslovak citizens but rather defined them according to the Nuremberg Laws, and deemed them unworthy of citizenship.

Subsequent regulations attached to the Nuremberg Laws defined a Jew as someone with at least three Jewish grandparents (according to their religious affiliation), someone descended from two Jewish grandparents who practiced the Jewish religion or who was married to a Jew, or the child of an intermarriage (referred to as a *Geltungsjude*). A person with two Jewish grandparents, but without Jewish religious affiliations and not married to a Jew, came to be defined as a *Mischling* (literally, a mutt), a cross- or half-breed of mixed blood. Legally, had I been alive at that time, I would have been classified as a "*Mischling* of the first degree" or *Mischling ersten Grades*.

Up until 1939, my father chose to self-identify on census and other official forms as Czech rather than as a Jew. Many others within the population thought of Judaism as an ethnic designation, as opposed to a religious faith, and on these same forms identified as Jewish. At the time, some in my father's group may have been contradicting the predominant way of thinking—creating twists and turns that forever changed their lives and the lives of those who followed.

As I waded into unfamiliar (and emotionally dangerous) territory, I was swept away. I was the religiously non-Jewish heir to the ethnic persecution of Jews in a context that recognized Jewishness as a religious category only. Simply adjusting your avenue of faith provided no safe protection from the Nazi atrocities that followed.

I decided to drop the topic and asked Katka to pick up the threads of the story told in Karel's letters. She graciously agreed, weaving together the details of their prewar lives and their harrowing flight to freedom.

Their train from Prague was "the last sealed train, one way through Germany to the west. You could not get out along the way." At the station, a Nazi policeman pushed a rifle in her face, demanding that she give him her wedding ring. She refused. Her eyes filled with sorrow as she described Karel's mother, Hedvička, coming to see them off, carrying overflowing bags of food that she insisted they take on the train. Soon after, the German Army marched into Prague.

When Karel and Katka arrived in London, they discovered the money they'd wired there had never arrived. They tried to sell a gold cigarette case to a man who refused to take it, saying it was not gold. Later they found out the case was indeed gold.

Like most immigrants, Katka had some difficulty understanding a new culture and suffered anxiety. She remembered in Haverford, Pennsylvania being asked to pour tea at the Quaker Circle and thinking it seemed demeaning, only to learn later that the group had meant to give her an honor.

While living in London, Katka saw her mother Margaret (Mitzi) when she came in need of her daughter's signature in order to sell their family business. Margaret returned to the Protectorate and continued to live there during the war and throughout most of the period of Communist rule. She left when she was smuggled out of the country in the trunk of her son-in-law Gustav's car and died a free woman on January 2, 1974, at eighty-three years of age.

In August 1940, once again on short notice, Katka packed their few belongings and left with Karel in a convoy of ships that assembled in Liverpool for the trip to Ecuador. As they sailed away, they saw a ship explode behind them as it hit a mine in the water. Obviously this was one of the adventures Karel had alluded to in his letter to my father. Karel's uncle, Emil Schoenbaum, met them when they arrived in Ecuador. Emil's contributions to the actuarial profession would become known worldwide. Before the war, he was a famous Charles University mathematician, responsible for the Two Year Cycle of Insurance Mathematics and Mathematical Statistics. Smarter than most, Emil left Prague a few days before the German occupation. When Karel and Katka arrived in Ecuador, Emil was working for the International Labor Office. After they left for America, he worked for the Social Insurance Commission of Mexico, essentially creating a Social Security system. Emil's contribution in 1942 to the reform of miners' insurance in Bolivia was well documented. He returned to Prague after the war, but left again after the Communist takeover in 1948 and became a citizen of Mexico, where he died in 1967.

In coming to America, Karel and Katka followed Karel's sister Anka, who had emigrated before the war with her husband, Dr. Kamil Neuman. Anka brought Katka's fine china and Karel's favorite tailcoat and collection of 78-rpm records. She mailed the tailcoat to London for Karel to wear when he accompanied Czechoslovak President-in-Exile Edvard Beneš to visit the Queen. Karel was at Oxford University at the time, active with the Masaryk Society. I thought about how objects have lives; often they seem to have witnessed important things and carry with them the shadows of experiences. The desk my father made the year I was born held such meaning for me. Some may say old letters are simply objects; I would not.

In spite of having two PhDs, Karel sold underwear in Macy's department store after arriving in America. For a short while in 1942, Karel and Katka shared a home with my parents in Forest Hills, New York, while my father worked for Dr. J. J. Eller on First Avenue. Katka recalled the friendship she developed with my young, effervescent mother as they rode the subway together to their jobs.

During and after the war, Karel was the head of the Czech Desk of the Voice of America (VOA) and a Czech commentator for their broadcasts. He was also an editor of one of the New York Czech newspapers. In 1945, Katka gave birth to her only child, Carol, who was featured on the newspaper's cover, crawling into New Year's 1946.

The young family relocated to the Palisades section of Washington, DC, in 1951, when the VOA moved from New York City to Washington. Encouraged by US Senator Joseph McCarthy and his infamous Communist witch hunt, some members of Congress launched attacks to discredit the State Department, claiming the VOA could never be the true voice of America while the State Department managed it.

This was a time in America when McCarthy enthusiasts dramatically increased the burden of proof placed on Americans whom they suspected to be subversives, making people not only responsible to prove their own innocence but also to prove that their friends and coworkers weren't Communists. As Czech Desk Chief, Karel ended up in the spotlight of Communist paranoia; an odd position because, by then, the Communist Party had taken over his homeland and Karel clearly wasn't supportive of that.

Caught in the midst of political debate, Karel was cited as holding too high a position for a foreign-born national. He had a choice of bumping someone ranked below him in position or leaving. He chose to leave and spent the last years of his life selling real estate in Washington, DC. Katka worked as a senior research analyst at the Library of Congress from 1951 until 1969. The Sheldons and the Holzers remained friends, visiting periodically in Washington and Florida.

Katka and Karel had been married almost twenty years when Karel died in 1958 of multiple myeloma in the prime of his life, three weeks shy of his fifty-second birthday. Katka was left alone to support her teenage daughter. She met her second husband, George Pughe, at the Library of Congress.

Among the languages Katka spoke were Hungarian, Czech, Slovak, German, French, English, and Spanish. Her appreciation for democracy and the freedoms America afforded was exemplified in a story her daughter Carol shared with me about how, even at her advanced age, Katka ardently followed the debate over how the United States treated detainees at Guantanamo during the Iraq War. She wanted to ensure that the rights we wrote into our constitution were available to all, equally.

The biggest disappointment in my puzzle-solving attempts with Katka was that she had no memory of a man named Bála, commenting only that his name sounded Hungarian. Two months later, I asked her again, after I'd learned his full name. She still did not recognize it. Thinking about the situation that unfolded in those letters, I felt as though I were standing over the carcass of a failed friendship between two men who obviously had been good friends before war drew out the complexities in each man's character. Their obvious rancor must have been disheartening to this kind and cultured woman who adored her husband. Over Katka's long life, I believe she simply erased the thorny recollections of Bála from her mind. I was glad that the memories she retained of my parents were still positive and enduring.

And there was more. Carol told me, "Joseph Korbel, Madeleine Albright's father, was one of my father's best friends from Czechoslovakia and their friendship continued in America."

During our conversation, when stumped for answers, Carol often repeated, "Oh, Jerry will know that." Kamil and Anka Neuman had settled in Schenectady, New York, with their daughters, Věra and Jarmila, known as Jerry. Věra had passed away but Jerry was "the cousin with all the family information," according to Carol. She would become my critical contact in discovering information about another Schoenbaum letter writer—Franta.

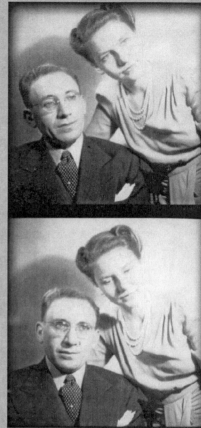

LEFT COLUMN TOP TO BOTTOM: KAREL SCHOENBAUM (LATER SHELDON); SCHOENBAUM CHILDREN (KAREL, FRANTA, ANKA, HONZA) WITH UNIDENTIFIED OTHERS.

RIGHT COLUMN TOP TO BOTTOM: KAREL AND KATKA/K. CHARLES SHELDON; KATKA

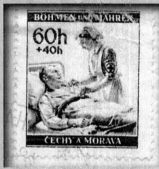

Left column: top left, Karel and Katka in Ecuador w/Karel's Uncle Emil Schoenbaum & wife; Carol Sheldon Hylton & son Kevin; Katka, K. Charles & daughter Carol.

Right column: Carol Sheldon, K. Charles Sheldon. (Photos courtesy of family)

Praha, leden 15., 1940

Milý Valdo,

Když jsem Ti posledně psal, nadhodil jsem, zda bys měl možnost sehnat mi místo šoféra, komorníka nebo něčeho podobného. Dnes jsem mluvil s nějakým člověkem, který jede do Číny a říkal, že se tam možno dostat; buď s 400 $ nebo s pracovní smlouvou. Vzhledem k tomu, že zmíněný obnos nemám, zbývá naděje č. 2, jež byla ovšem sám — ev. s Horsou neb Bratrem, pokud by to odneslo. Je-li něco podobného možné, buď tak laskav a napiš mi upřímně jsou-li pro mne možnosti.

Od Tvých rodičů mám o Tobě zprávy věčně s příznivé. Vaši jsou zdrávi a zcela v pořádku a chovají se ke mně velmi laskavě. Žijí s Andulou,

K Praha... Honzy v Jvanelle. Je ... ale všichni pohromadě ... tam je klid, což nám ... Praze za účelem ocko... ... den jedeme ... Andula chce připsat, tak sebe končí

Chapter 4:

František "Franta" Schoenbaum

Dramatis Personae

František "Franta" Schoenbaum

(Valdik's friend)

Paternal grandfather:	Mořic Schoenbaum
Parents:	Rudolf and Hedvička Schoenbaum
Uncles:	Karel Schoenbaum, Emil Schoenbaum
Brothers:	Karel Schoenbaum (married to Katka), Honza Schoenbaum (married to Míša)
Sister:	Anka Neuman (née Schoenbaum)
Brother-in-law:	Kamil Neuman (originally Neumann)
Sister-in-law:	Míša Šeba) and Katka Schoenbaum
Wife:	Andula "Anna" Schoenbaum (née Nejedlá; later Mrs.Pepík Lekner)
Sons:	Honza Schoenbaum (later John Lekner) Martin Schoenbaum (later Lekner)
Nieces:	Carol Sheldon Hylton (Karel's daughter), Jarmila "Jerry" Held-Kovell and Věra Neuman (Anka's daughters)
Nephew:	Michal Šeba (Honza's son)
Grandnephews:	Andy Held (Jarmila's son) and Steven Charles Held (Jarmila's sons) and Kevin Hylton (Carol's son)

I can hardly believe that I ever laughed.

—Franta Schoenbaum, December 1, 1945

Swept up in a maelstrom of war and genocide, my father's generation lost more than most of us can fathom, but Karel's brother, Franta Schoenbaum, didn't lose his sense of humor.

One of the first letters I read from the collection was from Franta. Writing from Prague just after the war, on December 1, 1945, he summed up the devastation of his homeland and his people.

> It wasn't pretty. I think it is best depicted by this joke: Three Hebrews meet in 1938, and one says he is going to Brazil. The other is going to Canada. The third says he is staying home. The two others nod their heads and say, "Yes, you were always such an adventurer."

The joke wasn't original, but it was typical of Franta's dry and inexhaustible wit—as I learned when the long process of translating and studying the letters finally reached the point where I could figure out Franta's unique place in the puzzle that was my father's life.

Because of the sheer volume of letters, I divided them among five different translators. As a result, I didn't receive the English versions in chronological order or sorted by author. Reading them was like listening to the random voices of strangers, one after another, as if flipping among radio stations. To bring sense to the process, I created a large database that captured not only details—dates, locations, and relationships—but also every name mentioned in each letter. The list eventually totaled more than three hundred names. At first these souls were strangers, but after two years, I knew them all and how they were connected.

Like Karel, Franta Schoenbaum shared both Benešov roots and a family friendship with my father's kin. There were four Schoenbaum siblings: Karel was born in 1906; the only girl, Anka, followed in 1908; then came Franta in 1910; and Honza in 1913. Franta was five months older than my father. I suspect that helps explain why their letters show a more playful, even rowdy, tone than the ones Dad exchanged with Karel. It's also clear that Valdik and Franta enjoyed the traditional, earthy Czech male sense of humor, often referencing various anatomy parts to make an off-color joke, no matter how desperate their situation was. Valdik and Franta wrote with enduring hope, believing that a better day would come, even when they faced horrors and atrocities.

Unlike Karel and Anka, Franta and his little brother Honza stayed behind in Czechoslovakia during the German occupation, experiencing a grim and tenuous existence that makes Franta's good humor all the more remarkable. As I read through the entire collection of letters, Franta and his wife, Andula, became my favorite characters in my father's wartime dialogue. Franta was one of the first people my father heard from when he reached the exotic Chinese port of Shanghai, and their close friendship enriches all their letters.

One sent by my father from Shanghai, on July 20, 1939, to Franta in Mezimostí in Southern Bohemia, was apparently a reply to a letter that has been lost. It included an uncharacteristically detailed account of my father's new life.

> ...If some of you are in a bad way perhaps, come here, as it is better here, despite all the misery, than in Prague or in Europe in general. Especially, one can work here, and I will be already sitting someplace with a medical practice by that time, so I could help you. One would not stay here forever, but it's somewhat easier to get to other countries from here.
>
> You have no idea how happy you made me with that letter of yours. You know, when a man does

not hear that dialect of ours anymore, at least he can have something enjoyable to read again.

To tell you the truth: the distance is not so big and it does not seem so huge, but I am damn homesick for everyone and for everything, particularly when a man is almost totally without news and when he does not know when, and if at all, he will return. Such thoughts develop in your head only after some time. Do not be angry that I am responding to your cheerful letter with such sentimental jabbering, but it is called "S'ai depression" here and supposedly everybody goes through it during the initial phase. After all, you know that is not my nature.

I hope that in your literary hellhole you will also mention the good physician Osvald Holzer who left his mother country to treat poor little Chinese. In order for you to elaborate on this topic better, I am sending you the following contribution:

So already for three days, I have been partially pummeled by malaria, I caught it somewhere in Saigon, stupid French Indochina, but it is better than tuberculosis. Hey, one must always be content. I am curing it by myself, chiefly with whiskey, which is dreadfully cheap here...

Otherwise, it is possible to catch in this beautiful but crappy country everything from measles to leprosy. Hey, so that I won't forget, if you happen by any chance to talk with my family, do not tell them anything about these nice things, they would be unnecessarily worried. It is not so bad...

In a week here, you set aside all European social prejudices, you let yourself ride in a rickshaw,

The next letter, from Franta on July 28, 1939, was a reply to a previous note. Two missives apparently crossed in the mail.

> ...I got your letter from June 18 that you wrote from the ship, and I am answering immediately...

> We are all now in Bechyně [a city in the Southern Bohemian region] and you are missing out on our party. Kantas, Jiri, Honza, Andula, and similar beasts are here. We are wonderfully vulgar, already nobody is speaking to us because "ass" is what we usually start our conversations with; what we end them with I will not even mention because, of course, I cannot write about [genitals].

> Yesterday, I was in Prague, so I immediately spoke with your father and learned how you are doing and where I should write to you. Of course, as far as the immigration drought is concerned, we are so far, so to speak, screwed [without prospects]...

There is a nearly six-month gap before the next letter from Franta, on January 11, 1940. It's clear that at least one exchange is missing because of Franta's reference to a previous request for work in China.

> ...When I wrote to you last time, I asked whether you would be able to obtain a position as a driver, butler, or something like that for me. Today I spoke to someone who is going to China and he said that it is only possible to get there either with 400 pounds or with an employment contract. Considering the fact that I do not have the aforementioned sum, what remains is no hope. I would however travel alone, or perhaps with [my younger brother] Honza or [my friend] Brabčák. If something like that is possible, be so kind and write to me frankly about whether there are options for me.

Your folks are healthy and completely fine and treat me very kindly. I am living with Andula, the boy [my son, Honza] and my parents, including Honza [my younger brother], in Jevany. It is cold as hell there, but we are all together and there aren't many people so it is peaceful, which suits us just fine. We are now in Prague for the purposes of inoculation against diphtheria (for the boy) and toward the end of the week we will return to Jevany.

The 400 British pounds that Franta needed to get to China was a considerable sum—about $26,000 in 2010 US dollars. The letter's reference to moving to yet another new location was something his family and most Jewish families that remained in Czechoslovakia experienced repeatedly as they tried to stay a step ahead of the Nazis. Because Franta was married to Andula, who wasn't Jewish, he was able to avoid early repercussions, but both he and his brother Honza were still wary of the occupying authorities, as Andula wrote so eloquently in the note she attached to Franta's letter.

...We are all really happy that you are doing well and mainly, that we can learn something about you, as the others...are missing, completely. This place reminds me of an island where ships never dock. I am really sorry that Franta and [our son] Honza cannot go outside but I can't do anything about it, and from selfish reasons I am happy that we are all together.

Yesterday, Milena Bálová [Ballenberger] and Viktor Schüch were here, so we remembered you vividly. Will we ever see each other again? Probably not. Valda, I am ceasing to believe it. Do you have a nice girlfriend there? Friends? We are left with two in total...

Now I am at this "should I leave" thing. Look, Valda, you are very kind to look after me, but I doubt that it will work out—the obstacles are quite substantial. I will write about it to you as soon as I manage to get this moving a bit...

A Bolivian visa was secured from America by [Franta's in-laws] Kamil and Pepik [Wiener, later Winn], unfortunately we haven't heard from them for a long time now. The last letter from them dates to Christmas, so it is not exactly fresh.

I will likely throw myself at some agricultural works [forced labor] somewhere in the south of Bohemia, but keep writing to me at this [Jevany] address. I am also quite often in contact with your folks, and I don't think you have to worry about them any more than they worry about you. Your mother has already realized that by missing you she will not be helping you and that you are lucky that you can practice your medicine and live freely.

I just read Dr. V. Heiser's An American Doctor's Odyssey. And I congratulate you from the bottom of my heart that you selected such a top-notch career—the only one, aside from the creative arts, in which one can perform the same services anywhere in the world...

Look, you old crock, this is not supposed to be some kind of sermon; I know that you are sensible anyway, but I think there is no harm in realizing other people's problems. As far as I am concerned, I would like to hit the road with abandon... Thank you for your efforts, if you have something already, you know; it can't hurt...

You really helped me a lot and mostly just by the fact that I can see your goodwill. Maybe I am being unnecessarily sentimental, but these days I am, thanks to all the circumstances, far more sensitive than I had been before. The feeling that one true friend joined the modest number of friends rigorously selected from a number of "acquaintances" and true freeloaders, is greatly invigorating.

Valda, I am ending this letter; I'm not in my old form because there is so little in terms of asses, [genitals], and [intercourse] that it almost scares me, it almost embarrasses me. Maybe it will enrich Andula; Honza it definitely will. Many greetings, ty vole!

Franta's closing term, *ty vole*, literally means "you bull," or "you old bull," but here, with a certain sense of irony, could translate to "you stud."

An added note from "Big Honza," Franta's brother, made reference to the effect of new laws restricting which foods Jewish families could buy.

...So you are allegedly featured in an ad for corsets, otherwise where else would your considerable belly go? Here we are copiously learning the Chinese ways, so you would feel at home among us, particularly Andula's and Franta's burps, lip smacking, etc...

Sorry that I am writing so discomposedly, but Franta's active little boy slammed my head with a log of wood. Otherwise we play cards here and I have just won ten one-crown banknotes. Valda, send some photograph of those Chinese girls as well (of above forty years of age).

Franta's humor became even drier as the situation in Czechoslovakia grew worse and his prospects for leaving the country diminished. On April 4, 1940, he wrote to Valdik from Prague.

> ...As soon as I wrote to you that I have a visa for Bolivia, I received the news that it is valid only until April 20 of this year and the last ship that could effectively be used will be steaming toward there in just fourteen days...this cannot be accomplished even theoretically, so I am [screwed] again...

> Valdo, you are very kind to take care of me but if you have difficulties obtaining a permit for me, then do nothing. You will get it with difficulty and laboriously (like Kamil has with the Bolivian one) and then they will tell you to wipe your...bottom with it. However, should coincidence bring into your path someone who could help, then I would be grateful if you didn't forget me.

> Otherwise everything is as it used to be. Sometimes it is greatly jolly, to the point of discomfort; usually however, we live in relative calm. It will be a year now since I was given my walking papers at the store. Time is flying, [Little Honza] is growing, and everything else can kiss my bottom.

> And so once again I had a chat with you, if only on paper. I hope one day it will be in person. And now that I've finished, I am not going to take a dump as you would probably assume, but I am going to pay my rent, which is a pleasure somewhat lower than the abovementioned act. I wish you manifold European (and in case of total scarcity, also Asian) ladies...

Big Honza's added note showed he would not be one-upped by his brother in either vulgarity or attempted humor.

> …Since winter has struck again, I am writing to you very briefly, until my ink freezes. Seriously, even though it is April already and we should be rejoicing in the meadows, it is so cold here at night that Franta, when he needs to urinate, prefers to do it on the spot rather than going downstairs. How Andula does it, I don't know.
>
> Many greetings, Honza
>
> P.S. Bring me a live Chinese man (not a Chinese woman, since I switched my orientation.)

My father took Franta's request for help very seriously when he wrote to him from Ping Ting Hsien on June 26, 1940.

> …First of all, thank you for stopping by my mom's on Mother's Day. That was really great of you. Don't be angry with me that I am only answering your April letter now; I was waiting until I could write something positive to you regarding your request. You don't even know how sorry I am about your setback with Bolivia; it is damn bad luck.
>
> With my heart heavy, I managed to get you a contract with a hardware firm in Shanghai. The contract was recently presented by my friends to the municipality, with all the formalities, etc., and they have just returned it all to me with the information that it is necessary to submit a guarantee in the amount of $400 US. Landing permits are no longer given on the basis of contracts alone. You don't even know how sorry I am about it. I would so much like to get it for you. I am holding on to the contract for now and I will still try something.

Maybe North China? I think these days it is the only possible destination from the Protectorate. Whatever can still be done, I will do.

Next month I will go shopping again to Tientsin and possibly even to Shanghai and so maybe I will get some advice—otherwise I am still in regular touch with all the relevant institutions. Just like many people turn to me with requests for information, I too am passing this on.

I can't really write much about myself; everything is, to put it bluntly, so crappy you can't even imagine. I had a high fever again for several days, probably malaria. It has stopped now, after the shots.

In the hospital [where I work], they bother me no end. It is really not a hospital; rather it is a mess where everyone does whatever he pleases. Any discipline? None whatsoever. In the beginning it annoyed me terribly, now I don't give a damn about it.

Whatever it looks like, I should be happy just to have a decent existence, employment, and even though this is the middle of nowhere, at least it is peaceful here. Imagine my luck: last month my radio broke; and what a relief that is. The most up-to-date news I received ten days late, so it is really no longer news anymore but history. In the evenings, shrieking Chinese music can sometimes be heard in the distance, at other times machine-gunfire, so these are the only sounds I get to hear.

As far as dirty talk is concerned, I managed to teach our doorman to greet me with "kiss my a_ _"; our missionary Ford is now called "fart-fart" and the smallest of boys at the mission can now say "crap" and "ass," backwards as well, and so now I am really starting to feel like I am among my own…

I see that for now (and at other times too), I am babbling and so I'll use Honza's excuse (his ink is frozen) with a modification: the keys on my typewriter are melting because of the heat, and so I will finish here.

I greet you all wholeheartedly and I scream: Write!!

Franta's letter from Prague, on September 20, 1940, is the first of many written over the following months that showed that the stress and persecution was finally wearing him down.

…Thank you for your letter from August 14. This time it took a bit longer to arrive here…we moved several times within a short period and so cumbersomely (thanks to the moving company), that I did not even have time to write.

Thank you for taking care of me. I don't even know how I will be able to repay you. Maybe I could do a bit of sweeping for you or something, if I actually manage to reach you some day. But the way it looks now, there isn't much hope, particularly if it is as you write. I am really happy that your folks like to see me; I haven't visited them for some time as I was helping my parents to move and settle into their apartment…

I have developed these idiotic mental conditions that are so bad I could probably substitute for ten lunatics. Those close to me naturally suffer because of this, which I realize, and that makes me even angrier with myself. I am coarse even with my dad, with whom I have always gotten along well, and I regret it. But then the next day he says something and we are in a fight all over again.

I think you managed to escape it. Otherwise, it would probably catch up with you, too. Everyone I speak to feels the same way I do. Milena has it worse thanks to her mother, who has always been annoying. I passed your letter on to her. So far Zetlata behaves the best from out of all our acquaintances; also Jůla is now decent. But Jarda W. is a moron, though I cannot say that he is evil or that he would do anything wrong to anyone.

Jarda Padovec is now going out with Hanka, Pavel Körper is now at home [in Prague], and Milena is busy with the children and knits some belts; I don't know for what…

On November 10, 1940, when he responded to news of my parents' marriage, Franta's mood was even more somber.

…Thank you for your letter from September 30 and most of all I want to congratulate you on your marriage. This isn't a cliché. Rather, I mean it completely genuinely, since there is nothing more sensible than when two people who share the same interests and are mutually congenial, both spiritually and physically, unite and go through life together. It becomes easier for both and I wish you and your partner so much happiness and as few troubles as possible.

As you know me, I am better at BS than serious talk and so I am thinking that maybe I haven't really expressed everything the way I had intended to write it to you. I hope that you know what I likely wanted to tell you and mainly, don't be angry for my writing only now.

I now have plenty of various worries and so I will admit to you that right after I received your letter, I literally sweated out several letters that, after reading them again, I tore up. A wire, even congratulatory, could not be sent and so I am saving a present for you, also called a wedding present, the main characteristic of which is that the giver takes advantage of the turmoil associated with the wedding and gets rid of some atrocious object.

You are at an advantage, because when I will hand you my wedding gift you will most certainly no longer be distracted by the wedding and what's more, I will likely be a wise and august old man surrounded by numerous grandchildren. Considering the fact that I will likely also indulge in a pensioner's philosophizing, I probably won't give you a penny, so don't thank me yet.

As [our friend] Jiří has already noted in his letter, we missed out on the wedding feast, so at least, you bull, write to us how the wedding went and all that you can about your wife. All of us here are as curious as cats. I am hoping your letter will be full of photos. I will tease your former female admirers a bit.

Everything is the same here. I went to visit your folks, and they are living in a smaller apartment, but a nice one, which is a thing of utmost importance nowadays, for one to be at home.

On this occasion I remember those beautiful times when we decided, together with [our friend] Rudla, that one day we would get ourselves a beautiful brothel, and Andula immediately wanted to reserve the position of booking clerk for herself. (You know her, always money hungry.) And then Honza wanted to be a woman and wanted silk stockings and a garter belt from me for his birthday. So I am babbling here and will probably tear this up again, since I wanted to write to you a letter full of noble thoughts and great ideas, and I am instead concluding it with the desire to own a brothel.

Andula showed her own biting wit in this appended note:

> …That's great news that you got married. I hope that you arrive in America soon and scold our relatives who are already banking their money (as they themselves write) but whose "help" consists of mailing us restaurant menus. I am not envious, just sad that my lifelong desire for travel is not being fulfilled.

By the time of their next communication two months later, on January 4, 1941, Franta and Andula were on the move again. Franta wrote about sharing an apartment with his parents in Garden City outside of Prague.

> …In that "Garden City" I haven't seen a single garden, not to mention a little tree, however, it takes 1-1/4 hours to get there by tram and we will live in one room surrounded by the thoughtful care of mommy and daddy.

> I judge from all this that our marriage will become free of intercourse and I will probably be hunting down that reputed anti-copulation treatment. Andula certainly would be happy with that because she read in an intimacy column for women that mating leads to rolls of the belly…

I write in a pleasingly silly fashion. Do not be surprised by that, everything in my head is concerned with moving. Winter is in full swing, therefore I have no idea how we are going to transport everything to different places as even one room's worth of stuff will only fit with difficulty into my parents' place.

Andula added to the letter.

...As I can see, moving is affecting Franta in a tremendously negative way. On the contrary, I am in my element: I sleep long hours, I pretend to pack, and I await the day when the movers come and find the apartment awash in doilies and carpets.

In all my life, I would never have guessed what such sober people like Franta and I have in terms of junk. Follow my advice: buy Ruth Alice at the most a slip or a pair of stockings and immediately throw out her old ones. But never buy statues, albums, vases, doilies, toys, and various trinkets because then, during an eventual persecution, you'll have no idea what to pack first.

Do not read books at all—and if you do, only borrowed ones, and return them immediately. You will have a smaller number of trunks. Do not take photographs. You will discover during the move how many bad photos you took and how much talent you have in continuing to find the non-photogenic aspects of your wife...

I spoke with your dear mother the other day. She was very kind and she invited me for a visit even with Honzik, so I will go there when the freezing temperatures improve...

Send us the photo of your wife already in order for me to criticize her honestly to you. I am glad that we now have among our relatives a real American woman; I am sufficiently proud of that. Is she at least American looking? And does she have those shoes with high heels and a toe sticking out? And does she have those properly well-shaped legs? And what kind of underwear do American women wear? And what kind of hairdo? So you see, Valda, I just destroyed your illusion. You go prepare a huge piece of paper, take it with you to the bathroom if you prefer, and start describing her precisely and faithfully.

Those were the last words from either Franta or Andula for the duration of the war, and at first I thought my blossoming friendship with them had come to an abrupt end. But then I received one more translated letter, which Franta had sent right after the war, on December 1, 1945, from Prague to my father in Ecuador. Its power is undeniable.

… All in all, we haven't seen each other for six years, but to me it seems like sixty.

My congratulations on your son; I cannot even imagine you as the father of a family. Remember how we used to chase our highly esteemed professors into a ditch with that ancient vehicle of yours? Or some of our other jokes? I can hardly believe that I ever laughed. I certainly don't mean to dwell on tragedy; I already dumped that on those who were in correspondence with me immediately after the war. But, somehow, we unlearned humor, and we also got older.

After relating the joke about the adventurer who stayed home during the war, Franta went on to tell of what befell him and his brother, Honza.

> …In short, the whole thing was a SOB, and if someone is still alive, he can damn well rejoice because it is nothing but a coincidence. It was indeed a devilish system, but unfortunately it cannot be said that people will learn anything. If we watch the Nuremberg Trials from the viewpoint of a previous inhabitant of the German Lebensraum we have every reason to be pessimistic about the future. [Lebensraum, literally "living space," was Eastern European territory seized by Germany; its ethnic populations were killed or deported to provide room for future development of the German people.] Most people lack the gift of imagination, and what they haven't experienced for themselves seems nothing but propaganda to them.
>
> I don't have to explain this to you; you lost enough people, even without mentioning your parents. I visited them up until their departure. They stayed in their apartment. They lived in a mixture of fear and hope. They were happy that you made it out and hoped they could join you.
>
> As you know, our Benešov friends, Dr. Karel [coincidentally also named Karel] and his family, have been lost. I survived thanks to my so-called mixed marriage and went to Terezín only in January of this year. I went there with myocarditis [chronic inflammation of the heart muscle] and tried to hang on.

The Nazis developed Terezín (Theresienstadt in German) concentration camp in a beautiful region in northeastern Czechoslovakia, 90 miles north of Prague. It was originally built as a military garrison in 1780 by the Austrian Emperor Joseph II and named for his mother, the Empress Maria Theresa. Surrounded by green hills and quiet rivers, Terezín's role in World War II was deliberately deceptive. Although it was not an extermination camp, Terezín was used as a transfer camp for Jews from all over Europe, especially from Bohemia and Moravia, on their way to other ghettos or Nazi death and concentration camps, and many Jewish prisoners were killed in this terrible place or died there from starvation or disease.

Franta speculated that he benefitted from slightly improved conditions because the camp commander realized the Nazi regime was headed for defeat:

> …I somehow muddled through until May 5, when I learned that I had a second son.

By then, the Czech resistance had initiated a full-scale uprising in Prague. Within days, the Allies declared victory in Europe, and the Russian Army entered the city.

> …I don't intend to continue the family tradition, which is a mild allusion to [my brother] Karel and his enthusiastic odes to his Katka's merits, but I am convinced that I wouldn't have been able to write this stupid and unremitting continuous message to you if it hadn't been for my gal. She did what she could. Little Honza was to be deported with me, but thanks to good friends, he made it—they hid him in Southern Bohemia. I then kept telling the idiots in Terezín that I had no son and that there must have been a mistake. Fortunately, they didn't have enough time to verify that. Before that I dug air shelters in Střešovice [an area in Prague].

Our Honza [Franta's brother] was sent away in a "labor detail" transport for two-and-a-half years, where only a third survived the day after they arrived in Auschwitz. Then he was in Gleiwitz [a subcamp of Auschwitz], and when the front approached, he ran with a friend of his over to the Russians. The friend was shot by the Germans.

After that, Honza joined the Russians and fought against the Germans. It was an achievement, if one considers that he had weighed 85 kg [187 lbs.] when he went to the concentration camp, but only 45 kg [99 lbs.] when he escaped. Well, he was then transferred from the Russians to a Czechoslovak Army officer training school and now, after a difficult three-month job search, he is employed as a French film agent.

I missed a job opportunity because of my heart trouble, so after much suffering I obtained employment with Báňská a Hutní [a mining and metal company]. They don't pay much, so I'm hoping to have a chance to talk to Rudla Brabec [Brabčák] and start a small business. That is, if I don't emigrate out of here. I have completely lost a feeling of home here. The reason might be that my parents are dead and the rest are gone.

Don't get me wrong, nothing evil is happening to me here now. It's just that there are some remnants of anti-Semitism. It's not a big deal, although it's hard to take, and it only has to do with the repercussions of brainwashing people, property transfers, etc. Also, the situation is not improved by the fact that the Czech Jews, with some exceptions, are gone, while the German and Polish Jews are coming back. The German Jews were after all Germans (not all of course), and the Polish Jews had vitality and were spineless enough to fare better than we.

You asked about our acquaintances: Jarda W., I think, perished in Poland; Jiri Glas returned in poor health, but he is back on the job; Pavel Körper and his wife had lived illegally in Kamenice, where he worked as a doctor—he is Dr. Urban now and works in a German health insurance company in Kolín; I don't seek out Jula [Julius] Lankaš. He is not bad, but he is a chicken. Jarda Padovec is fine, but many others have perished. For lack of paper and time I am not able to name them.

I must finish now, otherwise I will soil myself. Surely I won't refuse your offer of canned goods. The food situation is pretty grim here. I assume by sending them you are not depriving yourself and your family, to which I send many, many warm greetings. Andula and Honza say hi to you. There is nobody who can really clean this place, so I never get a break.

Valda, you big stud, take care and write, but with Czech diacritics [language marks like accents].

Franta's pessimistic view of the future contrasted with most of the Western world, which basked in victory over fascism. Within three years, however, his predictions came true as the Iron Curtain descended and Czechs endured the brutal reality of Communism.

One of the most difficult aspects of dealing with the massive letter collection was keeping in my head all that was contained there. Even with my extensive database, with four hundred multi-paged letters, I sometimes forgot what was there. As I wrote this chapter on Franta, I reviewed a myriad of old letters and emails about the subjects.

When I re-read the following letter (translated in December 2008), I felt it too should be shared. It is to my father in Ecuador from the older Honza, the uncle Franta's son is named after. Written from Prague in 1945, just after the war ended, it shows that Big Honza's humor was still intact.

> ...We were very happy to receive your letter; less happy with the fact that you don't use diacritics, in which way you resemble our Karel a bit. I cannot even imagine you as a father. As you may not be able to imagine me as semi-adult, that settles the score.
>
> It's great that you are doing well even though you are married, and mainly I envy you the warmth—not of the family hearth, but the tropical kind, about which I often dream when I am freezing in the room at night. But so far it is above zero out there and I have already had a sufficiently long training, both from Germany and the military. I served in a small hamlet under the Tatras [mountains], where the highest temperature in July was about 18 degrees Centigrade [64 degrees Fahrenheit].
>
> You have traveled much; I too, actually—but as per that Prague joke, it is I who is the adventurer, since I stayed here. And it is not far from the truth. Very often I feel completely adventurous—for example, today I only narrowly escaped a couple of slaps that I could have received from Andula. I do not want to complain, but she beats me very often; and Franta too. On the other hand, she cooks well. And for a small fee, she even makes my bed. I should stop talking nonsense.
>
> What about movies over there? Wouldn't they want some Czech ones? You know, now that I am kind

of in that line of work, I have to try. So, farewell.
Send us, from time to time, *The Ecuadorian Word*
or the *Paper of Ladies and Girls of Guayaquil.*

I knew that discovering what happened to Franta and Andula
after the war meant I had to find their son, Little Honza, wherever
he might be. Luckily, I got help from a new-old friend—Karel's
daughter and Franta's niece, Carol Sheldon Hylton.

Carol unlocked many doors when she introduced me via email to
her cousin and unofficial family historian, Jerry Held-Kovell. Jerry,
whose Czech name was Jarmila, was born in Prague in 1935. The
daughter of Franta's sister, Anka, Jerry wasn't quite four when her
family escaped the Nazi onslaught in 1939 and made their way to
America. Her father, Kamil Neuman, was a successful doctor. He
was the Kamil mentioned in Franta's letters, who tried to obtain
paperwork for Franta and his family to immigrate to Bolivia.

In our first telephone conversation, Jerry revealed the pain her
parents felt when hearing news of Nazi atrocities. Through my
research, I'd read the graphic descriptions that appeared in American
newspapers and the sporadic accounts of rumored massacres of
Eastern European Jews. Jerry's mother was rarely able to sleep
during the war because she was so worried about her parents and her
brothers, Franta and Honza.

Jerry knew how hard her mother tried to get information
about her brothers because, like me, she found a collection of
correspondence from relatives overseas that ended when mail to
the occupied Czech territory was cut off in late 1941. I suggested
Jerry join me in donating the letters to the United States Holocaust
Memorial Museum. She agreed the letters needed an audience.
As the world approaches a time when Holocaust survivors and
eyewitnesses are no longer alive to speak about what occurred, such
letters can continue to bear witness.

Jerry enthusiastically helped in my information-gathering quest. She filled in details about Little Honza and the second child mentioned in Franta's final letter. Honza was born May 13, 1938, five months before the Munich Agreement, which allowed Germany to annex the Sudetenland. Martin, the couple's second son, arrived on May 4, 1945, as the war was about to end for the Czechs. Because I'd read his postwar letter, I knew before speaking to Jerry that Franta had survived, so she fast-forwarded to 2001, when Franta died, at age 90, having visited his family in America several times. His brother Honza died in Prague in his fifties of stomach cancer, leaving a widow named Míša, "who might still be alive." Honza and Míša had one son, Michal Šeba, who lived in Prague. I was excited by this news, as my husband and I planned to travel to Prague.

The big surprise was that Franta lived the postwar half of his life without Andula. Jerry told me that Andula moved to New Zealand, "probably sometime in late 1949." She left with a man named Pepík Lekner. Lekner had secured emigration papers for New Zealand in February 1939, but lost his family in the Holocaust before he could leave the country. Lekner, his first wife, Růžena Nováková, and their children were transported to Terezín in July 1943 and five months later to Auschwitz. Later separated from her children, Růžena died at Treblinka. Their two young sons, Petr, 11, and Honzík, 9, died at Auschwitz. Pepík somehow managed to survive. He offered to take Andula to New Zealand, married her, and raised her sons as his own.

I felt a rush of sorrow as I thought of Franta alone, but I also remembered Andula's devotion to Franta during the war. I had come to know and admire her, a strong woman with a lot of patience. Marriage is a complicated thing. When you add fear and multiple displacements to that equation, I knew that there had to be a story behind her leaving her husband and country and taking their two boys halfway across the world.

Little Honza was the only person who might know.

From Jerry, I learned that Honza and his brother Martin still lived in New Zealand and that Martin was married to Gillian (née Knox), a New Zealand girl with Scottish roots. I found out even more when Jerry put me in touch with her son, Andy Held. Andy, who lives in Washington State, maintained a family website with a section devoted to old photographs, many of them featuring the people we were discussing. Thrilled with the prospect of putting faces to the names in the letters, I was soon staring at the section of Andy's site entitled "Neuman-Schoenbaum Family Photographs."

Andy's introduction explained that the pictures had belonged to his grandmother, Anka, who died at age ninety-three in 2001. Many were battered and worn, and he'd attempted to restore them. He offered to make copies for family members scattered across the globe. Next to his words was an image of an elegantly dressed woman with dark curls gently circling a Renaissance-like face bearing a very slight smile and penetrating eyes, touched off by what looked like a garnet teardrop necklace. Below was this warning: "Some of the family history here is painful. It is the family history as I remember it from my grandmother's stories, with help from my mother."

I hesitated for a moment before entering Andy's photo gallery. I knew it would provide a window to the world I'd been looking for, but it might also bring sorrow. Reading the letters of a few of my relatives who perished had been excruciating for me. With resolve, I followed Andy's directions: "Click here to begin."

The first black-and-white photo was astonishing. There, sitting around a large black stool that supported a child of perhaps one year, were two boys in matching sailor suits. They looked to be about three and five years old. Beside them stood a girl wearing a dark dress, with a white bow in her hair, along with four other girls in white dresses. I was startled because one of my favorite pictures of my father was taken when he was perhaps three, his little hands placed solidly on the starched white pants of a sailor suit.

Later I asked Lukáš Přibyl, an award-winning documentary filmmaker from Prague and translator of many of the letters, about the sailor-suited boys. He told me that it was very common attire for photographs of wealthy and upper-middle-class children. Andy identified the three boys in the photo as Karel, Franta, and Honza, and the girl in the white-bibbed dark dress and large white hair bow as his grandmother, Anka. He did not know who the other children were—but at last I had faces to match to the Schoenbaum brothers' letters. Franta sat in the front on what appeared to be a fluffed-up wooly bearskin rug, hands placed together, with the impish, innocent face of a three-year-old. I could already see in his eyes the mischievous humor that lay within.

The next photo was of the woman featured on the introduction page: Andy's great-grandmother, Hedvička Schoenbaum. Her piercing eyes entranced me. Her husband's picture followed. Rudolf Schoenbaum stared seriously into the camera lens; he too had penetrating light-colored eyes. Wearing a tweed woolen suit with vest, handkerchief, and dark tie, with a large-brimmed hat resting on his forehead, Rudolf was a contemporary of my grandfather, Arnošt. I imagined their friendship.

The next picture was of Kamil Neuman's family—a formal photograph of seventeen people taken around 1928, perhaps at the time of Anka and Kamil's July 12, 1928, wedding. It showed Kamil's six sisters lined up in the front row, with Kamil in the middle. With the same serious smile she wore with her sailor suit, Anka, twenty years of age, sat behind Kamil.

With the next photo, I saw Little Honza for the first time. Andy's caption, "John Lekner," announced the side-view image of a smiling, suited boy with a handkerchief. He was no more than two years old, sitting on Rudolf Schoenbaum's lap as his grandfather stared at the tiny boy with adoration.

Andy's note explained: "This snapshot was mailed to my grandmother in the United States after she and Kamil and their daughters had left Praha [Prague]. Rudolf was killed in the Holocaust. This was the last photograph of her father that my grandmother ever received."

Next was a picture of Hedvička Schoenbaum and John Lekner, still named Honza Schoenbaum, looking like all was perfect in their world, even though at the time the Nazis were already compiling names and addresses so they could schedule transports. The boy's face took an immediate place in my heart, as I thought of how his life would explode in the next few years. In his tiny hand, he held what looked to be a silver bell. This was the last photograph Anka ever received from her mother before the Nazis killed her.

I asked Andy if he knew how to find John Lekner. He responded: "I met John Lekner when he was here in Seattle working at the University of Washington. I believe it was during a sabbatical from his position at Victoria University of Wellington. I've included him on this email and here's a link with additional information."

I was almost ready to meet Little Honza—but first, before using his direct email link, I did what I had done when I went in search of other relatives or letter-writer descendants: I used the Google search engine. Up popped "John Lekner, School of Chemical and Physical Properties, Victoria University of Wellington, New Zealand." It was the same link Andy had given me. With one click, I was looking at Lekner, professor of physics. I had absolutely no doubt this was the seventy-one-year-old version of the little boy I had just seen. His receding gray hairline, tinted eyeglasses, and collared shirt did not perfectly match the picture of Honza at age two on his grandmother's lap, but his eyes, nose, and lips gave him away.

Chicago, Cornell, Cambridge and Oxford among others, and the pleasures of a lovely family."

He told me more about what happened to his family when the war ended in Prague.

"As the war's end approached, Mother was in the last month of pregnancy; my younger brother Martin was born on the May 4. Hitler's death was announced on German radio on May 1; general surrender was on May 7, but the liberation of Prague was not complete until May 11. Known as the Prague Uprising, during this period there was fierce fighting going on all over the city, in which over one thousand barricades had been set up in the uprising of civilians. Mother found her way to a clinic and had a safe delivery. I know at around this time the gates of Terezín were opened but I'm not sure if Franta escaped just before. He found his way back to Prague and Andula and baby Martin."

John continued about his own circumstance. "Meanwhile I was in the country with the family who protected me, who owned the pub. As the Russian tank crews passed the pub on their way to Prague, I was helping serve beer to them and came down with sunstroke. The Germans were retreating along the same road and the publican then raised the Czech flag. With it they hung the Russian flag as well. It was too soon, as troops of a German rear-guard saw the Russian flag and had us lined up against the pub boundary wall. Even as a young boy I remember the event well. Fortunately, a German officer riding in a motorcycle sidecar came by and stopped the impending execution. Mother and I were reunited a few days later, when the trains started running again. For a while after that I would not let her out of my sight. According to Mother, I would sit outside the toilet, waiting until she came out. Later when I returned to school, it was no use feeding me breakfast because I would throw it up from the stress of separation."

When I dug deeper about Franta's reaction to Andula taking his sons away to New Zealand, John responded it was hard for him to know. "There were occasional letters. He and I loved each other, in our own way."

Later, John sent a photo of Andula's best friend, Mima Lowenbach Bala. When Mima fell terminally ill in 1992, Andula flew from New Zealand to Canada to be with her. She stayed to the end. Mima was the second wife of Karel Bala—a new mystery to explore.

Left column, top to bottom: František "Franta" Schoenbaum (later Šeba); Hedvička & Rudolf Schoenbaum;

Right column, top to bottom: Andula and son Honza (John); Hedvička Schoenbaum & Honza; Rudolf Schoenbaum; Honza & Rudolf

LEFT: HONZA/JOHN LEKNER, DAUGHTER POPPY & GRANDDAUGHTERS; MÍŠA ŠEBA; JOHN LEKNER & SON DAYTON

RIGHT: ANDULA, HONZA, FRANTA; KAMIL & ANKA (NÉE SCHOENBAUM) NEUMAN; JOHN LEKNER & GRANDDAUGHTERS (PHOTOS COURTESY OF FAMILY)

Dramatis Personae

Karel Charles "Bála" Ballenberger/Karel Bala, JUDr.

(Valdik's friend)

Parents:	Leopold and Hermína (also Hermine and Hermínka; née Lustig) Ballenberger
Sister:	Anči (Anna) Ballenberger
Brother:	Zdeněk Ballenberger
First wife:	Milena Ballenberger (née Langer)
Children (with Milena):	Alena Ballenberger, Jan "Honza" (later John) Ballenberger
Father-in-law:	Leopold Langer, JUDr.
Second wife:	Věra Judith ("Mima") Bala (née Lowenbach)
Children (with Mima):	Ann Bala Matyas, Nicholas "Nick" Bala
Son (with Joan Thompson):	Hugh Thompson
Nieces:	Hana Žantovský and Soňa Kuber (Anči's daughters)
Grandnieces:	Irena Žantovský (Hana's daughter), Jitka Deyl (Soňa's daughter)
Grandnephew:	Michael Žantovský (Hana's son)

I did all I could and every time it went awry.

—Karel Ballenberger, April 14, 1940

Dear Valdik,

...I am truly happy that you too managed to escape from Prague. It is a pitiful sight to see all our acquaintances setting out for the seven seas, and you in particular I would not imagine on the road from Mánes to Shanghai, but then, Hitler has us where he wanted to have us...write to [tell] me whether [my wife] Milena wants to, or doesn't want to come here. It is a question I am greatly interested in...

The letter was signed simply "Bála." Written in a clear masculine hand, it was mailed from London in May 1939 and was waiting for my father when he arrived two months later in Shanghai, China, at the end of his 8,000-mile journey from Prague.

Solving the mystery of "Bála" became my mission, not only because the letter came first in the collection's chronology, but because Bála's name turned up so often, as both letter writer and as subject of curiosity and frustration in Karel Schoenbaum's correspondence. I was certain that learning about Bála would tell me more about my father, because their exchanges revealed both close friendship and a deepening anguish over the calamity in their homeland.

The relationship between Bála and Milena, the wife he left behind in Prague when he fled to England, also piqued my interest. As the translation progressed, details of the Nazi terror intensified, and I became gripped by questions about her fate as well as the fate of their marriage.

What I learned turned out to be more meaningful and more complex than I'd imagined. Bála's story of loss is heartbreaking, made worse by his guilt over irrevocable decisions. Getting to know him, even after his death, made me alternately sad and angry—but helped me to understand the overwhelming challenges faced by people who are forced to leave their homeland.

Translator Lukáš Přibyl became as intrigued by Bála and Milena as I was. Lukáš uncovered Bála's identity and traced his path from wartime Prague to England. In late 2008, Lukáš wrote that he'd "checked some records in London and likely Bála is Dr. Karel Ballenberger." The British records noted that this Czechoslovak attorney was born in 1908, making him a contemporary of my father, who was born in 1911. The rest of the picture began to develop as I interviewed Bala family members and cross-checked other sources, including a taped conversation with my father.

Bála was the third child of Leopold and Hermína Ballenberger (née Lustig). The family exemplified Jewish assimilation, blending into the diverse population, proud to have a country to call their own. They identified themselves as Czechs. When Bála was seven, his father died of lead poisoning. After the loss, the Boy Scouts played a mentoring role in Bála's life. The scouts taught him to be vigilant and to always have a plan. His dedication and intelligence won him a place at Charles University, where he studied law.

That is where Bála's path intersected with my father's. Both craved the company of other smart, intellectually curious young people, and they found it at the Mánes Café. Brimming with ideas and social concerns, he took his place among the group, where he went by "Bála" and not by his given name of Karel. Always dressed in tailored suits and ties, the handsome Bála wore his hair closely trimmed with a jaunty, off-center part.

Another member of the Mánes circle was the high-spirited Milena Langer, who had grown up pampered as the daughter of a prominent lawyer. In 1933, Bála and Milena traveled in a group from Prague to a Fabian Society summer camp in London. The socialist debating group attracted young activists from around the world. It was there that Bála began his romance with Milena. Bála and Milena married young, a few years after Bála's law school graduation. Later, Bála got a job at the law firm headed by his prosperous father-in-law, Leopold Langer. Bála worked with labor unions in addition to Jewish clientele. Leopold's cousin was František Langer, the well-respected Czech writer and military doctor, who was politically involved as well.

My apolitical father was drawn into Bála's activism when Bála asked Dad to provide some cartoonish caricature drawings for publication in a popular left-leaning Social Democratic Party newspaper. Dad obliged. His drawings of a little man with a funny head were caricatures of Adolf Hitler. These casual, seemingly innocent drawings heightened my father's anxiety as he slipped aboard a train on March 31, 1939, two weeks after the Nazi occupation of Czechoslovakia, and made his escape from the Czechoslovak Army. One week earlier, under the orders of the German high command, his fully armed division had been incorporated into the German Wehrmacht. Soon he contrived a daring defection. As the doctor for the unit, he could write his own orders for inspection of the meat supply. My father wrote an order in Czech, then translated what he had written into German for the guard, and the guard let him leave. Once through the gate, he proceeded in his car to Brno, Moravia, and boarded a train for Prague.

Wearing army-issued gray riding britches and a shirt borrowed from a friend, he was trying to blend in on the train. German military guards walked through the car, inspecting credentials. My father had none. He thought he'd be gunned down on the spot if he were found without discharge papers. (What was more likely was that he would have been taken away, charged as a deserter, and given capital punishment, but he feared a more immediate on-the-spot retribution.)

As he held the Brno daily newspaper in front of his face, the thought of the caricatures flooded his mind. Convinced that those unflattering cartoons and his Jewish heritage made him a wanted man, twenty-seven-year-old Valdik pushed his face forward into the protective fold of the newspaper. Suddenly, a man leaned across the aisle and whispered in his ear in Czech, "I see you are wearing army boots. Do you have your discharge papers?"

Valdik realized that the man was a Czech railroad conductor and shook his head no. The conductor responded, "All the trains have Gestapo who enter at the front of the train when we make a station stop. They work their way back and if you stay toward the rear, you will likely evade them." Thanks to the brave conductor's advice, Valdik was not discovered.

By the time Valdik reached Prague amid the turmoil of the occupation, Arnošt and Olga had not heard from their son for several weeks. Overjoyed, they greeted him at the door of their home in the Vinohrady residential district. But Prague was no longer the warm and inviting city he remembered. Immense German banners emblazoned with swastikas hung from prominent buildings. Armed patrols in tanks and jeeps swarmed the streets.

Arnošt described Hitler's arrival, telling my father that the Nazi Führer spent the night of March 14 in Prague Castle, former home to the kings of Bohemia, followed the next day by his proclamation of the Protectorate of Bohemia and Moravia. Arnošt might have been describing Valdik's cartoon as he spoke of Hitler's beady eyes, resembling those of a rat, as he stood on the balcony proclaiming the end of their country.

Britain and France both protested the German invasion, to no effect. Barely six months earlier, the two countries had signed the Munich Agreement, allowing Hitler to occupy the Sudetenland in exchange for his hollow promise to leave the rest of Czechoslovakia alone. As a citizen, my father knew that in handing over the Sudetenland, Czechoslovakia lost the strategically valuable heavy fortifications and natural mountain boundaries that had protected it from Germany. The Czechoslovaks had envisioned their line of fortifications delaying any German attack, allowing time for British or French troops to launch a counterattack.

The betrayal by those two countries destroyed any notion that defense of Czech Lands was possible. The major powers of Europe had virtually handed Czechoslovakia over to the goose-stepping Germans. The foolishness of appeasement was obvious to Dad, who, as a Czechoslovak soldier, was ordered to help with the handover of the Sudetenland. It was now clear to him that Hitler was no longer a cartoon figure. Valdik was determined to escape the tyrant's grip.

Over the next few weeks, he sought out his close friends and found that several had already left Prague. Karel "Bála" Ballenberger was one of them. As German troops massed along the border in mid-March, Bála secured a seat on one of the last flights the Social Democratic Party arranged out of Prague to London. Bála knew that if he stayed, he would face arrest—or worse—because he was Jewish and a Social Democrat. Milena and their children did not leave with Bála. Milena's parents, still grieving over her brother's suicide after a disastrous love affair with an older woman, pressured her to stay. Her parents had a house and resources, and her father had served in the Austro-Hungarian Army in the First World War. Like so many others, he wrongly believed that his status as a veteran would ensure their safety.

Milena was also concerned about the uncertain situation in London, where Bála had neither a job waiting nor any prospects. Believing that she could always leave if conditions in Prague worsened, she decided to stay behind with Alena, 4, and Jan, 2, whom they called Honza. Milena and the children moved to her parents' home, and she began working as a German-language tutor and translator, also making belts in the evening to provide additional income.

Upon my father's return to Prague from Brno, he met his friends at Mánes Café. These would be his last visits. They discussed what their futures might hold if they stayed or left. Despite diverse ethnic backgrounds and religions, they all felt in danger. By April 15, Mánes had posted a sign refusing service to Jews. Shortly afterward, Milena converted to Catholicism, believing that might provide some protection. Over the next eight weeks, Milena helped my father complete the voluminous bureaucratic paperwork necessary to leave the country. Serving as a translator of the German language appointed by the High Magistrate of the Czech Court (similar to a notary), she verified his Nazi-required proof-of-residence document. Several times before he departed for China, Dad and his friend Jiří Glas met with Milena at her father's home.

With the menacing sight of Hitler's thugs in the streets, my father attempted to persuade Arnošt and Olga to leave Prague with him, but they declined. They did not want to be a burden to anyone or any country.

By the time Dad reached China alone, Bála was in London, assisting other Czech refugees through the Czechoslovak Refuge Committee. In return, Bála received a small stipend. He encountered desperate people in a chaotic situation that he described to my father in the letter that awaited Dad's arrival in China.

> …The mood among émigrés here is altogether gloomy, no prospects and the possibility of emigrating totally negligible…in spite of the care the local organizations give the immigrants, to a

truly admirable degree, one can observe an obvious cooling of their interest in us.

Having seen the Nazi war machine up close, my father almost certainly had a more realistic view of coming events than Bála, who like so many in Europe was still hoping the troubles were temporary. Bála did not doubt that Germany would invade Poland, but from his comments he seemed certain Britain would be no more willing to go to Poland's aid than it had been to stop Czechoslovakia from being dismantled.

> ...I think that unless Adolf goes nuts there will be no war, the English certainly won't even think about going to fight for Gdańsk.

As Valdik settled into his strange new life in China, more letters from Bála brought secondhand news from home, relayed by other émigrés. The tone became increasingly ominous, and so did his references to Milena's situation, as in this letter sent to Valdik on July 12, 1939.

> ...As far as Milena and the children are concerned, she does have a visa for England and a two-year permit, however she cannot obtain a permit from the Gestapo...

By the time of their next exchange, there was no need for speculation about Europe's future. England and France had defied Bála's prediction by declaring war when the Nazis invaded Poland in September 1939. Travel anywhere became less likely and far more dangerous, as Bála acknowledged in his next letter from London on December 19, 1939.

> ...From Prague I have sad news. Milena is, in vain, trying to get to Yugoslavia with the children. I would have great trouble getting them here and it might possibly be better if they stay at home.

In that same December letter, Bála relayed even more worries.

> …About how the Nazis are faring in Prague you surely know, from our acquaintances, Zdeněk Thon was tortured to death…

> I know one thing that we have to do, at any cost, uproot Nazism and chase the Germans out of Prague. What Hitler did to us is so terrible that we hardly realize it…

Bála closed with hopes that the two would meet at Berlin's Brandenburg Gate after the war and celebrate victory by feasting on goulash (guláš). In his response mailed from Ping Ting Hsien, Shansi, on March 3, 1940, Valdik was clearly appreciative of Bála's continued contact.

> …A few days ago your December letter was forwarded to me…you can't imagine how happy it made me. When I count it, I get approximately one letter a month from somebody from our gang. It is therefore not much but it is the only Czech conversation I get to lead here, apart from letters from my parents. I am almost afraid that I will forget how to speak Czech…

The same letter explained why Bála's mail would sometimes take a while to reach its destination, as my father recapped his dizzying shuffle from job to job, and city to city.

> …I worked as a nurse for one old guy in Tsingtao [Qingdao], then was chief of an emergency room of the Red Cross for Chinese refugees in Shanghai, I had a private medical office in Shanghai as a plastic surgeon and then accepted a position in a missionary hospital in Shansi…

He also betrayed frustration at being so far removed from friends and family in a place where there was little he could do to impact events.

> …I am waiting for an immigration visa to the USA and though I have a job, I keep writing all over the place, chasing something else…Sometimes I am terribly angry at everything, I kick my rickshaw and in five minutes I regret it…I think this is some emigrant psychopathy, when one gives in to all kinds of things. Thankfully we have cheap whiskey here, a good medicine that always helps. When you get this letter, you will actually be a refugee for one year and I will be one when I receive your answer.

The letter reveals anxiety about the events in Prague, and uncertainty about the future.

> …I cannot even believe the fate of Zdeněk Thon. It is terrible. Also they wrote me from home that several acquaintances were killed in a similar fashion, you wouldn't know these people; they were mostly from Benešov—among them this Benešov character, a little Jewish simpleton, whom they also sent to a concentration camp. They must already even fear idiots.

> I cannot imagine what it looks like at home. What the Nazis did is terrible but I am scared of what they are yet to do when they will be withdrawing, for which I firmly hope. But for us it is already all quite defiled. I don't even know whether I will ever be able to come back home. I have no clue what I will do.

Valdik received another bit of gossip about Milena in a December 1940 letter from his mother, who referred to Bála's wife by a shortened Slavic-style surname.

...About your acquaintance I don't know much, only that Prague dames gossip a lot about Mrs. Bálová. She allegedly has some beau.

As the year progressed, Bála's letters revealed an increasing intensity and determination to do more than monitor far-off events. He wrote from London to Valdik in Ping Ting Hsien, Shansi, on March 20, 1940.

...I was already drafted in November. Every week we hear that already, already it is coming—and still nothing has come.

I am in the grips of bad forebodings. Our emigration is like every emigration—everyone is fighting helter-skelter—it makes one sick. News from Prague is dismal. The information about the killing of Zdeněk Thon was not confirmed, luckily. He is at the Gestapo in Berlin, I don't know if that isn't worse than death...kissing you on your forehead, your disgruntled Bála.

He wrote again on April 14, 1940.

...Finally they started to call up volunteers for the Czechoslovak Army and so probably within 4–5 weeks I will be a new recruit in France...I think the only way to go into that filth is with a machine gun in hand. I don't have any illusions, I am no warrior, but I am going in out of conviction that it is necessary to give—not only the Nazis but the Germans in general—a good spanking, so they will remember the lesson for at least one human lifetime...

Regardless of events to come on the battlefield, Bála now seemed almost resigned to life without Milena and the frustration Karel Schoenbaum had with him appeared to be reciprocal.

...I am still attempting at this twelfth hour to bring Milena and the children here, but I don't know, I don't know. It seems Europe has caught on fire, in any case by the time you get this letter you will have known this already. It is distressing that I had so much bad luck with Milena. I did all I could and every time it went awry.

Write to her from China here and there and she will be happy—at home it is allegedly totally mad. It is most of all a matter of nerves and people don't have steady ones there, thanks to the past two years...According to the last news Zdeněk isn't dead but is in bad shape in a concentration camp.

From our local acquaintances I am the only one going to war, as far as I know. I haven't heard yet that Karel S. would be pushing himself forward much in this. He is searching for connections in Oxford, ties that no one else would get there and he poses as a philosopher, and consorts with Katuška [Katka]. Here everyone already sees through him. Me he treats like a poor relative, but I don't care. When in need you get to know your friends and Karel most definitely isn't one, to the contrary...

So, write again very soon, give my greetings to Chinese girls and have a drink to my health. No, better, get wasted to my health. I am already like that Job. I had a wife, children, employment, money, a house, clothes, a car—and now I am setting off against Adolf as a recruit, without cash and not even knowing what is happening with my family.

Yours, charging through the field, Bála

Valdik's frustration with his own circumstances in China showed in his reply, written from Ping Ting Hsien on May 17, 1940.

> …I was just in such a crappy mood, I was swearing at the Chinese, naturally in Czech, so they pleasantly smiled at me, and I generally felt to be such a frustrated and abandoned soul. And then I received a bunch of letters from all quarters of the world and found your kind letter which improved my mood a little, even though it itself does not excel in optimism.

And soon, on August 14, 1940, my father took up Bála's challenge to write directly to Milena in Prague.

> …I trust that you are not angry that I haven't written until now. You probably know how I am from Franta [Schoenbaum].
>
> A few days ago I received a letter from Bála dated April 14. It got sidetracked to somewhere in southern China, so that I received it only now. Otherwise we correspond fairly regularly. He writes that he is relatively well and that he lives in modest circumstances. He misses his family very much.
>
> He has all kinds of plans for how to become reunited with the family. That is about all that could be of interest to you from his letter. As soon as I receive fresh news from him, I'll summarize them for you.

I found one last letter from Bála in London sent to my father in Peking, on September 10, 1940.

> …Here this world of ours is heading quickly and surely to hell. You in your Ting-ping-hseing [Ping

136

Ting Hsien] probably cannot imagine what it is like when Mr. Göring lets loose his fliers who drop bombs on us wildly, aim or no aim.

But one gets used to everything and except for the fact that we sleep in all kinds of underground shelters and various holes, life goes on as usual, if you don't mind that for example your favorite cinema is trashed by a bomb, there is no gas, and six to seven times a day there is an air raid with all it entails.

You wouldn't guess how well one can adapt and when you manage to get some sleep, you actually don't even miss anything. We go to the movies, with girls, as if nothing were happening…Now imagine our situation, when it explodes all around you and you don't know whether in an hour you will have a head on your shoulders…

About the development of things I have no great illusions. I know however that the Hitlerian terror has to be fought and that is also what all people at home expect from us.

I have not had any news from Milena for a long time. Hopefully she and the children will somehow manage to get through this horrific time…and yet, I wish you Merry Christmas and Happy New Year since this will just about reach you then. God be with you…

The following month, my parents were married in Peking. China had already been at war with Japan for several years, with provinces shifting from control of one country by the other. As the fighting closed in, the young couple succeeded in moving to the United States in early 1941. A letter from Milena, dated June 4 of that year, reached them in Long Beach, California. It is the only correspondence from her that I found.

...First of all I want to most wholeheartedly congratulate you on your married status and I wish you all good things. I hope that you have already learned that there is also something nice about being married, while I have completely forgotten by now, I can't even imagine it anymore.

And now I will start to swear! Why don't you write to me at all; have you completely forgotten that I sit here, weary and awaiting news? I am terribly lonely; I spend days and nights with the children and my parents. I have now by chance of fate become a desperate mother and I have my hands completely full. I shop, cook a bit, scold the children until my jaw hurts, and during the night I earn money, though not the way you think. Rather, I do translations, which are now highly in demand. (Though I should not undo it by saying it!)

The children are growing—I should say there's no stopping them from growing. Alena is a grown girl now and I have put her to work quite a bit already. She has to dry the dishes, dress herself and Honza, sweep and go shopping. Honza is a brat, his knees are always scraped, and he gets into fights and is hungry from morning until evening. He is quite big and strong. And I am blonde.

I terribly miss everyone and that man of mine in particular; it is his birthday just today, so you can imagine what a rosy mood I am in today.

All my acquaintances greet you most wholeheartedly and I hope that...you can make a bit of free

time to write to me. I am interested in everything,
how you live and what about all the acquaintances,
as well as your wife whom I greet wholeheartedly,
as well as you.

Sixty-seven years after Milena mailed that melancholy mix of
exuberance and trepidation, I learned of her fate in an email from
Lukáš. Working together, although an ocean separated us, Lukáš
and I followed Bála's trail from London to Canada after the war.
Soon after that discovery, Lukáš learned on December 23, 2008,
that Milena never escaped. She and the children were deported to
a concentration camp in Poland a few months after she wrote to my
father.

"I have positively identified Milena and her children—checked
the concentration camp transport records. Milena Ballenbergová,
born June 20, 1912; Alena Ballenbergová, born October 10, 1935;
and Jan Ballenberger, born December 4, 1937, were deported from
Prague by Transport B, to Łódź (on October 21, 1941). This was
(if I discount the first early transports in 1939) only the second
deportation from the Protectorate. This was one of the very early
ones, which went directly and not through Terezín. All three
perished. I checked the available Łódź death records, but none of
them died there, meaning they were deported further, to Auschwitz,
and perished there. It would be interesting to find his Canadian
family, I am pretty sure Bála had children after the war."

Thoughts of Milena and her last letter consumed me. When did
Bála learn that his family was lost?

I woke up early on New Year's Day 2009—the ninth anniversary
of my dearly loved mother's death—aching to know more about
Milena, Bála, and Bála's postwar family. With coffee in hand, I
typed "Karel Bala Canada" into the Google search engine. The first
item that appeared was titled "Canada Treaty Information." On the

second line, staring back at me in darkened letters, was "Karel Bala." Scrolling down the document, I came to the line on which, in 1947, Karel Bala signed as a document witness for a government financial loan from Canada to the Czechoslovak Republic. Below that search result on Google were two other results that verified Karel Bala's employment by the Czech government in Canada in the late 1940s.

I continued scrolling and came to: "Canadian Who's Who— Google Book Results." My immediate thought was that Bála had written a book. Could he still be alive? My heart was pumping wildly. But the link referenced a Nicholas Bala. Upon further review, I saw within the notation: "S[on] Karel Charles and Vera Judith Bala." Feeling my father's presence, I wondered with amazement: Could my search for Bála's children have been that easy? Could Nicholas really be the son of Valdik's long-lost friend, the mysterious character known to me as Bála?

And who was Vera Judith?

The electronic search led me next to the Web page of Nicholas Bala, a member of the Faculty of Law at Queen's University in Kingston, Ontario. Staring back at me from the computer screen was the photo of a man I thought to be around my age. My inner voice cried out: *This must be Bála's son!* The site included his email address, and on a bright, sunny Florida morning at 9:14 a.m., January 1, 2009, our acquaintance began as I typed, "Dear Mr. Bala..."

> ...First, Happy New Year. I hope your new year is a fine one for you. I am writing with a question rather out of the blue but wondered if perhaps you might be related to a man named Karel Bala (Ballenberger) who was a Czech immigrant just after World War II? My late father, Dr. Oswald Holzer, was a friend of his. I am doing research for a book I am writing. I would appreciate hearing

from you in this regard. Sincerely, Joanie Holzer Schirm, Orlando, Florida

Then I pretty much held my breath until I heard the "ping" sound of an incoming email at 9:25 a.m.

…I am the son of Karel, who died January 1, 1996, at age 87. He was born Ballenberger but changed his name to Bala during or after the war when he immigrated to Canada. I am afraid I do not remember hearing the name Dr. Oswald Holzer.

Nick Bala had no idea he had made one of my dreams come true. Through the letters, I had become intimate with relatives and friends from almost seventy years earlier, some of whom survived the war and others who did not. Now, with the miracle of modern-day electronic detective work, I had found someone just like me with inherited letter-writer blood pumping through his veins. As I read and reread Nick's email, I kept looking at the date of his father's death: January 1. I thought about my mother, whose missionary spirit rose to the sky that same day, four years after Bála. January 1, a day for new beginnings. For Nick Bala and me, January 1, 2009, would mark just that—the first of many examples of the human spirit that went on to thrive despite an evil Nazi "solution" crafted to end it all.

I emailed Nick and asked if he would share his phone number. He responded that same day and the friendship between a new generation of Holzer and Bala families began. I soon learned about Nick's wife and four children, all very accomplished lovers of the outdoors and higher education. Nick introduced me to his sister, Ann Matyas. Without fear of censors, we communicated in real time through email and telephone connections that never failed us. After reading the letters I shared with them, Nick and Ann revealed some puzzle pieces I had been missing. Nick sent me two pictures of his father. One showed a young man of about thirty, dressed in tie and coat, gazing seriously to the side, as if weighing the grave news that he was being forced to leave his homeland. A handsome man with dark hair, distinctive brooding eyes, and full lips, he shared a slight resemblance to the picture of his son Nick on the university website.

The second picture, solemn enough for a funeral portrait, had the caption "Karel C. Bala 1908-1996" beneath the image of a serious-looking man with close-cut white hair, wearing a tailored black suit, gray-striped silk tie, handkerchief, and boutonnière, much like my finely dressed father wore to formal events. Gazing at the picture, I reflected on what might have been if my father and Bála had been able to sit together in their old age.

The fates of the two friends had taken them to different worlds, but some similarities between their postwar lives were stunning. Over the next few weeks, I would learn that for both men, many truths were unspoken. Much like the father of Marie Jana Korbelová, later known as US Secretary of State Madeleine Albright, both men withheld the full facts of their Jewish heritage to some extent. During the war, in addition to his first wife and children, Bála lost his mother, Hermína, and brother, Zdeněk. His sister, Anči (Anna), survived Terezín. "My father's loss from the Holocaust left him scarred," Nick said.

From the revelations of painful secrets I had discovered in the hidden letters, I realized how deeply my father was also scarred. And he, like Bála, kept the depth of his suffering hidden from his children. As it turned out, the most important information was not in stories told, but in those untold. It was their way of protecting us from a past they did not want us to relive with them.

In our initial conversation, Nick told me he didn't know of his father's first wife and children until he was eighteen. I later learned that he didn't even know the nickname—Bála—that his father used to sign his letters to my father. Many of the details I've already shared about Milena were passed along to me by Nick and his sister, Ann, who uncovered them after they learned about their father's early life and turned up his own secret letters. There were more surprises to come. After Bála left Prague, still unaware of the danger approaching, Milena sold the ticket to Yugoslavia that Bála had arranged for her before he left. Later she wrote about wanting to emigrate but did not decide to take action until it was too late—the Nazi's human extermination plan was underway.

Ann also confirmed the rumor of a "beau" relayed by my grandmother sixty-nine years earlier: Milena had an affair with a non-Jewish diplomat. It was clear something was already amiss in their marriage by comments made in Bála's letters. I imagined that perhaps Milena's unhappiness earlier, along with her loneliness after Bála left, led her to find comfort in the arms of someone else.

I believed that a clue to Karel Schoenbaum's anger with Bála's behavior in London involved his reference to Bála's newfound "freedom." I wondered what Karel would have thought had he known of Milena's reciprocal action. Sympathetic to what everyone endured during this horrific period in history, I only wished that somehow their friendship could have been repaired after the war.

In 2010, from archived copies of Bála's military records, I saw that his 1940 petition to use the surname Bala was approved by the Czechoslovak authorities in exile on September 11, 1940. I learned from a translator that such name changes were a common practice intended to protect soldiers with Jewish-sounding names from being sent to concentration camps if they became German prisoners, as well as to protect family members left behind in Czech Lands.

Ann filled in what happened to Bála during the war.

> ...He served in England for much of the war, eventually going to Officer School after being called up in April 1940. After the Allied invasion

of Normandy (June 6, 1944), my father was sent to France as an officer with the Free Czechoslovak Army. In the fall, his arm was seriously injured when a truck he was riding in detonated a mine. He was sent to a hospital in England for treatment. There, to his delight, some of his nurses were Czech friends from Prague.

My father was released from active military service in March 1945 and went to London, where he began working with the Czechoslovak Ministry of Economic Reconstruction. He was appointed Minister of Foreign Trade responsible for Czechoslovak supplies to England and Secretary of the Czechoslovak Delegation of UNRRA (United Nations Relief and Rehabilitation Administration).

Across the world, thousands displaced by Nazi terror began rebuilding their lives by helping others. In June 1946, my own father joined UNRRA, leaving his young family behind in America while he worked for a year in relief operations to China. His service was chiefly in Peking and in North Anhui Province. He organized the surgical services at the Peiping Municipal Hospital and was an instructor in general surgery at Pei Ta University. He also worked as a consulting surgeon for the National Health Administration at Wuhu General Hospital. After a year, UNRRA's massive humanitarian relief effort ended when the Communists drove them out of China. I learned from a letter that my father and mother had wanted to return to China to build a charity hospital for the needy. Their China dreams were dashed twice—first by the Japanese and then by the Communists.

Bála returned to Prague after the war ended in 1945 and learned the fate of his family. He was told that Milena and the children were believed to have been killed at Auschwitz. His two nieces, Soňa and Hana, had survived in a Catholic convent under false names. The convent in Adelholtzen was a hospital for German soldiers and a factory for bottled mineral water. Bála did not receive official declaration of the deaths of Milena and his children until May 15, 1946, around the time my father received official declaration of the deaths of his parents. With modern technology and sophisticated Holocaust record-keeping databases, Lukáš was able to sit at his computer and quickly retrieve the detailed records of their death transports.

Four days before he learned the news of his family, on May 11, Bála became engaged to his second wife, who would become Nick and Ann's mother. He presented her with an emerald-and-diamond ring that had belonged to his mother, and later to Milena. "Near the start of the war, it was buried in their family garden in Prague," Ann told me. "After the war, his sister...found it hidden there and kept it for him. When he came to Prague looking for his family after the war, she gave it to him and encouraged him to remarry and have more children."

He didn't need an introduction to Vera Judith (Věra Judith) Lowenbach. Known to friends as "Mima," she had been a part of the circle of girlfriends in Prague. Bála encountered her again by chance. Guided by a prescient relative, many of Mima's extended family left Prague before the German invasion in 1939. Mima and her parents managed to leave Prague soon after the invasion, making their way to the United States via Switzerland, England, and Cuba. After attending Temple University and Columbia, Mima joined UNRRA and was sent to Germany to work with Holocaust survivors.

As Ann described the fateful moment: "On her way to Germany, my mother had a one-night stopover in London. She immediately began to look for someone who could help her transfer her UNRRA posting from Germany to Czechoslovakia. A friend suggested she contact her old friend Karel Ballenberger, then officially Karel Bala."

Mima's reunion with Bála occurred as he was dealing with the terrible reality of the death of his wife and children and many of his relatives. The couple met several more times before he gave her the ring. By then, Bála was working for the Czechoslovak Foreign Service in London and Prague. In 1947, he was posted as the Commercial Attaché to the Czechoslovak Legation in Ottawa (after WWII legation offices were designated as embassies or high commissions) and Mima and Bála married on February 8, 1947, in New York City on the way to Canada. He worked for the Czechoslovak Legation until February 1948 when the Communist Party, supported by the Soviet Union, took over Czechoslovakia. The whole Czech Legation resigned their posts; once again, just as my father experienced on multiple occasions, Bála was forced to begin anew. It was at this traumatic moment—when Bála lost his homeland and livelihood for the second time—that his daughter Ann was conceived.

Bála and Mima adjusted to life in Canada and did well financially. Under the name Karel C. Bala, he worked as an Alcan company executive in Montreal from 1948 to 1976, using his legal training but never again practicing law, because his foreign credentials were not recognized. Ann was born in 1948, and Nick four years later. Nick said their parents spoke Czech, but Ann and he did not learn it. Bála and Mima were at the center of the Czech community in Canada and sent emotional and financial support to relatives and friends under the thumb of the Communist regime. They contributed money to future Czech Republic President Václav Havel when he was imprisoned for speaking out in support of human rights. Over the years, the couple's house was often filled with Czech refugees, including many who managed to escape in 1968 and 1969 after the Soviet-led invasion and occupation that crushed the Prague Spring, a brief period of political and cultural liberalization in Czechoslovakia led by progressives within the Communist Party.

By all appearances, my father's old friend had overcome tremendous obstacles to achieve a respectable and satisfying life. However, he was haunted by the loss of his family and friends, and his own experiences on the battlefield. Nick said Mima was "less scarred" than her sister and mother, who left Europe just before the war broke out, but she shared her husband's fear of a resurgence of virulent anti-Semitism. Their fears were realized in Czechoslovakia after the Communists came to power and they learned that in *Rudé Právo (The Red Law),* the official Communist party newspaper, people were described by the dangerously divisive words, "of Jewish origin." Once again, people were segregated into Jews and non-Jews.

In 1951, it became even clearer that immense danger lurked in their homeland as Rudolf Slánský, General Secretary of the Communist Party of Czechoslovakia, and thirteen other Communist leaders (eleven of them Jews) were falsely accused of high treason in a proclaimed "Trotskyite-Titoist-Zionist" conspiracy. Under torture or great pressure, the defendants confessed to the bogus charges. In 1952, after an orchestrated Soviet-style show trial with obvious anti-Semitic overtones, eleven were sentenced to death. Slánský, a Jew, was hanged in Pankrác Prison.

Bála and Mima's defense against the possibility of such danger pursuing them to their new country was to swear a pact to keep their Jewish origins a secret. "Partly because Karel [Bála] did not want to lose another family, he made my mother promise never to tell the truth," Ann said. Nick and Ann were raised Unitarian and did not learn of their Jewish background, or of the existence of Milena and their half-siblings, until they were young adults. Nick told me one relative on Mima's side of the family became Catholic and had thirteen children, including one priest and one nun. He knew of others who became agnostics or atheists. Ann married a Jewish man and later she and her younger son converted to Judaism. And, as Nick described, Ann "proudly held for her son the first Bar Mitzvah in the Bala family in over seventy years."

My father never kept his Jewish heritage a secret, but he lived as a proclaimed agnostic after he settled in Florida after the war. He supported my mother's continuing dedication to her faith and service at the Eastminster Presbyterian Church and his children's embrace of religion. I remember his friendship with a local Episcopalian priest and the lively debates they held. I always came away impressed by my father's knowledge of the world's religions. In 2009, I learned from my father's longtime nurse, Sue Barge, a steadfast Baptist, that my father once told her the only religion he would consider joining was the Bahá'í faith. When I read the words of its divine messenger, Bahá'u'lláh, "The earth is but one country and mankind its citizens," I understood why my father felt this way—it reflected his desire for humanity to live in unity.

In our first phone conversation, Nick told me he looked forward to reading his father's letters but that I should know his family "had some complexities." At the time, I simply thought to myself, "Don't we all?" I later discovered what he meant.

After their mother died, and about three years after Bála's death, Nick received a letter from Hugh Thompson in England. As a young university graduate in 1968, Hugh had spent two weeks with the Bala family in Montreal. Bála had introduced him only as a family friend. Nick, then sixteen, recalled being surprised when he observed his father taking what seemed like a rather large sum from his wallet and giving it to Hugh to help with travel expenses. "I was introduced to Hugh by email in July 2010." He explained the "complexity" of their bond and the likely reason for Bála's generosity many years before: Bála was Hugh's father.

Hugh wrote, "I was born June 15, 1946, the son of Karel Bala and Joan Thompson, though I was not aware of my relationship to Karel [Bála] or the circumstances of my conception until much later in life. My parents' relationship occurred in the tumultuous period just before, during and immediately after World War II. As far as I can make out, Karel [Bála] and my mother first became friends just before the war in 1939 at a Fabian summer camp in England."

Hugh speculated that his mother's lifelong socialism was an act of rebellion against her upper-middle-class upbringing. He suspected her affair with Bála didn't begin at their first encounter, because she was married then to Dick Thompson, whom she'd met when they were both students at Oxford. Thompson went on to have a distinguished legal career, for which he was awarded Commander of the Most Excellent Order of the British Empire (CBE), but Hugh said their marriage faced challenges during the war when Thompson was stationed abroad with the military. The affair must have been sparked when Bála was demobilized from the military and returned to London. "I was conceived in October 1945," Hugh explained. "Dick was still in the Army training Belgian officers in the fall of 1945 and there is a letter from Joan to Dick admitting that she and Karel had slept together but saying that it was just one of those things."

Joan and Dick Thompson's marriage ended in an ugly divorce after she had another child, a daughter, by another suitor. Thompson dropped all claims to paternity of the girl, but disputed his wife's admission that someone else had fathered Hugh—although his "absence from England at the time of my conception meant he must have known this fact," Hugh wrote. "Until I was forty, I believed that Dick Thompson...was my father." Then his older sister shared the family secret she'd discovered in the divorce file. "We now fast-forward to 1987 and my mother's seventieth birthday party. In between courses, for reasons I still do not know, I asked my mother: 'What is this story about someone in Canada being my father?' Without missing a beat, she replied: 'Why didn't you ask earlier? Don't you know? It's Karel Bala.'"

Hugh knew Karel Bala only as his mother's longtime friend. She had never told Bála the truth about Hugh. By then married and himself a father, Hugh asked her to write a letter to Bála. Bála wrote back warmly, but did not acknowledge that he was Hugh's father. "At the time, he was in his early eighties, no longer fit, and any admission of paternity would have complicated the already complex, dramatic story of his family life," Hugh said. "He had kept the secret of his Jewish identity and his first family from his two Canadian children, Ann and Nick, until they were adults, and he may have worried that to add another sibling so late in life would have strained relationships with his wife or his children." Bála may not have been certain Hugh was his son, as Joan didn't tell him for more than forty years. Hugh didn't press the issue. "It didn't upset me as I was secure in my own family," Hugh wrote, "and was not some dramatic soap opera character in search of some missing emotional or biological link. At the time, I felt sorry for Karel missing out on two lovely grandchildren."

After Bála died, Hugh reached out to the brother and sister he'd known only for those two weeks in 1968. Nick and Ann knew about the letter their father had received but didn't realize the depth of his feelings toward Joan until Bála died. "Apparently, among the papers in his bedside table when he died, Karel [Bála] had pictures of three women: his first wife, Milena; his second wife, Mima; and my mother, Joan." Soon after, Hugh flew to Canada. Any doubt about Bála's paternity was dispelled at first sight. "I look (and reportedly act) much more like Karel than either of his other children, who take after their mother," he said. "The family joke has become that it is Nick who should have to take a DNA test to have his paternity established. Ann and Nick have accepted me as the long-lost brother that I am and have shared some of Karel's things with me."

It was already very clear to me from reading the multitude of letters that the time leading up to and during World War II and its aftermath was an era of many difficult and unimaginable choices. Some people were prepared for the consequences or temptations and rose to the moment, and others could not. After Bála's death, Ann and Nick discovered a few letters from his past. They found a letter from Milena in an old wallet. Inside were clippings of his children's hair. It is distressing to imagine what Milena felt as her situation deteriorated and she may have believed that she and her children had been abandoned, or what Bála was thinking as he recovered from his war injury and heard rumors that his wife and children had been taken away. With my own comfortable American upbringing, I feel inadequate to grasp what it was like to survive in a world at war in which the individual had little or no control over destiny, where so many were victims of horrific atrocities. How could anyone ever escape that shadow—the guilt of decisions made in desperate situations and the guilt of survival when others perished?

After I sent the first letters to Nick, he forwarded them to relatives. Within two weeks, I received a call from Jitka Deyl, a grandniece of Bála, who was living in Ottawa. Jitka's mother, Soňa, born in 1924, was Bála's niece. She lives six months of the year in Ottawa with Jitka, and then returns for the remainder of the year to her hometown of Prague. Both women were very moved by the letters. Though it pained her, Soňa wanted to help me by sharing her very vivid memories.

When the Nazis occupied Czechoslovakia in 1939, Soňa was fifteen. In the horrible years that followed, she and her sister Hana, born in 1921, grew up very fast. They were "non-practicing Jews" and she remembered the anti-Semitism as she grew up. Soňa did not recall meeting my father, but she recognized the names of some common friends who skied together in the Krkonoše Mountains. I asked Soňa if she recognized the name Julius Lankaš, a well-known artist mentioned in several old letters, who frequented the Mánes Café with Bála and his friends. Soňa told me that Julius had made a plaster bust of Mima and that it was now in Nick's country cottage.

Soňa's most moving recollections were of Bála and Milena. Bála was extremely bright; a Boy Scout at heart, true and dutiful, individualistic, much attached to friends, socially active, ebullient, fun and a girl-loving young man. During her visits with him in Canada, Soňa said Bála never failed to blame himself for underestimating the political situation in Prague, which caused the imprisonment of his family in a concentration camp and the inevitable death of his first wife, two children, his in-laws, and his own mother and brother. Bála's older sister, Anči, and her daughters, Hana and Soňa, noted his loyalty through all the years of the Communist regime in Prague: "He stretched his financial and moral support to our children after their emigration to Canada. His deep interest in their well-being and further development was demonstrated on a daily basis, and so was his grief and pain for what he lost."

She remembered Milena's beautiful family home, with servants and a garden. "The last memory—the family was removed from their house to a small flat, packing for the departure to Łódź to an unknown future, and I was helping them get ready for the trip and talking to the kids, advising them to be good to their mother and grandparents." The same transport took Soňa's maternal grandmother and Bála's older brother. "My grandmother was debating if she should take her hats and which would be suitable... nobody knew anything of the nearest future. They all died in Łódź; only Milena and her kids were moved to Auschwitz. I have many more memories of them which I have tried all my life to forget." Soňa continued, nonetheless, "The last time I saw Milena was at my father's funeral in early October 1941. It is the saddest picture of Milena in my mind…Milena looked beautiful and she came bearing a big flower bouquet of red roses. She told us she had received her notice for deportation to the concentration camp." Soňa paused and then added, "The memory is always there, I keep it hidden. Otherwise I couldn't live with it."

It was clear to me that many of my father's dispersed friends had been helped to some degree by their privileged class—mostly through contacts abroad. But for those Jews who stayed behind, this same privileged past was responsible for their demise. Many of the early deportations by the Nazis and their Czech collaborators were driven purely by the desire to acquire—or more appropriately, confiscate—these people's property, a motivation later described by my father as "pure thievery."

Soňa reminisced about her uncle Bála and my father Valdik. "Their lives before the war had been so happy, so joyous. They were completely different after the war. Yes, they adjusted to new lives, new practices, but they were never the same. All that happened is so hard to explain to the generation of today. It is like speaking a foreign language when you try to tell them of the atmosphere of the 1930s and '40s and all we went through. The letters make it all so real; they provide the connection to the past." As Soňa aptly pointed out, after seventy years their newly freed words allowed us to understand what they and millions of others endured and be sympathetic.

I knew the letters might also hold meaning for Hana's son. In February 2009, I reached out to Michael Žantovský, who served as the Czech Ambassador to Washington in the early 1990s. At the time of my contact, he was the Czech Ambassador to Israel and soon after became Czech Ambassador to the United Kingdom. With appreciation of the past, Michael responded: "I was fascinated and more than a little moved by reading about your odyssey in retracing the footsteps of your late father and finding about his friends, including my late great-uncle Karel Bala. I got to know him as a student in Montreal, enjoying his hospitality and generosity in the turbulent years of 1968-1969. Although we did not see eye to eye on my eventual return to Czechoslovakia—I was a typically wild and rather rebellious child of the era—I remember him fondly and I appreciated the opportunity of seeing him again shortly before his death in Ottawa."

While conversations with Karel's relatives went back and forth, Nick visited his country house to look at his father's old collection of address cards. There, amid many heirlooms, including the bust of his mother by now-famous Czech artist Julius Lankaš, he found a card for Dr. O. A. Holzer, P. O. Box 998, Melbourne, Florida. It triggered Nick's memory of his father's trip to Florida long ago to see an old friend. When Nick told me the big news, I realized that Valdik and Bála did meet again; not as they had hoped at Mánes Café nor at the Brandenburg Gate, but in the bright sunshine of Florida where I grew up.

In January 2009, Bála's daughter Ann said, "My father never told the most important story. He never shared the details of what happened with the attempts to get Milena out." Two-and-a-half years later, I received correspondence that provided critical information to Bála's narrative.

Indicative of the way my retirement sleuthing unfolded, with puzzle pieces suddenly appearing, was the receipt of this surprise email on August 3, 2011, from a total stranger named Carol Provisor. The information she provided felt like another gift on my journey of discovery.

Dear Joanie Schirm,

I am in possession of a photocopy of a letter written by Karel Ballenberger to Carl Ballenberger in Cleveland, Ohio, who I believe is a nephew of my grandmother, Clara Ballenberger Kraus, a first cousin to my father, Arthur E. Kraus. My father gave me the original letter long ago and recently I gave it to my brother, Arthur D. Kraus, to keep in the Kraus family. I am sending a translated copy to you because I suspect some descendent of Karel Ballenberger (now Bala) will want to read his eloquent, desperate plea for help in emigrating from Czechoslovakia in 1939.

I had not conducted a Google search for Karel Ballenberger in a long time, so I was surprised and intrigued when your article in *Shemot* [the magazine of the Jewish Genealogical Society of Great Britain] December 2010 came up. I had learned via the Internet the fate of Milena and her children, but not that of Karel. And now I know. Your article was not only informative for me but extremely moving in all respects. I am contacting you because you may want to forward the copy of Karel's letter and its legacy to his family, with whom you have been in touch.

Bála's letter, sent from Prague, was dated March 6, 1939.

Dear Sir,

It is to Mrs. Šťastná-Eksteinová that I am indebted for your address. I am a son of Leopold and Hermína Ballenberger from Praha-Blaník/Smíchov, who was a cousin of yours. This relationship authorizes me to ask you a great kindness, to grant me an affidavit of support and enable me thus to go with my wife and family to immigrate to USA.

I hope you are informed about the political and economic situation of the actual Republic of Czecho-Slovakia {so called Second Republic}. The growing anti-Jewish trend and the general economic circumstances seem not to allow in the next future any Jews to work and live in Central Europe.

I am 30 years old, my wife Milena, whose maiden name was Langer, daughter of Dr. Leopold Langer, is 26 years old. We have two children, Alena, who is 3 years old and John, who is only 1 year old. I am enclosing their photographs.

At present I am running a barristers' office in Prague, but I am afraid I shall not be allowed to act as a barrister any longer, should anti-Jewish measures come into force, and shall therefore have to try my chances somewhere else.

I studied law at the Czech University in Prague, am Doctor of Laws and have had great experience in commerce. Besides Czech, I speak rather well, English, French, German and Spanish. My wife speaks the same languages, and possesses commercial experience too. She is a chartered nurse. The personal particulars of my whole family are enclosed.

I assure you, Dear Mr. Ballenberger, that, should you make up your mind and send [unreadable— copy is on the fold of the letter] any member of our family affidavits, that we are prepared to do anything to earn our living. I have no other relatives in the USA and am sending you this depressing letter with my greatest reluctance, forced only by the present strained circumstances.

I hope you will kindly do what is in your power and thank you together with my wife from all my heart for whatever you will be kind enough to do for us.

Yours very respectfully,

[signed:] Karel Ballenberger

1 photo, 1 enclosure.

Dr. Karel Ballenberger, Prague XVIII. Vořechovka, Slunná 4.

Czecho-Slovakia.

In 1939, an affidavit of support was required by every would-be immigrant to the United States, with the exception of persons of means who arrived on specific visas as "capitalists." The notarized affidavit statement contained information about the person's salary, bank account, and employment verification to ensure, if need be, the sponsor could support this person. Quotas for US immigration were determined by a formula for each European nationality. For the government fiscal year ending June 30, 1939, the limit was 2,874 for Czechoslovakians. Unbeknownst to Karel "Bála" Ballenberger, enough Czechoslovakians had already applied for US visas to fill the quota for the next year.

As fate would have it, the forwarded translated letter I received from Carol reached Nick and his sister when both their lives were being filled with happy events. Ann had just become a first-time grandmother of a healthy baby girl. Nick was on vacation and immediately responded:

"It is painful to read, but important to know more about his life. Although formal in tone and translated, his voice still comes through. Coincidentally I am at present in Maine on a vacation with Jitka, and my (half) brother, Hugh Thompson...so it is good to be able to share the letter in person."

After reading this letter written seventy years ago, I have no doubt that Bála desperately attempted to ensure his first wife and children would be safe. Had Milena's father not convinced her to wait, perhaps all would have ended differently. But in the end, providence chose Nick, Ann, and Hugh to carry forward their father's legacy.

KAREL C. BALA
1908 - 1996

LEFT TOP: KAREL (BALLENBERGER) BALA; RIGHT: TOP: KAREL BALA; BOTTOM RIGHT: First wife Milena (née Langer) Ballenberger, children: Alena and Honza "Jan" Ballenberger, circa 1939

2 PHOTOS OF KAREL BALA WITH SECOND WIFE VĚRA JUDITH "MIMA" (NÉE LOWENBACH);
BOTTOM: CHILDREN: ANN AND NICHOLAS "NICK" BALA, 1957

Left: Nicholas "Nick" Bala; below: Hugh Thompson; right: Ann & Bob Matyas family, 2011; middle: Nick Bala family; bottom right: Bob and Ann Matyas and Joanie Holzer Schirm, 2012 (Photos courtesy of family)

H. Fürtenöh
For Mr. Lenfurth, Park House,
Rugeley, Staffs.

H. W.

Rugeley dne 9. VI. 1939.

Milý Valdíčku!

Děkuji Ti za Tvůj milý dopis, který jsem před několika dny obdržela. Máš to věru dobře, že si tam poteš hezkým časem ani nevíš jak dobře máš a až se Ti dobře daří. Aneb přece dopsila jsem včera psaní Tvého dopisu, kde vlastně nyní jsi zdali střídavě v Hong - Kongu a Šanghaji nebo zda-li si nyní již v Šanghaji, tak bych byla ráda, kdyby mi o sobě více napsala. Také píšeš, že máme pojedeš do Evropy apod. Máš to ještě jisté v úmyslu? Ja bych vědět že Táňa když tu byl jiz plán. Protož jsem nyní tak bláznivě a každým dnem se situace mění úplně naruby, že člověk věru těžko může dělat nějaké rozhodnutí nyní. Ale i kdyby se ve světě budou dít nějaké změny k lepšímu a činí velice pochybný, my řekl to budeme mít velice těžké dostat se zpátky do starých kolejí a začít nějakou slušnou existenci, ať už to bude všude venku, nebo zase doma. Nejhorší nyní ale je jak v tom případě tak v tom, že naše rodiče jsou tam a my venku. Jsi s nimi ve spojení normálně tak jako dříve, nebo Ti psaní od nich dochází pomaleji? Já si s našimi a Vilíkem Dubským, který je také v Belgii nyní pravidelně dopisuji.

Já tu jsem již od prvního tohoto měsíce v místě co by panská. Je to pro mne sice poněkud neobyklá práce, jak si můžeš představit ale ne jsem si na to ze cela zvykla, nejsem ta normálně zdravá ale přece jen jsem měla účaší. Přišla jsem k moc slušným lidem, kteří se ke mně moc dobře chovají a práce nemám také přespříliš mnoha odpoledne mám dost času na odpočinek tak myslím že tu nějaký čas ráda zůstanu, přišla jsem sem do Anglie tato úmyslem zůstat jako panská jen krátce a pak si najít místo k dětem, co by mně bylo přijemnější zaměstnání když mi v tom zdejším čase, to není nic normi přijemna...

... všech obtíží s tím spojených, tedí ačkoliv mám ráznějši ... ve stavnění chůze práce jen dostala. Měla jsem tedí ... se 14 tidenně lhůta ten platný do 31. června, ne ale ... dostala se sem. V domově se právě jaká ... dověti se poručíkud víc a víc jsem si právě ... (Praině mně) má a mou přítelkyni ... od vypuknutí války. Event nejpři jsem U.S.A. i ... před jeden dopis, tak v těch dvou dopisech jsem se vše ... chtěl Ti dva mně sdělit jak to tam nyní vypadá a ... ně nejpíš, při pomůchad to bě, že je rozhodl ... otěžínnýny neudály. O krizech mi táteňka píše, že je ... dam Fürerové, strýčka Fürtha, strýčka Ehrensteina ... nebo, jsta hraní, celé serie, to se také dá přivít

Chapter 6:

Hana Winternitz (Bell)

Dramatis Personae

Hana Winternitz (Bell)

(Valdik's first cousin)

Maternal grandparents:	Alois and Marie (née Porges) Holzer
Parents:	Rudolf "Rudi" and Olga (née Holzer) Winternitz
Uncles:	Arnošt Holzer (married to Olga, Valdik's father) Leo "Lenda" Holzer (married to Elsa) Emil Kraus (married to "Ritscha") Fritz Winternitz (married to Leo Lilling's sister)
Aunts:	Valerie "Valda" (née Holzer) Mařík (married to Jaroslav "Sláva") Marie "Ritscha" Kraus (married to Emil)
First cousins:	Valdik Holzer, Hanuš Holzer, Jiří Mařík, Pavel Mařík, Pavel Kraus (later Paul), Franzl Kraus (later Frank), Fritz Kraus, Anny Godsey-Carman (née Kraus)
Husband:	Christopher "Idris" Bell
Daughters:	Jennifer Bell, Stephanie Bell
Grandchildren:	Joanna Bell, Penny Bell, Christopher Bell
Nephew:	Owain Bell
Second and third Cousins:	Tomáš Mařík, Martin Matějka, Leo Lilling (by marriage)

I would be content here, if one can be content at all in these times.

—Hana Winternitz, July 9, 1940

The letters by my father's cousin, Hana Winternitz, read like a script from the longest-running prime-time drama in American television, *Masterpiece Theatre*, or a tale by Charlotte Brontë: An earnest young woman toils through a series of jobs working as a humble domestic in the English countryside while dreaming of a better life.

> …I came here with the intention of being a maid only for a short time and then planned to find a job as an au pair. Then the war came and I thought that in such insecure times, it would be better not to move unless I have to. Now I am nonetheless rethinking that and in the nearest future I am going to start looking for a job with children. Nothing is keeping me here, and if I choose well and with deliberation, my life will be a bit easier.

Nothing captures the uneasy yet determined spirit of my letter-writing adventurers like these words from Hana. Her grace revealed in the sixteen letters in my father's collection was all the more remarkable to me because I knew that her leap—from being a privileged teenage Czech girl who attended Swiss boarding schools, vacationed on the French Riviera, and was active as a Girl Guide, to being only nineteen and alone, working as a maid in a foreign country where she barely spoke the language—was made all the more harrowing by the burden of anguish she bore over the perils facing her family back home. And there was far greater grief to come when she learned their fate.

I never met Hana, and I knew little about her while my father was alive. I recalled my mother and father visiting a Czech relative, Hana

Bell, perhaps three or four times on trips they took to Great Britain and Prague beginning in the 1960s. Fortunately, my introduction to Hana didn't have to wait for the translation of her letters. Tucked into a thick file of my father's, I discovered a 1990 memoir handwritten by Hana in English.

> …I had a normal happy childhood in Prague… I was too young to be aware of the Depression years. My father, Rudolf Winternitz, was a builder and had some difficult years, but he became a successful and prosperous businessman in the 1930s. He was not allowed to carry on his business after the Germans occupied and divided Czechoslovakia in March 1939, because he was a Jew.

I recognized her father as my great-uncle Rudolf. His wife, Olga, was one of my grandfather Arnošt's two sisters. When I saw their names, I realized that the unfolding story of Cousin Hana was a continuation of the saga that I inadvertently began to uncover in 1993 when I naively asked my father if he'd like to come along to see *Schindler's List*. My father's refusal was swift and vehement, but also deeply revealing. Without speaking, he sat down and typed what I came to call Valdik's List: the names of forty-four relatives who died in the Holocaust. I was forty-four years old, and this was the first time my brother, sister, and I learned the true extent of our family's loss. To say I was stunned would be an understatement.

The devastation made clear from the list reached evenly through both maternal and paternal lines. Using his own codes for additional details, my father noted the years when he thought each relative had died and where the death occurred. Overwhelmingly, most were forced from their homes into Nazi transports in 1942. Two names later took on significantly more meaning when I began studying the letters:

Chapter 6: Hana Winternitz (Bell)

Rudolf Winternitz (O) TZ 1942; +A 1942
Olga (Holzer) Winternitz (A) TZ 1942; +A 1942

In his code, O stood for uncle, I assume from the German word *Onkel*, and A meant aunt; TZ referred to the concentration camp Terezín, and +A meant later relocation to Auschwitz. I believe that most of his information was acquired just after the war from Aunt Valda (Valerie Mařík, his one surviving aunt). With modern resources and research, I learned that in a few instances some details, such as where or when the death occurred, were wrong, but never the crucial one: in every instance, I confirmed that the people on Valdik's list had perished at one death camp or another.

Rudolf Winternitz, born September 24, 1882, and his wife Olga, born November 26, 1892, were both deported with a thousand people from Prague aboard Transport Bd on September 4, 1942, to Terezín. With them on the transport was Olga's mother, Marie Holzer, my great-great-grandmother. She was eighty years old. Just before Rudolf and Olga arrived at the camp, several prisoners were charged with having attempted to smuggle out letters and were sentenced to death by hanging. In another document, I read that a friend of my father's from Mánes had been hanged from the Terezín gallows for the crime of storing in his pocket a gold inlay that had fallen from his tooth. It was forbidden for Jews to have anything gold on them—even a stray filling meant death.

Records show that Olga was in Terezín not only with her husband and mother Marie, but with her brother Leo "Lenda" Holzer, his wife Elsa, and their young son, Hanuš. Terezín records detail how Marie, 80, died of pneumonia three months after they arrived, on December 26, 1942. On October 16, 1944, along with 1,500 other people, Rudolf and Olga were sent on Transport Er to Auschwitz, where they perished.

Arnošt's sister, Valerie (Holzer) Mařík—known to us as Aunt Valda—wrote my father just after the war and told him that as the Allies advanced toward Terezín in 1945, Marie's ashes, along with the ashes of many others, were thrown in the nearby Ohře River in an attempt by the Nazis to eliminate the last remnants of the Jews and hide the extent of their atrocities.

Not until early April 2008, with the translation of my grandfather Arnošt's letter of love and farewell to my father—written three days before Arnošt and Olga were deported from Prague by the Nazis—did I discover the special place his brother-in-law, Rudolf, held in Arnošt's heart.

In this letter that changed everything for my father were three people's names: Rudolf Winternitz, Uncle Jaroslav "Sláva" Mařík, and Cousin Robert Fischer [my Grandmother Olga's nephew]. I knew I needed to know more about these men and their families; I had no idea how that would happen since I couldn't ask my father. From Hana's letters, I felt I understood Rudolf a little better but wanted to know more. Reading her account made me queasy, but I persevered.

> ...Troops were mobilized before the Munich agreement. There was a fear of air raids in Prague and I went to stay with my grandmother. After that I left school and started preparing for a new life. After experiencing the First World War, my mother, Olga, bought clothes including linen, etc. for my trousseau with no husband in sight. It came in useful after the war started. I even let neighbors have some of the bed sheets.
>
> I decided to immigrate to Britain because friends of our family had immigrated there. I found a job as housemaid with a family in Staffordshire.

With the assistance of a British organization that helped refugees I was able to get a visa. Getting an exit permit from the Gestapo proved to be more difficult...a local landowner from my father's birthplace was friendly with the Nazis. When I went with him in August 1939 to see a high-ranking officer of the regional Gestapo, I was very nervous. He said that things were getting difficult and that there was movement of troops on the Polish frontier but he gave me the visa.

I left Prague to travel on my own by train through Germany to Holland and then to Britain. My parents and many of my relatives came to the railroad station to say goodbye. Fortunately most of my cousins in my generation also left, some for Belgium, some for the States, and some [like Valdik] for China. One [Hanuš] even survived in Terezín camp in Bohemia.

Out of all of my uncles and aunts, only my mother's sister, Valerie (Aunt Valda) survived, because she was sent to a different place, as her husband wasn't a Jew. My father was one of six and my mother was one of four and the Germans killed all but one in concentration camps.

Hana's chronicle was reminiscent of how my father sounded in his interviews. Both cousins wrote in a matter-of-fact style, alternating between safe and hugely tragic stories as if this were normal. Sitting in my soft chair, I thought about these two young cousins whose parents were murdered by the Nazis. I thought about how it would feel to say, "My parents were murdered," to have many friends and relatives whose parents had been murdered. I could not imagine friends being gassed, or seeing ships loaded with innocent passengers being blown out of the ocean just as I walked away. And yet as I stared at Hana's handwriting, I felt relief, as miraculously both she and her cousin Valdik made it through those troubled times.

A year after I read her mini-memoir, I received Hana's translated letters, along with three letters written to her by my father. Her terse summary developed into a full picture of the uncertainty this young woman encountered as she tried to find her footing in war-torn Great Britain while she worried about the safety of the parents she left behind. She endured air raids and bomb shelters, blackouts, food rationing, and loneliness. As I began to read the letters, I conjured up an image of her, imagining a petite woman with a pretty smile and a thick Czech accent cast amid proper, crisp British voices, as she set out alone to find a safer world.

Upon reading the first letter in the series from my father to Hana, dated September 15, 1939, I realized how far the Mánes circle of friends reached, when he offered her the London addresses of Dr. Karel "Bála" Ballenberger and Dr. Karel Schoenbaum:

> …I think both have connections to leading Czechoslovak people; they could possibly be helpful to you.

Nineteen-year-old Hana led a rather vagabond life during the war, I soon realized as I read her words, beginning with a November 9, 1939, letter to my father from Rugeley, Staffordshire, England.

> …I have already been here since the beginning of August, working as a maid. It is a bit of a strange job for me, as you can imagine, but I have already gotten quite used to it. It isn't particularly entertaining but nonetheless I was lucky. I am working for very nice people who are treating me very well and don't really have too much work to do. I have time in the afternoon to rest and so I think I will stay here for a while…

My translator and researcher, Lukáš, noted that domestic work was perhaps the only path to a British visa for Hana, who was too old for the Czech *Kindertransport* to Great Britain. This heroic mission, led by British stockbroker Nicholas Winton, saved 699 Jewish children from Czechoslovakia from the Holocaust in 1938 and 1939, until the invasion of Poland. However, older refugees found it almost impossible to qualify for entry to Great Britain before the war. The only exceptions were for those willing to work at jobs the British couldn't or wouldn't fill. Domestic servants were in high demand, and permits were issued even for those with no experience. Hana's decision to pursue this course almost undoubtedly saved her life.

Even knowing little about Hana's background, I felt sure this wasn't the sort of work she'd aimed for, and I scoured each letter for a clue to her real aspirations. Every letter began with "on the day of," a formality I found charming and one that somehow helped me melt into her world long ago, like this one from Rugeley, England to my father.

On the day of January 7, 1940:

As far as our [more distant] relatives at home are concerned, I am also adding Uncle Ohrenstein to the long line of deaths. He died the same week as Uncle Fürth and Mrs. Maříková. It was quite a long succession of them, but they were better off than those in a concentration camp. About them I don't know, even about a single one of them, but my parents are probably not bold enough to write about it as your parents are. Ota Porges was locked up while I was still at home, of course in a concentration camp, as was Erna Fürth and Franta Ohrenstein—but him they must have arrested by sheer chance.

In your letter you write that I should write in case I needed something. Naturally I would be happier if I weren't here without money and if I had something extra for unforeseeable circumstances (I of course save a little bit of my monthly salary but of course not very much) but I don't need anything urgently and therefore do only as you find convenient.

Grim as this was, I added each of the names to my database. My father's reply from Peking, dated March 8, 1940, indicated he'd already heard the sad family news, and understood the danger in writing openly from the homeland and the unsteady conditions for his parents in Prague:

...With the news from your letter I am actually mostly familiar already, through letters from home. It is not that my folks are more courageous in writing, but they are writing in a rather smart way, so for example when they mention that someone is going to a spa, it means he is in a concentration camp, etc. Of course they don't write much detail to me, but nevertheless I am at least a little bit informed about what the situation is like there already now. At one point it must have been quite threatening since some of the family wanted to get out but now, as far as I have news, the situation calmed down again...

It is natural that you are looking for something better and for an easier job; in any case you are not used to such work. I sincerely hope and wish for you that you have already found something suitable. So much to your letter; now I will write to you something about my recent fate. I will write about it as it really is and I ask you not to pass on all of the information.

I have to admit that my medical office in Shanghai, which went just so-so, bored me terribly. Understandably, I was constantly on the lookout for something better and well, maybe I found something. Before Christmas one of my numerous applications was finally answered and with it came a position—as the head of the hospital of the American Brethren mission in Ping Ting Hsien, Shansi. It is nothing spectacular. The pay is that of our surgery-room attendant (4 pounds), but considering the local conditions it is good enough and most of all, one has some livelihood and work which pleases them, with plenty of tremendous professional experience gained.

In a letter from Anglesey, written on March 24, 1940, Hana responded with more news of yet another adventurer.

> …As to what I know now about the family and acquaintances: Pavel Kraus, my cousin (he used to be in Pernegg and from there went in your direction to China). I don't know exactly where, whether to Shanghai. With the huge distances there you most probably won't meet him, since you are now in the North. Maybe he'll write to you. Father must have surely given him your address. I am eager to hear what he will report. One cannot make for oneself a true picture from these reports and I never know whether it is true or it is an exaggeration.

It was from this letter that Pavel Kraus made it into my database of unknown names. It would take another year to discover fully how he fit into my paternal family tree. My father's letter, written on May 24, 1940, indicates that he was already in touch with Pavel when Hana's letter arrived.

…I hope that you have found a nice job already, with a decent air-raid shelter, though I strongly believe that you will not need it, as I hope that there will be an end to all this stupidity soon and that you will be on your way to Prague again. Otherwise I am not sure whether being in London is to your advantage in these insecure times…

Pavel Kraus is in Shanghai. He would like to study here, preferably chemistry, and so I have been chasing after this in Peking a bit. It is however terribly difficult as the lectures at most schools are held in Chinese. I don't want to take him here with me yet, since I don't know how long I will be staying. If it becomes clear that I will stay in one location for some time, he will be able to join me, should he want to live in the interior. But there is no future here. Otherwise, however, I am already in frequent written contact with him. His news isn't greatly alarming but also isn't overly cheerful. I think he was the last one to arrive to Shanghai from Bohemia, since it is now exceedingly difficult to get out of there.

I have been in the interior again for a month and I am rather stuck in a foul mood. I don't have much work, I act like a big lord but my income is that of a petty one, no prospects and so it is all getting on my nerves a bit. Nonetheless, I have to be content with what I have. I am concluding for today. You can write to me in Shansi or Shanghai. To save on mail charges, you can include the letter to me in one to Pavel Kraus, his address is: c/o Dr. Braun, W. 11 Park Road, Shanghai, or to Mr. Lilling, both will forward it to me.

The name Leo Lilling was another that appeared and reappeared in the file of correspondence. When I began organizing the letters, I was especially drawn to the ones he and my father exchanged. There were fifty in all and several were in English, written by Leo to my father when he moved to interior China from Shanghai. I learned they used English because Japanese censors in some areas of China would throw letters away written in Czech because they could not decipher them, so the two men chose the safer language, which both understood. I listened again to the interview with my father I'd recorded about his arrival in June 1939 at Hong Kong Harbor and realized a "distant relative named Leo Lilling" had met him at the port. His only additional details about Leo were that he was a successful importer/exporter and an Austrian Czech who had lived in China for perhaps ten years by the time my father arrived.

From the letters it was apparent that Leo was older, wiser, and knew how to survive in war-torn China, where Japanese, Chinese Nationalists, and Communists all vied for control. Leo was both protective and helpful to my father when he needed it most and obviously knew my father's relatives, including Hana. I learned from Hana's letter from Southport, Lancashire, written on July 9, 1940, that she too found kind help along the way.

> …Thank you for your letter from the 21st of May. I was happy to see the handwriting of my parents once again, after a long time, though dated such a long time ago. I haven't written to you for an awfully long time but these days one doesn't have much time, nor mood or inclination for writing.
>
> I was employed in London for over 2 months. It was a Jewish family, very rational and decent people—I was really happy with them. But when this history with Belgium and Holland came about

[the German occupation], they decided to send the children to school in the countryside, away from London.

I myself—though all my acquaintances are there— of course preferred to leave London and I found a job here in Southport. It is a place that is half spa, nice beyond all expectations, by the sea, a bit north of Liverpool. They are Jews again, the children are behaved, and the girl (she is six) is very cute. Except for the fact that on the weekends they always have lots of guests and that's a lot of work, I would be content here, if one can be content at all in these times.

The Graffs however decided to leave, they still don't know exactly where to, they wanted to go to Cape Town, but that is impossible. The lady is going with the two children, so if it were possible, I would go with them. I am doubtful that it will be possible but maybe it will work out, I can try. Work conditions here are becoming increasingly worse for foreigners. A number of districts are off-limits to foreigners and elsewhere the conditions are better. To find employment however isn't easy anywhere and if I can't get away, I will search for a job here again.

Franzl Kraus wrote to me about my parents, that they are fine; it takes a while before I can find out about them and nothing can be done. In short, one has to be patient and let's hope that they will endure it there, in peace, until the end of the war.

I wondered if Franzl Kraus was related to the mysterious Pavel, whose name continued to pop up in the back-and-forth letters between my father and Hana, like this one from Valdik in Ping Ting Hsien, written on August 2, 1940.

> ...Yesterday I got a letter from your dear parents, which I am enclosing. Like to you, I wrote to them through addresses of friends in neutral countries. How they can also serve as intermediaries you can see from the enclosure. I wrote to both friends simultaneously but so far I have not received any answers. I believe it will be best for now if you send some letters to me and I will mediate the connection for you. It will take a bit longer, but they will be calmer at home if they get something at least. Anyway, I think you don't have to feel completely abandoned, as you have a number of relatives in England...

> My parents were expelled from their apartment, since the building was "Aryanized." They moved to Slezská Street on July 1. They didn't give me the address for whatever reason; every little stupidity now worries one. It seems they get together with your parents very often and so at least both don't miss us so. This month I got two letters from Šebířov [township]. It seems all is well there.

> Pavel Kraus has not called on me for about three months now, I therefore don't know how and what he is doing.

> Did you ever look up my friends in London whose addresses I sent you? [Dr. Karel "Bála" Ballenberger and Dr. Karel Schoenbaum.]

The comment my father made about his parents being expelled from their "Aryanized" apartment building referred to the National Socialist government's transfer of ownership of real-estate and businesses in occupied lands from Jewish to non-Jewish hands. Under the 1933 Aryan Paragraph and the 1935 Nuremberg Laws, Jews were classified as racially inferior, which set in motion the banning of Jews from the practice of certain professions as well as the racially biased confiscation of property.

During the first years of Nazi occupation (and earlier in Germany, the Sudetenland, and Austria), mass transfers of Jewish properties into "Aryan" hands occurred, along with the liquidation of law and medical offices, factories, department stores, banks, and other businesses. Over time, the policy swelled to allow the confiscation of everything of value, including houses, land, stamp collections, books, jewelry, art, and more. The plunder took place in the open and was no secret to anyone.

By her next letter, written from Southport on September 26, 1940, Hana had moved on yet again.

> ...I have...been searching for a new job and had to move, I hope for the last time while in England. I am already fed up with all this moving from place to place. However, I am content here and let's hope it will stay this way.
>
> The job with the Graff family did not work out the way I imagined. I spent little time with children but had a lot of work in the household, often with an absurd number of guests, and since Mrs. Graff wasn't an exactly pleasant person I decided not to stay there. Now I am not with children. To find a good job dealing with children isn't that easy and at the time I also didn't want to go to London and start searching from there.
>
> But I got lucky and found a job here in Southport with a Jewish couple who have a ten-week-old baby.

However, Mrs. Goldberg takes care of it; she also cooks. I don't have much to do here, plenty of time to myself and they are very decent people, I am almost a family member to them. And so hopefully everything will finally be OK.

I nevertheless still have some hazy moving plans. The Hermanns are trying to get a visa to Australia and they attached me to their application, however I doubt that anything will come of it. I would be happy if I could get out of here and start something decent, but I will probably have to be patient and wait. But I share with you the opinion that even if this war ends quickly—it is hard to say whether it will or will not be so, probably only a few privy individuals know that and maybe even they don't—but even if the war ended quickly, everything in Europe will be so upside-down and fragmented that it will be difficult to start a new existence.

Australia would be a good way out of this, but I don't hang high hopes on that request and so my plans for the future are even hazier than they had been before the beginning of the war. But it will all somehow end, for now peace and tranquility are of utmost importance. We luckily still have this calmness here and I hope that will last.

Thanks for the regards from my parents. I don't have an idea about the way it really looks there now, regarding the atmosphere and the like. The letters talk about hens and the cow and at most about the visit by Uncle Lenda [Leo Holzer]. My folks at least have a distraction from that atrocious countryside drabness and life without some respectable employment.

After receiving the news that Valdik had gotten married in Peking, Hana wrote from Southport on February 14, 1941.

> ...I just learned from my parents' letter the surprising news about the change of your status and so, even though a bit belatedly, I wish you and your wife all the best in the future, that you have plenty of luck, and all your plans and wishes come true and that you live in harmony and health and most of all contentment.

> I can imagine how surprised your parents must have been when you surprised them so suddenly, just as I was surprised. I wasn't surprised by you with two people together; things are easier, if you know that you have someone close by your side, rather than being alone in a foreign country. Write to me something about your wife so I can make some sort of an image of her, or do you have an extra picture of her?

> I am starting to think in English. My folks only wrote to me that she was studying there in China and that she comes from America. And what other events concerning you happened in the meantime? Where are you now—back again at that north China hospital?

> I am still here in Southport, in my second job; I am satisfied with both the Goldbergs and with Southport, but, there is one "but." I am once again of the mind to change my location and profession. With the Goldbergs I get along very well and in time I even got into a very good friendly relationship with them. I like the baby, too. She is a very cute creature with large eyes and round cheeks and she likes me, if one can talk about that at her age. She is seven months old.

Southport is also OK. It is a calm and pretty town with a fine movie theater, two theaters! I saw Richard Tauber here in *The Land of Smiles*, Robert Donat in a wonderful play by Shaw, and the day after tomorrow I am going to see *Rebecca*, which was an excellent movie, and so considering that I am in the middle of a war I don't have a bad life.

However, I think it would be a waste of time to work as a housekeeper for the duration of the entire war. God knows how long this will drag on and since in addition I have resources, thanks to [distant relative] Uncle Rainer, I think I will go for a six-month secretarial course. The lack of workforce is becoming apparent here and so after a thorough training I hope to be able to find a decent position.

I will hardly make it to the US in the foreseeable future, as it is too difficult and I don't even know when my quota number will come up. I don't yet have an answer from the consulate, so I cannot count on it...

Uncle Lenda [Leo Holzer] wanted to go to the US; he attempted to get there through Russia and Japan, as Otta Fischer [Leo's father-in-law] wrote. It seems like a wild plan. Through Lisbon it would be simpler, and I don't know which part didn't work out.

Soon after, as Japan escalated its assault on China, my father and mother left for the United States. Hana's next letter, dated June 5, 1941, reached them in California.

...I am still at school, I am doing well, and I am still with the Goldbergs. However, last week it was announced that all foreigners have to register in the next fourteen days for work either in the war industry or enlist in the Air Force or the Army. So I don't know whether there will be any exceptions and whether I will be allowed to complete the course at school.

It would be a waste of time and money, to stop halfway through the course; I would most prefer to finish it and then go to work in an office of some munitions factory. I will see what I will be able to do.

Uncle Rainer is taking care of my affidavit. He wants to give it to me and so I still have a glimmer of hope to get to the States. That's why I will try to avoid going to the Air Force or the Army. If the only option were to work as a manual worker, then maybe I would nonetheless put on a uniform. In the next letter I will be able to tell you more about it or perhaps even give you my new address. Otherwise everything is OK here; there are no air raids right here...

The last letter from my parents that I received was written a week before Easter; everything is fine with them...My folks allegedly asked Franzl whether he could get an affidavit for them in order to get out. I don't think there is much hope, but nonetheless I am hoping for it.

Hana, meanwhile, continued her steady, determined march toward a better life, which she described to Valdik in California on July 31, 1941.

>...At school I had to take the final exam in shorthand this week; French I am already done with. Our term ends on Friday. After two more

terms I hope to be writing 110 words per minute and I will also attain good speed in typing. I have to be finished by Easter—if everything goes well, if I am healthy and if they allow me to stay at school. I had to register for war work in June but for now they are not taking female students.

Last week I got a pleasant surprise since our Ministry of the Interior in London met my request and gave me a scholarship, they paid my school fees for the entire past quarter of a year, so that's great for me and I will be able to have some extra money for holidays. My plan is to go for a week with Hanka Hermannová to some student camp and to visit the Hermann's for a week in Chelsea. It will be my first vacation in two years and so I am naturally looking forward to it…

With that stipend I am now all right for some time and hopefully they will give me another one next term. Should your "pocket become too heavy" later, remember me but it definitely isn't urgent.

You must already speak English well or American by now, as your parents always write in fear, having such good practice with Ruth. Do you already say "first" in the American way [Europeans use their thumb to indicate "one," while Americans use their index fingers] and "swell" and "guy"? And how is Ruth doing with Czech? Will she be able to communicate when she meets your parents?

Let's hope it won't take too much time now. I think that next spring we will really be able to make plans for a reunion and I hope that I am not mistaken this time that it is about time.

Rather than coming to a close, the war spread to Valdik's new country—America. Hana wrote her next letter from Southport on December 13, 1941, just days after the Japanese attack on Pearl Harbor.

> ...I thought of you a lot in the last few days, how wise and lucky you were to get out of that Japanese melee on time, including Pavel too. What is Mr. Lilling doing? Is he still in Shanghai? Does he write to you?
>
> The events of the last week surprised us a lot, you too probably. I did not expect it so suddenly, I don't even know whether to be glad or not. It will definitely speed up the war but you are probably experiencing the first aggravating wartime days, the way we had it here, blackouts and similar treats.
>
> But you live outside of Los Angeles. You won't have air raids there. Anyway, it's only the first time. After the fourth air raid people calm down and no one pays much attention to them, unless it is a particularly sweeping one and those you will definitely not have there. Well, now that three such strong powers are at it full steam, Hitler and the Japanese will be finished soon, Mussolini is almost done for and so hopefully by next New Year's we will already be celebrating with the prospect of our return home.

This time, Hana added a note to Valdik's new wife, Ruth.

> ...I was very pleased to read all the good news from you and amused by Valdík's grumbling about the California sunny weather, but I know he doesn't mean it. I could do with it here as we have plenty of rain and dampness now, but I am satisfied with

it just the same; glad to be here as there must be plenty of trouble at home and all our relatives there are having a very trying time. But it will not be forever and I hope the coming year will bring the solution to all of the trouble.

The blackouts Hana referred to started in Great Britain even before the war began. Rules called for citizens to cover up their windows at night with dark fabric and streetlights were turned off, in an attempt to make it difficult for German bombers to find targets. As soon as an aircraft was spotted, the air raid sirens sounded. Some people had communal shelters on their streets; others hid underneath a table or under the stairs. In London, people sought shelter in underground railway stations.

As I read Hana's letter and thought about her optimism for the war's end, I knew it would not be realized. For the people of Czechoslovakia, the war would not be over until May 1945, nearly three-and-a-half years later. The accelerating conflicts caused other unforeseen problems, too. Hana described them to Valdik in a letter written from Southport on February 1, 1942.

> ...Before America entered the war [in December 1941], [distant relative] Uncle Spitzer got a letter from his parents in which they asked him to get them a Cuban visa and boat passage (which they later rescinded).
>
> He did what he could to get that visa but America's entry into the war ruined it all. It must have been a huge disappointment for them since they had been able to get all the complicated permits and then it all fell through.
>
> It made me very upset at the beginning. However it is partially their fault, they had an opportunity to

go to Palestine when the Poláks went. Partially it is my fault as well. After the fall of France, I should have been more energetic and left. Anywhere would have been fine. My parents would have followed me there. Now they can't.

Talking about it is easy; doing it is harder. What happened, it's done and now I will not have any news from them until the end of the war; I am not the only one, unfortunately.

In the meanwhile, I have the moving process behind me. I don't know whether I wrote about that in my last letter, that Mrs. Goldberg invited some acquaintances, a couple with a baby, for a while until they find a new apartment. Since this has now dragged on for over five weeks and they still show no inclination to move and I just started the last term of my course, I decided to end this situation. The work at home and at the same time for school has lately been too demanding. I thought about it this way and that, and this gave me the final impetus.

I parted with the Gs on good terms and I found a room with a decent, easygoing Jewish family, and I am now a "lady of leisure" for three months. I am in better health and at least I have more time for studying. It costs money but after Easter I shall, God willing, be earning again and everything will be OK.

After passing along a few more updates on family and friends, Hana added:

...You have more recent news about Franzl and Pavel than I. Franzl was moved to Louisville.

Hana then made another bold leap, this time to London, writing from Westbury on June 9, 1942.

> …I…first started to look for a job with the Czech bureaucracy since they provide good working conditions and pay well. By chance, however, there were no openings at any of our ministries. Mostly I was told that just a short time ago they got new staff but that they would put me on their list. Then I started to look for employment with the English and found it with producers of various shoe, floor, and furniture polishes.
>
> It is a small company; now during the war they don't have as much work as they used to. I am alone in their office, doing a little bit of everything, mainly accounting, and so I can at least learn something. The bosses are very decent and nice to me. They have already raised my pay to three pounds, from two pounds and ten shillings…
>
> I am happy to be in London among acquaintances again, in a Czech milieu…
>
> Otta Fischer with his wife produce leather belts and flowers; they are very industrious and are doing well. I told only Rena about Uncle Lenda, not Otta. There is nothing new with Aunt Porgesová. The Hermanns are also doing well…
>
> My last news about parents, through the Red Cross, is from the beginning of March from Vožice. They are writing that they are healthy and that Grandma celebrated her 80th birthday. Do you have any news from your parents?

There were no other saved letters from Hana until the end of World War II, after my brother Tommy had been born in June 1944 in Purdue, Indiana, where my father served his medical residency and became a naturalized citizen of the United States. He was completing his US military service as a physician to workers in the oil fields in Ecuador, following a similar stint in Peru, when he received a letter from Hana written on August 13, 1945.

> ... Thank you for your kind letter and the stockings, which made me tremendously happy. I have not seen such thin stockings since the beginning of the war. It is something sublime. They will come in handy, perfectly, for the wedding, thank you very much.

> I was very surprised that you were no longer in Peru. You will really see the world this way. Ancon has a very exotic name; is it close to Guayaquil by the ocean, or is it already in the mountains? Congratulations on your promotion; it is amazing that at your age you are already a chief surgeon. Do you already have an apartment? Thank you for the pictures. Tommy is a great boy; I would very much like to see him, but before his aunt gets to do this, he will already be a big boy and not a baby. How does he like all the traveling? He has already done quite a bit of it in his short life; he must get a kick out of it.

> Yesterday I received another letter from Aunt Valda, but unfortunately it does not contain any news about our family. Aunty is still not losing hope, but unfortunately very few are returning from the concentration camps. Jirka [Aunt Valda's oldest son] too added a few lines, and I was greatly surprised by how much humor he inherited from his father. He described his wanderings around the Protectorate and Germany in very funny terms. In the fall he will start attending technical college. Pavel

[Valda's youngest son] will finish the gymnasium [college-preparatory high school to which he was denied access under the Nazi occupation] and will go to a timber-management school.

Though the Neveklov sawmill, house, and garden are hardly recognizable (there was an SS school there), everything spread about and stolen, Aunt [Valda] and Uncle Jaroslav plan to return as soon as possible, i.e., when they receive the "méblák" to move the furniture. [*Möbel* is German for furniture. I think she meant a coupon allowing one to receive, free of charge, items of furniture. The furniture came from large warehouses where the Germans collected stolen Jewish furniture after the deportation of the owners, as well as furniture belonging to Germans (which in some cases also had been Jewish-owned before that) who were deported to Germany after the war by the Czechs.]

Hanuš [Holzer, Leo and Elsa's son, fourteen years old after four years at Terezín] left for some convalescent home, and Otta Fischer will try for him to come here to England and study.

I have already been in my new job for three weeks. I work with an organization that organizes summer camps for youth who want to help with work in the fields during vacations, to collect fruits, etc. It is such a funny, unconventional, merry office. In a week I am leaving to go on a holiday to Scotland for two weeks, I will walk around the Scottish mountains with a group of friends.

Written three months after the war ended in Czechoslovakia, this was the last letter from Hana included in my father's collection.

After that, Hana vanished for me as though her life had ended midstream. Although I learned much about her personality by reading her letters, I was left with many questions. She seemed less worldly than my father, and he came across as very protective of her—as one might treat a much-younger cousin—but I still didn't know her age. I was impressed with her confidence, as she bravely took on her tumultuous world while maintaining her optimism over their five-year correspondence. Left with a feeling of unfinished history, I yearned for more news. And then, as if through magical intervention, my understanding of how Hana had developed such a worldly view arrived.

On May 30, 2009, during a month-long trip to the Czech Republic, I met with eighteen relatives at a family reunion in Benešov. They ranged from six months to eighty years old. Knowing that I was writing a book, they arrived with old pictures, family tree diagrams, antiquarian books, and many stories waiting to be told. Among the shared treasures, I received five pictures of Hana and her parents Rudolf and Olga just before the war. At last, I could add the sweet face and dainty body to my imagined Hana. Her smile was much like I had pictured. It matched my father's. I could instantly see the Holzer resemblance through her mother, Olga. Her father Rudolf's bow tie and dark suit could have been in a modern photograph—he looked every bit the successful businessman, proud father, and husband. I realized that Rudolf and Olga were the unidentified couple in one of four small pictures my father carried in his brown leather notebook throughout China, now a possession I held along with the letter trove. Received at the reunion, two more old pictures showed Aunt Valda, likely in the 1960s; in one, standing at Neveklov, the family homestead, with her arm around the shoulder of an older Hana; another with an unknown, swarthy man standing stiffly next to her.

I treasured the photos, but it was a chance conversation at that reunion that resulted in an avalanche of information about Hana. My benefactor in that quest was Martin Matějka, another cousin of Hana. The day I met Martin, his great-uncle Pavel Mařík told the story of my father's 1937 stunt at the Lucerna Theater—the same tale Katka Schoenbaum Sheldon Pughe had told me. Pavel Mařík had heard it from his older brother, Jiří, who was also there. Throwing his head back with a laugh, Pavel described the prank as "a great act of self-promotion." It was Pavel's nephew, Tomas Mařík, another of Martin's uncles, who served as translator for the storytelling at Neveklov. His father, Jiří, was mentioned in Hana's last 1945 letter. The story of my father's life was coming full circle.

As fate would have it, Martin had worked for a year in Ireland. During his stay there, he met with Hana Winternitz's nephew by marriage, Owain Bell, on a mission to gather family information for his great-uncle Pavel. Martin promised to send me Owain's email address along with his informative note that had been added to the Bell family tree. My query to Owain drew an impressive response: another memoir by Hana, also handwritten but far more comprehensive at twenty-two pages. I also received a package of letters, including a four-page 1945 letter from Aunt Valda to Hana, three 1939 letters from Hana's father, and one 1939 letter from Uncle Leo Holzer. In Leo's letter I noticed a familiar name.

> …Valdik has been writing more often recently. His letters are very funny. He is getting himself into all sorts of amusing situations.

By this time I had read enough of my father's correspondence to know that he went to great lengths to write only pleasant things to his parents and relatives who were under Nazi oppression. He wrote as if he were doing great in China—no worries. Clearly it was not always the case as he expressed otherwise to friends outside

Czechoslovakia. But to think he had created amusement through his letters home made me so proud of him. It was much the way he protected me throughout my childhood by telling varnished stories of his life.

In a letter to Hana written in 1939, not long after she left her parents in Czechoslovakia, was a piece of advice from her father Rudolf.

> My dear Haničko, years ago I knew a woman who would say that "The kind of person you appear to be at the beginning, that is how you will be treated." Hana, be honest and polite to C. and they in return will treat you with honesty and politeness.

I assumed that C referred to the first family she worked for as a maid. Regardless, I thought of how this proud and successful man gave his cherished daughter his key to life's success. In addition to the advice, Rudolf included an engineer's sketch of her parents' new Prague apartment, forced upon them by the Nazis. It was small in size compared to the villa where Hana grew up.

In her own extended memoir, Hana answered my question about her age: she was born in Vienna, Austria, on November 5, 1920, two years after the end of World War I and the formation of Czechoslovakia. Rudolf's family owned a farm in Pernegg in the Mur Valley in eastern Austria. His brother Fritz married the sister of Leo Lilling, whose many letters I held. Finally, I knew the Lilling connection and understood Leo's involvement in my story.

Olga was a Czech patriot, as were the other Holzer children, all proud of their heritage. She was also a Zionist and along with many friends was a member of the Women's International Zionist Organization (WIZO). A passionate volunteer, Olga helped run a Prague home for girls waiting to immigrate to Palestine. Olga loved the theater and opera, and Rudolf was her constant, handsome escort. Rudolf became a civil engineer. After moving from Vienna in 1924, he formed a design and construction company with a partner in Prague. Over time they became very successful, building roads and several apartment houses, many of which still stand. The family lived in a villa with gardens, along with other wealthy neighbors. I later discovered that the last address of Rudolf and Olga Winternitz before they were transported to Terezín was on Pařížská ulice (Paris Avenue), one of the most prestigious locations in Prague since 1905.

Like many other assimilated Jews in Prague, the Winternitz family was not religiously observant, going to synagogue only on high holidays—the Jewish New Year and the Day of Atonement. Hana joined the Girl Guides, an organization like the American Girl Scouts, where she developed a friendship with Hanka Hermannová, whose mother came from Benešov. From Hana's letters, I realized the Hermanns made it safely to England before the war.

The Winternitz family's wealth allowed them vacations to the Adriatic coast and Venice, ski trips to the Krkonoše Mountains, and visits to Pernegg. Her father never learned to drive but had a car and driver to take the family on trips to the countryside. Her father arranged for Hana to study German along with Czech and French. During the summer of 1935, she attended boarding school in Switzerland to further her French at a beautiful spot above Geneva Lake. Most of the other girls were German and with Hana's fluent German she made new friends. Fifteen at the time, she was only slightly aware of the Nazis. Her mother came to visit and took her to the French Riviera.

In Prague, the Winternitz family often visited cafés (like Mánes), drinking coffee and beer, eating pastries and reading newspapers; dressmakers and tailors made their clothes. Rudolf was regarded as a wise man and relatives often sought his advice. Although Hana felt her father had Victorian ideas about women, he mellowed with Hana because of her mother's influence. While attending the Commercial Academy in Prague, Hana became interested in politics, combining her new interest with ski adventures.

> ...The Spanish Civil War was being fought and we sang songs about it in the evenings after skiing. We had a romantic notion of the fighting—siding with the Republicans against Fascism. We had no idea of the reality, of the Communist in-fighting in Spain.

In school and through the Girl Guides, Hana developed friendships with both Jews and non-Jews, one of whom was Lída Baarová, who later became a Czech film actress who performed in German films during the war and became a mistress to Nazi Joseph Goebbels, Reich Minister of Propaganda. Eva Pacovská was Hana's best friend; she was mentioned in Hana's letters to my father and in her memoir.

Then, in 2009, Hana's daughter, Stephanie Bell, sent me a San Marino address for Eva Pacovská Gould. Stephanie wasn't sure where San Marino was located in the US, and I was too busy to look. It would be two years before I decided to take a spin on the Internet to see if I could locate Hana's friend. To my amazement, a search led me to believe there was a chance that Eva was still living in San Marino, California.

I took a chance and wrote a letter to her on June 29, 2011. I asked if she'd be kind enough to share memories of Hana and others from her Prague youth. Perhaps she'd even known my father? I included my email address, and received this startling response.

> Dear Joanie,
>
> This past Saturday I received your letter addressed to my mother at the San Marino, California

address. My mother did indeed go by Pacovská and grew up in Prague, leaving for America in 1939.

It is a most remarkable thing that your letter reached me. My mother, Eva, passed away two years ago last month, but she and my father had moved from the San Marino address in 2003. I had become friends with the current residents of our former family home in San Marino. They are moving to Oregon next month, so I stopped by to say goodbye, and, believe it or not, the postman delivered your letter while I was there.

I am copying my sister (also affectionately known as Joanie) on this letter with your letter attached, as she is much more diligent than I on attending to family matters like these. She can tell you what information and photos we might have. Alas, my mother is not here to tell us what she may have remembered about Hana, but we may yet be able to piece some things together. I look forward to learning more about your family. It was very exciting to receive your letter.

Best regards, Don (Donald P. Gould)

I can only assume a higher power made sure the letter was delivered by the US Postal Service on the day that Don happened to stop by. How else can one explain it? Soon Joanie (Gould) Freed and I were sharing information.

Hana's friendships meant much in her life, then and later; her family meant even more. She wrote in her memoir that it was in Pernegg, in a beautiful Austrian valley twenty-four kilometers south of Graz, that she visited Rudolf's sister, her favorite Aunt Marie (known as Ritscha). She referred to Marie's husband as the "kind and even-tempered Uncle Emil Kraus," always present in their fun-filled home, which included three sons—Franzl (Frank), Pavel (Paul), and Fritz—and a daughter, Anny.

In this memoir, I was excited to find the information I had been searching for.

> ...Franzl, the eldest, studied chemistry and then worked with his father in charge of a liquor distillery...I was in Pernegg just after the assassination [by ten Austrian Nazis] of the Austrian Chancellor [Engelbert] Dollfuss. The main rail line from Vienna to Graz and Yugoslavia ran along the Mur River and I remember an engineer walking slowly along the tracks before a train was due in to examine them for bombs...

> Another year when the Kraus family was away and we stayed there with my mother, we had our midday meal on the veranda when the cupboard started shaking. It was an earthquake. We ran into the street. Anny stayed with us one winter to get to know the winter season. Three of the Kraus children are in the States. Unfortunately Auntie Ritscha didn't want to part with the youngest.

Could one of those children have been Pavel Kraus? I found a clue in a letter Hana wrote about the Germans invading Austria at the beginning of 1938 and several Austrian relatives coming to Czechoslovakia, among them her Aunt Ritscha, whose husband had retained his Czech citizenship after 1918.

> ...Aunt Ritscha took the situation quite well but she regretted leaving a particular wardrobe behind. Paul (Pavel) was in Prague already, apprenticing to a plumber to his great disgust. He wanted to study medicine but that was impossible (under the

Nazis). Anny, his sister, was in Palestine, married by then, and Frank (Franzl) had gone to the States where his knowledge and experience came in useful in making a career. Eventually he became Vice President of Jim Beam, a whiskey company. Paul too had an excellent job in that company.

Thrilled with Hana's longer memoir and letter, I reached out to Owain Bell in 2009 for even more detail. Canon Owain Bell was ordained in 1972 as an Anglican priest, and since 1997 had been the Vicar of St. Mary's, Kidderminster, where Richard Baxter, the famous seventeenth-century theologian, preached. Owain explained that Hana met his uncle, Christopher Idris Bell, at a Fabian summer school in Wales. They walked in the mountains and discovered they liked each other while "sitting in a pleasant garden in warm, sunny weather discussing postwar reconstruction." They were married in Middlesex County in 1945 after Hana became a British National. Since Idris was an agnostic and Hana a Jew, they chose a non-religious registrar office wedding, the equivalent of a city hall ceremony in America.

"Idris was the first son of Sir Idris (Harold Idris in England) and Lady Winifred Bell," Owain wrote. "Sir Idris was a very distinguished scholar, Keeper of the Manuscripts at the British Museum and President of the British Academy." Sir Idris, appointed Officer of the Most Excellent Order of the British Empire (OBE), was a British papyrologist specializing in Roman Egypt and a scholar of Welsh literature. He was knighted in 1946.

Hana's husband, Idris, was "a great character and taught economic history at the University of Wales, Swansea for many years." Hana and Idris adopted two girls. Jennifer was born on September 15, 1953, and then Stephanie arrived on March 28, 1956. "Jennifer...lives near Newport in South Wales. Stephanie lives near Chippenham in

Wiltshire and has three children, Joanna, Penny, and Christopher."

Sometime after Czechoslovakia's Velvet Revolution in the 1990s, Hana and my father relinquished their ownership in their grandparents' ancestral house and store on Benešov's small square. They arranged for the property to go to their cousin, Hanuš Holzer. Hana's only wish for the building was carried out during the historic renovation: the Holzer name was engraved just outside the room in which my father was born on a hot summer day in 1911 along with the dates of the building's purchase and sale (1897-1997).

Owain's admiration for his father's brother, Uncle Idris, ran deep and he was very pleased to share information about his eccentric uncle. One family tradition told how Idris, at the height of World War II, having been put on permanent latrine duty because he was such an inept soldier, was finally asked to leave altogether "to promote the war effort." Hana and Idris lived happily in Swansea, Wales, for many years before retiring to Chippenham, which is west of London. Idris died in 1995 and Hana died on March 25, 2004, at age 83. Upon learning of Hana's marriage into such a prestigious family, I cried for joy. After all she endured, Hana deserved a happy ending.

Rudolf, Hana, and Olga Winternitz, 1940

LEFT: OLGA (NÉE HOLZER) AND RUDOLF WINTERNITZ; VALERIE "VALDA" (NÉE HOLZER) MARIK WITH HANA'S HUSBAND CHRISTOPHER "IDRIS" BELL; VALERIE MARIK WITH NIECE HANA (NÉE WINTERNITZ) BELL

RIGHT: HANA WINTERNITZ

Rudolf and Olga Winternitz; Owain Bell and family.
(Photos courtesy of family)

American Brethren Hospital in Ping Ting Hsien in Shansi Province in northern China.

> …Thank you very much for your card from April 24. I have already gotten a leaflet from the University; unfortunately it did not tell me much. It contains only general prattle and about medicine only that it is very difficult for a foreigner to be accepted to that Institute…

> I got a very interesting letter from home today. They write the following: You wrote to your parents on March 1 that there is a prospect for me to work as a laboratory assistant or something like that, even without pay, that Leo Lilling knows about it but that I might already be in Peking. And since I am still sitting here, I would ask you if there is any possibility of something like that; I would even go to Hell just to be able to do something.

> And how are you doing there? What kind of a hospital is it? Are you there as a specialist or as a general practitioner? Also write to me in case you need me to get something done for you here. I have plenty of time and I would do it gladly.

> Otherwise I am unfortunately forced to hang around; I am learning English and that's all. Leo Lilling is all right again. Last time he was very nice to me.

I wondered about the mercurial Leo Lilling. Why was he so angry with Pavel at first but not later? Whatever the reason, Leo was surely in a better state of mind than my father. Dad's letter sent to Pavel from Shanghai on May 16, 1940, portrayed a bleak view of a young doctor's life in China, one that would discourage almost anyone from pursuing the path Pavel had been contemplating.

…Regarding your last letter. As you can see from the enclosed copy, I have a great "job" for you. I see you are interested in it but the situation has somewhat changed lately and so it is necessary to wait a little bit. So, the Mission is pressuring me to leave for our second hospital in the south of Shansi (at Liao Hsien), but for various reasons I don't feel like going. First of all, it is not safe there. Second, it is the hell-hole of the world. Third of all, there is absolutely nothing to do and so I presume I would be bored there big time. Altogether, there are two whites there now, one ancient missionary and a grandma teacher at the missionary school.

I am therefore intent on waging "my battle." It is therefore necessary to wait and see how the situation develops. As soon as it becomes clear what will come of it, I will write to you. Generally, I have been really pissed off lately. There isn't much work so I am studying Chinese and English—I am reading books about good missionaries. I have already drained all of the whiskey which I brought from Peking, smoked all of the tobacco and so I am foul with the Chinese. Thankfully they don't understand and are nice to me.

All that's left for me is to begin collecting Chinese nails or medicine bottles and I will completely have turned into a missionary. You can't really take everything I am writing to you completely seriously, as I am already going slightly mad from it all. Rebhun and I used to call this "depressions" and just ask him how they would end up.

But here such crappy moods are absolutely incurable, unless you start to spank your monkey.

of this BS; so once again, good wishes and as it is written in the book: let it stand day and night, St. Wenceslas to the rescue. I am almost afraid to be nasty to you already!

And so don't be angry with me that I haven't written to you for so long, I have your letters from April and May…they were great and I hope to have an opportunity to read your "exploits" until the age of 150. Just don't become "well-behaved overnight"!

Since this is the unofficial part of the letter, I ask you, what is she like? I hope she is pretty, so you don't put us to shame…

Otherwise I'd rather do it as Rudla did. He played poker, lost, got up and said: "So, boys, I am getting married." You should have seen all the fuss, until he gave me power of attorney. First, she was in a hospital, since love made her mad, but finally I took her away and all is fine these days—except that Rudla still hasn't paid up all the various expenses!

You surely know that when the [man is aroused, his] brain is screwed. So what will you do, or what do you intend to do, when you will have an opportunity to think? I hope that you will visit Shanghai…I wish you all the best in the New Year! Lilling said you would be getting married—you and not him! Then he got me, he asked me whether I was still a Jew. Adding to my bad luck, I said "yes," so I will have to go to church [synagogue] with him and do all those rites!

Rudla was just telling me that he has already written to you and that he will now go on such a "campaign"; I can't leave him alone. Kiss and a handshake from the representative of the Kraus family and I sincerely wish that you do really, really well and so does your wife; success and strength.

And so that was how I first got to know Pavel Kraus. Clearly he was an adventurer against his will, making the best of his circumstances in a very foreign land. As a young Jew, he had nowhere to go after the Nazis overwhelmed both Austria and Czechoslovakia. I could see he was confident, playful, and industrious, wishing to continue his university education in medicine or chemistry. He was willing to work at most anything available in a tumultuous country crowded with emigrants all looking for jobs, surrounded by Chinese under the control of the Japanese.

What I did not know was what happened to Pavel. I began my search where I almost always did, with Google. That's how I discovered Chicago lawyer Chuck Cowdery. A proud bourbon drinker, Chuck had been inducted into the Kentucky Bourbon Hall of Fame—not for his drinking skill, but as author of the book *Bourbon Straight*. His name was attached to a website link to an article about a "Doc Kraus."

Chuck confirmed that the Doc was Frank Kraus, former executive at Barton Distillery and Jim Beam, the company that was a leader in making Kentucky corn whiskey—bourbon—an international commercial success. He wrote to me saying, "Frank and Paul Kraus were important figures in the post-Prohibition distilled spirits industry." Soon I was reading newspaper articles and a detailed 2004 obituary of Frank (Franzl), 92, which referred to the town of Pernegg, Austria. Most important, it said his brother Paul (Pavel) worked with him. Frank ran the distillery for twenty years with Paul as his second in command, after which Paul took over. The obituary also included the names of family members.

I knew I had the right family. Now I needed to track down Pavel. I can barely imagine how detectives found missing persons before the Internet. My next move was as easy as clicking on the Facebook page of Marie Kraus Lerner-Sexton, Frank's daughter mentioned in the obituary. Soon we were conversing by telephone and email. By then I knew a little about her dad through Katherine "Kathy" Abelson, one of the daughters of the founders of Barton Brands.

Frank worked for Barton as general manager in Bardstown, Kentucky, for nearly twenty years. "A gentleman with beautiful manners and a very gentle soul" was how Kathy described Frank. She said his success with Barton Brands may have included working on their formula for a "light whiskey" called QT, with lower alcohol content, like a fortified wine. When the company moved its managerial offices to Chicago, Frank relocated his family to Lake Forest. He became vice president in charge of production for the company's distilleries worldwide. After Frank left Bardstown, Paul took over management of the Bardstown plant.

In 1969, Frank began work with Jim Beam Distilling Co., a division of American Brands, where he remained until he retired in 1984. During that time, Paul assumed the vice president position his brother had held at Barton Brands, and traveled the world. Although I had no letters in the collection directly from Marie's father, his name was mentioned often. I felt he was one of the gang so I inquired about his life. Marie, always using her regular sign-off of "Shalom," provided information that mirrored many other lives from those harsh times.

> ...My father was Franz Josef, named for the Austro-Hungarian emperor at the time of his birth in 1911. He and his sister Anny mostly identified with their Austrian heritage and felt they were Czechs by accident...

While my dad did very well in business here in the United States, and he was a prominent person in our community, he lived what he might have called a dream denied, or at least, a dream dashed. It was his vision all along to return to Austria with his family and run his family business.

In 1953, when he went back for the first time, he discovered that there was no distillery to run. Since Pernegg was in the Russian-occupied sector of Austria after the war, the place was subject to worse devastation than the war had caused. The Russians looted everything, including the woodwork in my grandfather's house, the huge vats that held distilled spirits in the plant (anything that wasn't literally cemented to the floor), and even the marble flooring in the downstairs of the house. My dad didn't have the financial resources at that time or, quite honestly, the heart to rebuild the place from scratch. He returned to the United States determined to make a good life for his family but haunted by what might have been an Austrian business empire.

The other shadow that hung over his life until the day he died was the guilt he felt for not being able to get his parents and his brother out of the country before it was too late. He had procured visas for all three of them to go to Cuba. Alas, my grandfather chose to return to Bohemia and his family instead of making his way west. My father felt wholly responsible for their fates and never really forgave himself...I think it is why my father was so reluctant for so long to discuss his life before the war, and why finally telling the tale on tape in 1994 was so painful for him.

Marie also shared that Franzl's sister, Anny Godsey-Carman, became the owner of a well-known women's clothing store in Salisbury, Maryland, before moving to Boca Raton, Florida, where she died in April 2000. Anny had married a merchant marine who left the seas to run a business in Princess Anne, near Salisbury.

Two days after I met Marie on Facebook, she made the introductory call to her uncle to let him know I wished to talk. Pavel Leopold Kraus, born in Austria on May 21, 1919, came to life for me on March 26, 2010, when I picked up the telephone and heard a serious, slightly accented male voice saying, "This is Paul Kraus. Is this the daughter of Valdik Holzer? I hear you are looking for me."

My heart skipped a beat as I heard my father's name pronounced "Vald-yik" in a perfect Czech intonation.

"Yes, I am Joanie Holzer Schirm and I'm so glad you called. Is it all right if I call you Pavel?"

"If you want, sure," he responded with a boyish laugh.

That hello touched off two hours of rapid-fire conversation painted bright by memories from his emerging recall. By the end of our first talk, we were like old friends who had not seen each other in a very long time but easily picked up where we'd left off some seventy years earlier.

But we had never been friends; Paul had not known I existed until two days before that telephone call. He was not even Paul to me but Pavel, his Czech name in my prized letter collection. Thirty years younger, I had never been to China, but I already knew the details of his early life. At age twenty, he fled Nazi-occupied Prague in April 1940 and sailed to Shanghai, China. And because of that journey, he survived to talk with me all these years later.

During our first telephone call, I lobbed question after question to Paul about "our" Shanghai friends, Leo Lilling and Rudla Rebhun. When he heard me say Rudla the first time, Paul laughed out loud.

"Funny you mention him. I hadn't thought about Rudla Rebhun in a hundred years."

Well, not quite—only seventy! Often Paul would pause after a question and then, as if a spotlight began to glow in the recesses of his mind, say with excitement, "It's coming back to me now." This exhilaration would be followed by a vivid story, revealing new information about the letter writers.

Describing Leo Lilling as about five feet ten with a slender build, balding head, mustache, and "the patience of a flea," Paul made clear the reason one of my father's letters includes an apology to the quick-tempered Leo for an unacceptable incident of youthful behavior. "Please excuse me for alarming you with that crazy letter from Tsingtao. I wrote it when I suffered from fever, which excuses me somewhat for my detailed bad conduct." Paul reacted in disbelief when I promised to send him the photo of my father and Leo on the dock in Hong Kong. With a boisterous sudden laugh, Paul shared a story about Rudla Rebhun, who often hung out in a Shanghai club for expatriates known as the "Czechoslovak Circle." Some had arrived early in the century, part of a Czech unit of the Austro-Hungarian Army fighting the Bolsheviks with White Russians in support of the Czar. They stayed in Russia and then moved on to Shanghai.

"I remember being in a bar with Rudla with an exotic pretty young woman who was speaking English. She was his date for the evening. Rudla turned to me and in German asked whether I would like to play cards later in the evening. I said yes and then Rudla walked off. The woman turned to me and said in perfect German, "If Rudla wants to play cards, he can just tell me so." Miffed, she left the bar. Turned out her mother was Japanese and her father was German, so she understood what Rudla thought he had said secretly."

Rudla, an engineer from Prague, arrived in Shanghai about the same time as my father. His letters revealed him to be desperate to find a lucrative livelihood in Shanghai. Rudla pursued several get-rich-quick schemes that failed, including a mechanical laundry, with business partner Walter Schiller. I grew very fond of Rudla even though some of the letter exchanges with my father in Ping Ting Hsien were the raunchiest in the collection. Together these young men sowed their fair share of wild oats. When my father hid the letters away, I do not think he thought ahead to the prospect of his youngest daughter later being privy to the graphic details of his coming of age, and I am confident he never translated these risqué letters for my mom.

After the first conversation, Paul and I shared five more telephone calls, each lasting an hour or two, during which I took copious notes. I used his memory to fill in some holes in my voluminous database, but sometimes he added new questions to what I already thought I knew. The conversations connected me to my father once again, and I never wanted our calls to end.

Paul revealed what happened to him during the remainder of the war. He discussed his successful life in the distillery business, his three grown children—Carole, Allen, and Ginny—and his divorce from their mother, Kathryn. He shared how, by chance, he met his partner of over twenty years, Sheila Burkhardt, 70, in Chicago's famous Pump Room restaurant. They struck up a conversation, found they shared a love of skiing and music, and the rest was history. I sent him pictures of the prewar Winternitz family and copies of his letters along with Hana's. I included my database containing the three hundred names referenced in the letters. He called me to review the ones he knew, their link to our common history, and what he thought happened to them. After our fourth call, I sent him my father's list of forty-four relatives who perished in the Holocaust. I knew it would be difficult for him to see. He responded with details about his family members who met a similar fate. He said he had photographs of the liberation of the Dachau concentration camp, sixteen kilometers (ten miles) northwest of Munich, when he was there as a US soldier. Then Paul said he would show me everything he had stored away from our related past if I would come to Chicago. It was an offer I couldn't refuse—an opportunity to meet one of only two living letter writers from my WWII trove.

In May, at the time of Paul's ninety-first birthday, I called to say my husband and I would love to meet him and see the mementoes he had left of lives lost during the Holocaust. I knew that if my father were alive, he would have jumped on a plane with us to renew this relationship that had been fleeting in his youth but dramatic in its outcome. Both adventurers made it out of Czechoslovakia and went on to have children and successful careers, living the American dream. It was in May 2010, three months after our first conversation, that Roger and I arrived from Orlando at Paul's Chicago home. He enthusiastically greeted me at his front door as if I were a young friend. His slim athletic build, penetrating clear blue eyes, and quick smile were instantly engaging. Despite the gray hair receding high on his forehead, he looked like his photo in the 1966 *Kentucky Standard* newspaper article where I first read about his American past. Only bulging, veined hands gave his age away.

Within minutes he brought out the ticket stub from his 1940 train trip out of Prague, the pass that kept him alive. As he traveled from Prague to Vienna, he was lucky enough to go through Pardubice, the Czech village where his family was living, and see his parents and youngest brother from the train. It was the last time. Paul told me of his decision to leave Prague after the Nazis beat a close friend to death. He knew it was time to get out. By luck, while walking near Wenceslas Square, he encountered another friend who told him he was going to Shanghai and explained how to do it.

Although the government claimed to encourage Jewish emigration, it created obstacles to the process. The Jews wishing to leave had to complete around sixteen separate forms (the number changed constantly), and supply certificates of good conduct and property tax payments, as well as health and other documents, many of which were difficult and time-consuming to obtain. Paul completed the necessary emigration forms, got his Protectorate passport, and paid the required money from his parents' "Sperrkonto," a restricted-use bank account. A November 1939 Nazi regulation prohibited Jews from disposing of income from property, requiring it to be placed in these blocked accounts and used for emigration fees. Pavel waited two months and then was suddenly given notice by the Nazis that he had three hours to leave the country.

After his train ride, he traveled in March 1940 on the Lloyd Triestino Italian ocean liner *Conte Verde* from Genoa, Italy, through the Suez Canal to Shanghai. My father had passed through the canal one year earlier on the ship *Chenonceaux* from Marseille, France. A friend of Paul's from Prague was on the *Conte Verde*, which made the trip less lonely. When they arrived in Shanghai, the two friends shared a room for a while.

Paul and I met several times over three hot days in Chicago, swapping stories about his and my father's past. I was now my father's storyteller, sharing information from our 1989 taped interviews. Paul gave me an extra "P.L. Kraus" business card from his Shanghai days when he worked in the offices of Leo Lilling at Lilling & Company, 133 Yuen Ming Yuen Road. I knew my father must have spent many hours there too, receiving Leo's coveted advice. It was also where he retrieved his mail, as Leo had him send it there for safekeeping while my father traipsed around China seeking paid work assignments.

The business card was printed in English on the front and Chinese on the back, something I had seen before on my father's Chinese business cards. I finally had an address for the office of the man who helped my dad in so many ways when he arrived as an "emmie" in Shanghai. Not the least of Leo's help was his role as a psychological lifeline as my father ventured alone into the interior of China, an adventurer against his will.

Paul told me that Leo Lilling was related to him through Leo's sister, Ida, who married Paul's Uncle Fritz. They had one young son, Pepík. Leo had tried to figure out how to get the boy out of the country and wanted Paul to meet with the family before he left to discuss this. With the short notice, Paul was unable to see them. This explained why Leo was so furious with Paul when he arrived in Shanghai. Leo's sister Ida, his brother-in-law Fritz, and his nephew Pepík all perished in the Holocaust.

From an old box, Paul drew out aged, sepia-toned photos and documentation of the lives of his family which changed dramatically after the Anschluss, Nazi Germany's 1938 annexation of Austria. Hitler had broken the Treaty of Versailles, which stated that Germany could not unite with Austria by simply declaring an Anschluss, or union, between the two countries. That historic moment introduced heightened and brutal persecution of Austria's Jews. Paul told me how he overheard one of his mother's cousins pleading with his father Emil to "sell whatever you have and get out, leave!" His eyes growing moist, Paul recalled his father's response: "How long can this foolishness last?"

His father Emil, his mother Marie (Hana's "favorite Aunt Ritscha," mentioned in her letters), and his twenty-year-old brother Bedřich, known as Fritz, were all sent to Auschwitz. Fritz, being the youngest, may have chosen to stay with his parents so they weren't alone. They all died on March 8, 1944, in one of the largest exterminations of Czech Jews during the war—almost 4,000 were murdered that day in the liquidation of the so-called "Czech family camp" of prisoners sent to Auschwitz on a special transport from Terezín.

Paul's photographs also showed his family at their home in Pernegg, smiling and innocent in the time before the war. I took photographs of his pictures, one after another of groups of happy people at Pernegg reunions, surrounded by the stunning natural landscape. He showed me his mother, father, and youngest brother's December 1942 transport papers: Cg and Cf from the village of Pardubice to Terezín concentration camp, and then their final documents nine months later for Transport Dm to Auschwitz.

After the war, an old Prague neighbor gave Paul several postcards from his parents written in German in late 1943 and sent from Auschwitz-Birkenau. Paul spread them out on a coffee table and translated a few. They talked about who they saw in the camp. Within the missives were coded messages, including references to their "empty stomachs." They used the word "leer," meaning empty and a "family name" that sounded like Stomak. Paul had not read the postcards in many years. I could see it was taking a toll on him as they brought back a dreadful past. I suggested we take a break but he wanted to press on. As I captured the documents in photographs, Paul pulled out a thick book he had previously told me about on the telephone, *The Auschwitz Chronicle 1939-1945*. Translated from original German records and containing eyewitness descriptions, it is a chilling account compiled by a former research head of the Auschwitz Museum. Sitting beside Paul on the couch, I read details of the group he thought included his family marching from quarantine B to the gas chamber, singing the Czech national anthem: 3,791 Jewish men, women, and children from Terezín in Crematorium 2 and 3, 1944. Looking at each other with knowing eyes, we uttered not a word. After all, what can be said in English, Czech, or German to make sense of something like that?

In early 1941, Paul met my mother for the only time; it was three months after my parents' wedding. The US Embassy was encouraging US citizens to exit China as danger had increased when the Japanese ratcheted up their attack. My father, now married to an American citizen, was able to secure an American "preference" visa. On their way to the *President Coolidge,* the US evacuation ship docked in Shanghai, my parents stopped to see Rudla and Paul. Paul recalled my father wearing an overcoat as my father, mother, and he rode a crowded bus. A thief cut out a piece of my father's coat pocket and stole his wallet.

Around that same time, Paul received official word from the US Embassy that his own visa was denied because "too many people want to go to America." Beyond the fact that anti-Semitism was prevalent in the US, it was also a period when both US government officials and ordinary citizens suspected that refugees from German-occupied Europe were possibly Axis spies. As Jewish refugees from Europe were known to have relatives held behind enemy lines, they were viewed with particular mistrust for their potential to be willing spies. As a result, the ability of Jewish refugees to gain entry to America grew even more restricted.

Paul thought he would be forced to remain in China, a country mired in civil war and war against the Japanese. He witnessed Japanese soldiers beating Chinese on the way to work, making them bow to them. But then a letter arrived, saying his visa had been approved. He had no idea how or why this happened but was relieved to be getting out of China to join his brother in America.

Paul arrived in San Francisco on June 28, 1941, on the Japanese ocean liner *Kamakura Maru.* From my research, I learned the ship manifest mentioned his ethnicity: he was one of 23,737 "Hebrew" admitted to the US between July 1, 1940 and June 30, 1941; my father was another one. Paul listed his brother, Frank F. Kraus, as his sponsor in America. When he arrived in Baltimore, where his brother was working for Joseph E. Seagram & Sons, he learned how his visa had been approved. In hopes of helping his brother, Frank had spoken to his boss, the brother of 1940 Republican Party presidential candidate Wendell Willkie, who lost to Franklin D. Roosevelt. Willkie's influence secured the visa. This likely saved Paul's life, because the situation for foreigners in China was turning desperate under Japanese control, and after Pearl Harbor it deteriorated even more.

In Baltimore, Paul went to work at Seagram. After six months, he applied to join the US Air Corps. After some confusion when his visa was lost and no record could be found in America of a Pavel Leopold Kraus, he ended up in the US Army as a linguist in the intelligence section and trained at Camp Ritchie. The Army was interested in his ability to speak German, Czech, and French. He graduated from Ritchie as Staff Sergeant. His naturalization as a US citizen came in April 1943, and soon after he was in Europe with the Army, attached to the 3rd Infantry Division.

At the war's end, around the time of Hitler's suicide, Paul was sent to Hitler's retreat, Eagle's Nest, near the town of Berchtesgaden, where he helped remove an extensive wine collection stored there by Field Marshall Göring. Paul arrived at Dachau concentration camp, with German guards still at their posts, as the Americans were liberating it. He somewhat reluctantly allowed me to snap a photo of a gruesome picture he took of male bodies lying on what looked like a row of deck chairs in the sun. It was graphic proof of the Nazi harvesting of body organs. The scene was so surreal that it looked faked, but I knew it had happened.

Paul described walking through a row of grain-storage trains at Dachau, unaware of what they held. Then a limp, dangling arm appeared through a train car's wooden sidings, tipping the soldiers off to open the door and look further. Inside were piles of corpses, left by the Germans because someone unexpectedly turned the gas off at the camp and they were unable to finish burning the bodies.

My stomach churned and my heart broke. This incident was enough for me to know why Paul did not want to revisit that part of his life. I felt great pain when Sheila told me later that our conversations triggered dark memories and caused him to suffer nightmares.

Although he had told me on the telephone, at our meeting Paul again recounted how he learned of his family's fate; this time, I could see the pain in his eyes. Near Salzburg on the day the war ended, he managed to return to Prague through a lucky opportunity. In Pilsen, he ran into a man he had known before the war, who gave him a Czech military uniform. The uniform allowed Paul to travel to Prague without formal approval or notice. The demarcation line between the Americans and the Russians was in Pilsen. An agreement between the two powers had allowed the Russians to be the ones to liberate Prague. A revolt, later to be known as the "Prague Uprising," surprised the Germans, pushing them into retreat while the Russian troops approached. The uprising galvanized the population of Prague and gave Paul a unique chance to sneak back into the city he had left in 1940.

On a train along the way, he encountered a woman he had not seen since he was a teenager. She recognized him and told him she worked for an agency in Prague that was seeking information about displaced citizens or those who perished at the hands of the Nazis. She said, "There are millions of names to contend with and I may be able to help you." When he arrived in Prague, he went to the official hotel for select US military men allowed in the city and changed back to an American uniform. He said the desk clerk looked quite surprised as he exited the hotel, having seen him arrive in a Czech uniform. The woman from the train met him again and took him to her office, where he found the information that his parents and brother had been transported to Auschwitz and had likely perished. (Like my father, Paul did not get formal Red Cross death notifications until the late 1940s.)

Paul then went to Werfen, Austria, near Salzburg, to oversee a prisoner-of-war camp—six soldiers were living there, "like God, overseeing prisoners." They were able to get a Viennese cook and had lunch on porcelain, with silverware and napkins. While there, Paul had a memorable experience, which he described to me.

"One day while we were eating, someone came in and said 'A German officer needs a pass.' Because I spoke German, they wanted my help. I first said, 'Tell him I am having lunch,' and the response was that the guy had to go somewhere. They brought me to the guy, who was well over six feet tall with a big scar on his cheek. I took one look and knew who he was—there was a $10,000 reward on his head as a wanted man. I looked at his papers and all were fake. He finally admitted he was SS Lieutenant Colonel Otto Skorzeny.

"Skorzeny at one point had been Hitler's personal bodyguard. He was known as Hitler's favorite commando, and as a master of deception. During the Battle of the Bulge, Skorzeny led a large group of English-speaking German soldiers behind Allied lines in France; they were wearing American uniforms as part of the subterfuge. He was also the guy who liberated Mussolini in September 1943 from the Italian successor government that was holding him in prison high in the Abruzzi Apennines. German radio called Skorzeny 'the most dangerous man in Europe' for his daring role in rescuing the ousted Benito Mussolini.

"Earning the title, Skorzeny led an airborne commando force to the hotel where Mussolini was held. He came in on a glider and got him out, flying Mussolini to freedom. For all his mischief, Skorzeny received a telegram from Hitler, awarding him the highest medal—before Hitler committed suicide." When Pavel met him, Skorzeny wore a watch that Mussolini had given him.

A friend of Paul's from Vienna interrogated Skorzeny. "He was Harry Freud, nephew of Sigmund," Paul said. "Skorzeny was turned over to the Austrians and soon he was gone, escaped." If anyone as alert as Pavel had been on duty at Darmstadt Prison on July 27,

1948, Skorzeny might not have eluded justice. Three men wearing American military police uniforms secured his release by presenting bogus orders for the prisoner to appear at a hearing. Skorzeny later admitted they were former SS officers.

"I think he went to Ireland, then Spain," Pavel continued. "A few years ago when I was skiing in Austria, I ran into an American doctor who knew that I had captured Skorzeny. He said his son was building roads in Spain. He said Germans had to approve the plans he was using and knew the truth about where Skorzeny was but never brought him to justice."

Not all the stories were dark. Paul told me how his brother Frank, already in America when Paul left Prague, insisted that he carry Frank's much-loved snow skis with him, which he did. He brought them to Shanghai and then on the boat to San Francisco. When they arrived at port and the various items of luggage were being lowered to the docks, he looked up and saw the skis dangling in the air. Beside him a stranger said loudly to his companion, "What idiot would carry snow skis from Shanghai?"

Surrounded by art and curios gathered during travels around the world, ninety-one-year-old Paul Kraus shared dozens of faded black-and-white photographs and tattered old documents with me. Our eyes were beginning to tire. Suddenly his weathered, veiny hand held up a small, yellowed piece of paper, blank except for three words neatly handwritten along the top of a torn edge: *papír snese všechno.*

From thin, parted lips, with a sly smile, Paul said, "You know what this old Czech saying means, don't you?" Since our recently developed relationship was based on a somewhat convoluted shared Czech family history, for a moment I think he forgot I didn't speak or read Czech.

"No, what does it mean?"

Paul read the words a couple of times to himself, then lamented, "It's difficult to say an exact English translation, but something like: You can put anything on paper and it will be there—it will last."

Curious, I reached for my laptop that rested next to me on the well-worn but comfortable couch we shared in Paul's living room. I typed the words into Google Translate, which instantly returned a translation I could understand: "Paper can withstand anything."

Goose bumps rose on my arms as I felt a chill run through my body. "Be there, last, withstand anything"—these words describe perfectly what the letters represented for the writers I had come to know so well. For over two years, I'd spent every waking hour with paper—a lot of it. I had been surrounded by nearly four hundred multi-page letters filled with voices that had "lasted" for some seventy years. All the authors, having overcome tremendous odds, had been waiting for me to read their words, and my father had ensured they would "be there."

It felt as if the writers had mysteriously offered their remarks as clues to understanding my father's life. I had developed a deep romance with the idea of finding every piece of the past to create a full picture of the father I grew up with. Because of the "withstand anything" paper, I was on the trail to the information I needed and Paul was the bridge.

For a moment, we simply stared at one another, he ninety-one and I sixty-one; the only sound around us a rumbling central air-conditioning unit cycling on and off on a stifling Chicago summer day. There we were, sitting in his high-rise condominium, not taking in the spectacular skyline view. Instead, we were poring over the history of his life, existing only on paper and in his memories, that I was trying to capture and preserve. The paper maze revealed who we had in common: Hana's father, Uncle Rudolf Winternitz— "Rudi"—an uncle to two men whose seventy-year-old conversation I had been privy to. Now I knew where I could place the puzzle piece. For Paul, Uncle Rudi was his mother's brother. For my father, Rudi became an uncle when he married my father's aunt, Olga Holzer.

Paul's clouded gray eyes peered at me as if he knew what I was thinking. We shared no genes, just a circuitous family relationship, but through some mysterious providence we knew the same people intimately, their words preserved in the everlasting paper letters. Now, we had a Czech phrase to describe our situation—written in hand by someone who would remain a mystery to both of us. For a long moment, we just smiled at each other. Then we went back to the task at hand—reviewing materials that would allow me to understand what Paul's life had been like before, during, and after the moments he met my father—once in 1939 in Prague and once in 1941 in Shanghai. Leaving an indelible imprint on my life as well as theirs, they were companions on a long-ago journey.

At the end of our final two-hour, videotaped conversation, I closed by asking Paul what his biggest achievement was. Knowing that he had led a rich life filled with senior executive-level business success around the world for Barton Brands, I expected an answer I did not receive. After barely a moment of hesitation, his face turned determined and he responded, "My biggest achievement in life is that I survived."

Postscript: Paul Kraus passed away September 22, 2014. The Chicago Sun-Times, October 1, 2014 article headline: Chicagoan Paul Krauss, WWII GI who nabbed 'most dangerous man in Europe, dead at 95' referred to his identification of Nazi Otto Skorzeny, credited with leading a daring WWII raid to rescue dictator Benito Mussolini from his mountaintop captivity in Italy. Staff Writer Maureen O'Donnell closed her article with a quote from Paul's long-time companion, Sheila Burkhardt:

Though he skied each year in his homeland, he didn't want his ashes scattered over the mountains of St. Anton, Burkhardt said. "He said 'Don't bring a part of me back to Austria. They didn't want me.' "

Top: Paul Kraus' WWII US Army dog tags

Middle left: Paul Kraus; right: Bedřich "Fritz" Kraus

Bottom: Paul Kraus army jeep at WWII ending

Top: Emil and Marie "Ritscha" (née Winternitz) Kraus with son Bedřich "Fritz"

Paul Kraus family photos, circa 1950's

TOP LEFT COLUMN: PAVEL KRAUS; PAUL KRAUS WITH SHEILA BURKHARDT; BOTTOM JOANIE
HOLZER SCHIRM WITH PAUL KRAUS, CHICAGO 2010

RIGHT COLUMN: SHEILA, PAUL, DAUGHTER CAROL KRAUS, JOANIE HOLZER SCHIRM, CHICAGO
2010

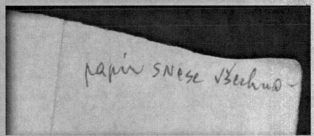

papir snese všechno

Top: Paul Kraus family; bottom: Carol Kraus, father Paul, and Sheila Burkhardt (Photos courtesy of family

RUDOLF FISCHER
ancien: / DIRIGENT
ANGLO-ČESKOSLOVÉNSKÉ A PRAŽSKÉ ÚVĚRNÍ BANKY
EXPOSITURY PRAHA V.
adresse actuelle:
Villa de Cytises,Parc des Rivalles,
Néris les Bains,Dep.Allier,France

Néris les Bains,le 4.novembr
1939.

Lieber Valdo!

Nach beinahe 2 motatigen Aufenthalt hier in Néris les Bains,
habe ich von Deinen Eltern Deine Adresse erhalten und ich beeile
mich Dir sofort zu schreiben.Vor Allem teile ich Dir mit,dass ich
nicht tschechisch schreibe,da ich annehme,dass bei der dortigen
Zensur,das niemand verstehen würde und dies vielleicht der Grund
sein könnte,dass Du den Brief nicht bekommst.Ichń weiss nicht
ob Du von Deinen Eltern bereits die Nachricht bekommen hast,dass
wir am 19.8.Praha verlassen haben,waren bis zum 10.9.in Italien
und seit dem 13.9 sind wir hier.Obzwar ich mich kurz vor meiner
Abreise aus Praha mit Deinen Eltern verabschiedet habe,wollte
ich vorsichtigerweise Deine Adresse nicht mitnehmen und durch die
schlechte Postverbindung,habe ich erst jetzt einen Brief vom
26.9. von Deinen Eltern erhalten.Ich soll Dir ausrichten,dass
Deine Eltern die ganzen Teppiche und Schmuck zurückerhalten haben,
worüber Sie sich sehr gefreut haben.Ich glaube,dass sie dort,ganz
gut leben,es sind zwar verschiedene Besohränkungen,aber es ist
lange nicht so arg,wie es ênwartet wurde.Wir leben hier in einem
kleinen Ort 250 km südlich von Paris,also sehr gut gelegen,ich
kann natürlich hier nicht arbeiten und muss abwarten,wie sich
die ganze Situation entwickelt.Sollten wir die Möglichkeit haben
nach Amerika zu fahren,dann werden wir es tun,aber wir kommen,
mit der Quote frühestens im März nächsten Jahres an die Ríhe,
und werý weiss was bis zu dieser Zeit Alles geschieht.Wie geht es
Dir?Arbeitest Du? Wie hast Du Dich dort an das Klima und den
Verhältnissen im Allgemeinen gewöhnt?Bitte schreibe uns recht
bald und ausführlich,denn ich möchte gerne mit Dir im Kontakt
bleiben.Leider kann ich Dir keinen Antwortschein einsenden,da
dieselben hier momentan nicht zu haben sind.Bitte mir auch die
Marken,mit denen ich frankiere zurückzusenden.
    Solltest Du etwas brauchen und sollte es von hier möglich
             reibe es mir.

Mit herzlichsten Grüssen u.Küsse

Dein

Chapter 8:

Rudolf "Rudla" Fischer

Dramatis Personae

Rudolf "Rudla" Fischer

(Valdik's first cousin)

Maternal grandparents:	Jakub (later Jacob) and Teresie/Teresia (née Vodička) Orlík
Parents:	Leopold and Karolína (née Orlík) Fischer
Brother:	Robert Fischer (married to Marie)
First wife:	Erna "Erny" Frenkel
Brother-in-law:	Walter Frenkel
Sister-in-law:	Marie Fischer (married to Robert)
Son:	Tom Hanuš Fischer (later Tom Weiss)
Niece:	Alenka (later Alena) Fischer Morgan (married to Alan)
Erny's second husband and Tom's stepfather:	Eugene Weiss
Second wife:	Hilda Marion Terry
Daughter-in-law:	Aurice Weiss
Grandchildren:	Max Weiss, Elisa Weiss, Eric Weiss

Only by a miracle am I still with my family.

But I don't know for how long.

— Rudolf "Rudla" Fischer, March 2, 1940

I consider my father's letters almost magical, a priceless gift allowing me to see him as few children get to see their parents—as a young man coming of age. Understanding the letters, understanding him, required more than translation from Czech into English. Reading the correspondence over and over again, I began to see through the haze of wartime censorship that spawned a language of analogies and euphemisms. Dad's references to storms that unleashed a "red flood," for example, had nothing to do with the weather; they meant the Chinese Communists were on the offensive.

I relished his brutal honesty in his conversations with his closest friends as he described bizarre and occasionally bawdy encounters in an alien culture wracked by war, poverty, and social upheaval. Some of my father's most frank and meaningful revelations were contained in his letters to Rudolf "Rudla" Fischer, his first cousin and confidante. Dad shared his deepest feelings about religion and national identity with Rudla—and by way of their letters, he then shared them with me.

Rudla's name jumped out as soon as I began sorting through the translations. His son, Tom Weiss, had visited my father in 1999 after he started his own investigation into family history. What I learned from Tom resonated when I read his father's words nearly a decade later, and we teamed up in our efforts to learn more. Much of what follows in this chapter comes directly from our conversations or from an extensive manuscript Tom sent me describing his family history.

For me, the journey since meeting Tom in 1999 has been challenging but exhilarating. What I've learned about my father has only confirmed his essential strength of character. For Tom, the lessons were harder. Rudla Fischer, it seems, was never as candid about his feelings or his circumstances as Valdik Holzer.

Born in Prague on June 25, 1901, Rudla was ten years older than Valdik. Their mothers were sisters, both members of the Orlík family. The entire clan was close, so the boys saw a lot of each other growing up, despite their age difference. They saw even more of each other when Valdik and his parents moved to Prague and he began his studies at Charles University.

Rudla, an athletic business-school graduate, had fallen in love by then with Erna "Erny" Frenkel, an enticing young Viennese woman he met while vacationing on the Adriatic Sea in Riccione, Italy. The only daughter of an upper-middle-class Jewish family, Erny had a very comfortable childhood. Rudla was the most attentive of her many suitors. Erny was attracted to the stocky, balding, ambitious young banker some eight years older than she. The courtship involved an exchange of letters and personal photographs that traversed the 150-mile rail route between Prague and Vienna.

While they were courting, they met in both summer and winter resorts and exchanged dashing photos—Rudla with brimmed hat and dark, smoky eyes gazing to the side; Erny almost in profile, jeweled hand supporting her chin and a dark, classic wavy hairstyle exhibiting her elegance and chic. Erny and Rudla married in Vienna on June 29, 1932, at the one synagogue out of fifty-five that some six years later survived the Nazi Kristallnacht rampage.

The couple took a three-week honeymoon, visiting sites in Italy, Switzerland, and Austria, ending in Munich, Germany. Tom described the German setting when he wrote, "Munich had been the center of the Nazi movement, which was gaining popularity. In the

July 1932 election, the Nazi party gained 230 out of 608 seats in the Reichstag (parliament). Not only was Erny and Rudla's honeymoon over, but shortly Europe's honeymoon would also be over."

Rudla and Erny settled in a Prague apartment in the same fashionable, modern Vinohrady district where my father and his parents lived. Rudla soon became an assistant manager for Anglobank in Prague, developing an expertise in international banking. He especially loved soccer and card games with friends, including my father. Rudla and Erny's son, Tom, was born on October 17, 1934, into a tranquil household where both Czech and German were spoken. Family members often visited, many traveling from Vienna.

Foreseeing the danger after the Nazi occupation of Prague in mid-March 1939, Rudla prepared to move his family to safety. He shipped five crates and six suitcases of belongings to a storage company in Paris on May 15, 1939. From his position as assistant manager at Anglobank, Rudla secretly enlisted his international banking connections to help Jews move their funds out of the country. As assets had been frozen after the German occupation, this was an illegal activity and a very dangerous undertaking by the young banker. After a few weeks, he was warned that the Nazis were monitoring his actions and he arranged for his family to leave Prague.

On August 19, 1939, weeks before Germany attacked Poland to ignite the European war, Rudla and Erny fled with their son. They became three of only 26,000 Bohemian and Moravian Jewish refugees who legally left before 1941, after which it became impossible for Jews to emigrate.

Rudla wrote to Valdik from Villa de Cytises in Néris-les-Bains, France, on November 4, 1939, as soon as he got word of Valdik's address.

...Although during my departure from Prague my goodbye with your parents was brief, I wanted to be careful to take your address with me and due to the poor postal service I just now obtained a letter from your parents dated September 26. I should tell you that your parents had their carpets and jewelry returned to them, which pleased them a great deal. I believe that they live quite well there although there are various restrictions but it is not as bad as anticipated.

We live here in a small town 250 km south of Paris and are also well situated. Of course I cannot work here and must wait to see how the whole situation develops. If we have the opportunity to go to America, we will do it. But our quota number will come up the earliest next March and who knows what will happen between now and then.

The US strictly limited immigration during the 1930s and 1940s. Potential immigrants—at least those without quota waivers—were assigned numbers and often waited for a long time with permits in hand for their quota number to come up. On grounds of national security, the US restricted immigration in 1940 by ordering US consuls to delay approvals. According to the United States Holocaust Memorial Museum, the US did not admit refugees as a special category until much later, when President Truman issued a December 1945 executive order allowing 16,000 Jewish refugees to enter the US during 1946-1948. With the 1948 Displaced Persons Act, around 400,000 visas to immigrants above the system number allowed were issued, including 80,000 for Jews.

Valdik's first reply to Rudla apparently failed to arrive, and another crossed in the mail with Rudla's next letter. Dad's second letter, sent from Shanghai on December 7, 1939, got to the heart of his almost otherworldly experiences in China.

...I am waiting for you to write to me some interesting things that the people in the Protectorate can't write. All the correspondence that arrives is inspected and mother writes some things that I am afraid for her that she'll get arrested and locked up.

Otherwise lately they did not write much. Their letters are full of optimism, which I do not believe. My father is working up until now. They write that they have enough food; who wants to believe that? I am concerned about them, especially after the last uprising, the news is that they are evacuating those who are not "dependable" to Poland.

I am not badly off; I have my own surgical practice, and I earn enough pocket money for a cup of tea for breakfast. In time it will get better. I am waiting, because I have applied for another position and perhaps will get it.

I had malaria and paratyphoid and I am not yet well. But please do not mention this when you write home. Here in Shanghai it is not at all pleasant; about 20,000 immigrants are here, mostly without any money. Out of them, 18,000 are living in the ghetto. You cannot imagine what it is like in the ghetto for escapees in the Orient. Most of them have died from different infections.

Altogether 500 doctors came here, of whom 300 have opened their own offices. Shanghai has its own population of five million. It is a small nest because there are only 80,000 white people, out of whom 20,000 are Russian émigrés and the rest one meets in two months. The Chinese people live separately and it is not suggested to be friendly with them.

Otherwise in every other building there is a nightclub or bordello, lots of cinemas and ladies of every race. So, one can't complain as a man about the entertainment. Of course, after a week it's enough, not to mention that it costs money. So I've prattled on a little much and must slowly end the letter.

Rudla and family found themselves in a very different set of uncomfortable circumstances, which he shared in his letter from Villa des Cytises on December 2, 1939.

> ...It is different with me. We had to voluntarily register and I have the impression that I will only stay with the family at most until the end of January. I like it here very much, the people are quite different. I wish I could stay here in peace until the end of my life. But I have no employment as I cannot get a work permit and I live in a small place where there is no prospect for work or some sort of beginning. I am trying to do business with stamps and I hope that I will earn a franc or two.
>
> I am not at all sure how long I will be able to stay here with my family. But at the present I am not unduly worried, because I have reserves of capital for our maintenance. But it is not pleasant to sit around without anything to do, not knowing what will happen next. We shall have to hope that the western states will destroy the regime, so that millions of people can feel free...I am thinking of moving to the U.S.A. next year, but of course, only if it will be possible. At the moment we are all learning to speak French, we are making progress—especially Tomáš, who attends French nursery school.

Heartily I greet and kiss you,

Yours, Rudla

Also with my best wishes,

Erny [Drawing of a heart]

This is his own handwriting; he is named Tom here.

Rudla's next letter, dated January 23, 1940, elaborated on the challenge of making a living as an immigrant.

> ...It is terrible that one creature has caused humanity such bad fortune. At present we are experiencing a frost—20-25° C. The room where Erny sleeps with Tom is without heating, so it is several degrees below zero. You can imagine how I feel when I put Tom to bed now and think how it was in the past. I sleep in the kitchen on a sofa and in comparison it is warm there. Good food to eat is available for those who have money.

> I am looking forward to the fact that you will write to me soon. Even if I will not be here, Erny with our child will send me your letter wherever I shall be. I wish to maintain our contact. Perhaps everything will change one day soon and fate will lead us somewhere where we shall be able to meet again.

Rudla dreamed of the far-off United States, but as he wrote on March 2, 1940, he seemed dubious about his chances of cutting through the red tape.

> ...As far as U.S.A. is concerned...the visas they are issuing now are for people who registered at the beginning of May. Accordingly, it could take

about two years before we are called. But one never knows. Sometimes one thinks that things are bad at the time and it may be better later. I think it would be nice for us if we could get into the U.S.A. Of course, I have different reasons than you.

Only by a miracle am I still with my family. But I don't know for how long. I am thinking that through some miracle of fate somewhere we shall stay together and that I will not be called up for the army. I don't know what the explanation is. I am not pushing anything. You know me as a modest person.

I am idle here, just learning French for about one hour a day, and in between taking Tommy to and from nursery school, I snooze for about two hours. Sometimes I play with stamps, write letters; I read *Baseler Zeitung*, other times French newspapers and twice a week I play cards. That is what I do. Starting tomorrow I will have one more lucrative job. I shall train men here to be soccer players. I might become a thin man yet…

Really I wish I could live here in peace. You would see what it means for people to live in France. I love this nation and I am sorry that the nation next door is inciting it into war. I am sure that if I knew the language, I could earn a living here. I seem to be making progress, but Tommy is doing much better. Tommy talks like an old Frenchman. I wish I could speak half as well as he does. He does not feel that he is an immigrant. He likes everything here.

The way things are, the war will not end soon. It gives me more than minor problems thinking about the future. But we must live for the present. Who knows what will happen. We are constantly fighting with our nerves. It is not easy to keep them at rest...

In his reply from Peking on March 4, 1940, my father revealed despair over the worsening situation in Czechoslovakia.

...I am really pleased that we have left "the madhouse." It must be horrible there. I have received a few letters from home. My parents indicate that they will have to leave the country eventually also. So you can imagine, I was upset and tried to get them out. In the meantime it seems that things are quieter again and so they are staying. So I don't really know what to do. My fate will be decided if my parents have to leave and they manage to come here. Then I will need to stay here so I can look after them.

So I obtained a job as a small consultant in an American mission in Shansi. I have a house with eight rooms, a Ford car, central heating, electricity, radio, and a modern comfortable hospital with a big X-ray machine and 170 beds. Only I am desperately lonely, although there are eight white persons, missionaries. But in the big house I am alone with two Chinese servants. Now I know why young people wish to get married before going out into the world. For someone like me it would have been much more pleasant if I were married.

When I decided that I would stay, an epidemic of typhus struck, during which one nurse who was my translator for Chinese to English caught the bug and sadly died. Now I can't understand the language. Because of that, the mission agreed with my proposal and sent me to Peking for three months to the College of Chinese Studies to learn Chinese at their expense. And now I am battling diligently with the hard language. It is the third language to pack into my brain. At the end of April, I shall return to Shansi, where I will be in charge of the hospital. As soon as my quota number will come up or some other possibility to reach the U.S.A., I shall take it so that I can continue my medical practice. So in short, this is my fate and my plans.

Please do not mention my difficulties when you write home.

While continuing to lament his inability to speak French or earn a living, on March 12, 1940, Rudla struck a melancholy tone regarding the Czechoslovak forces.

…Everyone who has arms and legs is in the army. As I told you before, Rudloušek is still with his family, but only by accident. Now at Easter holidays army friends came here on holiday. They have better times there, especially those officers. They have 1,800 francs a month. They can live on that beautifully. The prospect that they would wish to leave is small. They think that this lot will free the motherland and put things into order afterward; I think some of it is fantasy…I am hoping that I will last financially for two years, because comparatively living is cheap. But after that, I do not know what will happen.

Dad's next letter, one of his most eloquent, written on April 18, 1940, revealed his strong suspicion that the folks back home were self-censoring their true situation, just as he was.

...In the last letters my parents wrote that my aunt is happily making deals and that Cousin Robert Holzer is employed; Dad allegedly also still works. The question, however, is whether what they write is truthfully said or are they lying to us? I also don't write home the whole truth; why should they have an extra worry?

And so next week I am once again leaving Peking; you can't even imagine how I don't feel like doing so. I liked it here so much, I found plenty of good friends here, and I am frequently invited out into the society. I found so many beautiful secrets here that I would love most of all to start writing novels. The only thing that consoles me is that in the fall I will return here for some time.

I think that this time I have babbled enough and that it is advisable to finish with a poetic finale: I am influenced by the blossoming Sakura, the wind from Gobi bringing fine sand blinding the eyes, Japanese girls in colorful kimonos and Chinese girls on tiny feet, the smell of Mongolian dishes, thousands of different impressions, all in a colorful mixture; I am weeping; I am not a poet.

That letter, written one year after he left his homeland, is the one I call the Testament Letter. It is one of the most significant of the four hundred. In it, my father suddenly unfurled his anguish over the country that he'd embraced as his own—and that he had believed embraced him.

...I have learned enough Chinese as to be able to swear and so I believe in operating successfully among the yellow [skinned] people. As you can see from my previous letters, I am slowly getting out of

247

that émigré's hangover and I am again starting to think straight and surprisingly, also to work.

I think that each of us has to overcome this initial after-surgery shock, like when one's tumor is cut out, one which deprives your organism of much energy. This tumor was our unfailing trust in and love for a country which never really absorbed us Jews and even though we loved her and felt home within her, all others considered us strangers.

You know, recently I made up my mind about it all; I swept away my assimilation and fought for a new self-confidence. Maybe I am making a mistake but it is my truth, one I am not scared to stare in the eyes.

I don't want to recall all the old wrongs I felt from the moment when I began to meet children at school, even though I was raised in the spirit of the nation in which I lived and of which I felt a part—there was not an occasion when it wasn't made clear to me that I was an unwanted stranger, whether it was at primary school, high school, at the university, in the army—everywhere I met with the sneer, a scoff, though I tried to assimilate everything necessary to belong.

I didn't even know another language and thought exactly the same way as everyone else, but it was not enough: To get rid of us, to oust us from society, to make us second-class citizens. We shouldn't lie to ourselves, at least that's how I see it from the distance of one year, which I needed in order to digest it all.

Now I am in a colored country, I became a member of a white community, without differences of nationality, and I am assessed on the basis of my personal qualities and not of my curly hair.

Maybe I am facing a new lie and a new self-delusion but so far I don't know about it, so far I am evading it. We all have one enemy, the degenerate Nazism and racism, totalitarianism, the suppression of the free mind—in Peking we expelled all of the supporters of these pseudo-ideologies; we created a white front of cultured people.

When my father next wrote to Rudla, on June 2, 1940, his mood seemed brighter. He was clearly becoming more sanguine about life in China.

...I have already gotten quite used to the local substandard conditions, to the point that I am beginning to like them, or as one of my friends from Shanghai would say, "Far Eastern spoilt mentality," meaning I'm beginning to be spoiled by the Far East. You know that constant change is my thing, but those of you in Europe cannot complain about the lack thereof either. You are right saying that it is not easy for me but I at least have an opportunity to make a living—and I got through the tough start thanks to a sporting passion and a dose of humor.

I did not compromise on my living standard, on the contrary. Of course, we have all gone through periods of depression stemming from the shock of emigration and being in the Orient; everything is multiplied by the climate, distance from home, etc. Anyway, you sensed it from my letters. Now it is, thank God, all behind me and I am taking care to move on and in case of urgency, also to try to help my parents get out.

I do believe you that you like France, it is the most beautiful country and Paris the most splendid city I have seen. The land, people, climate, altogether everything is OK there, but it has one flaw, and that's the fact it is in Europe. Whoever once gets a taste of the colonies finds it hard to return to Europe for good; life out here is much easier. I think even my American trip will turn out to be only a temporary stay and that I will again return to some half-civilized country. It has a tremendous charm to it.

I also receive news from home, quite regularly; the most recent letter is once again a bit pessimistic. It is now official that physicians, lawyers, vets, and architects are banned from practicing. Only two percent are allowed to do so and only for Jewish customers. Otherwise I don't have direct news from anyone, I only learn about the family through my parents. But I also don't write to anyone, I don't even know what to write.

I don't really have much to write about myself. As you know from my last letter, I went back to Shansi at the end of April and I am now the absolute ruler of the hospital. It is a slightly different hospital than those we are used to in Central Europe. Altogether it is quite interesting and generally a very instructive experience. From time to time I am quite content with everything. Sometimes I swear like a heathen. I am completely isolated from the world, which, under current circumstances, should really be accepted with gratitude.

As far as the US is concerned, I am now working on several things at once, independently of relatives and acquaintances. Since I now speak and write

English quite decently, I can correspond with hospitals in the US directly and acting on advice of my American friends in Shanghai, I am turning to particular institutions—and so it is not impossible that I will set out for there soon. But as I say, only to gain some experience. The visa isn't an obstacle. Did you know that I have a Czechoslovak passport, issued by the Consulate in Paris, valid until '42?

Less than two weeks later, German troops marched into Paris. My father had no way of knowing Rudla was gone by then. He tried to reach Rudla a few months later, on September 11, 1940, and kept a carbon copy of his letter.

> …Thanks to the European circumstances I have had no news from you since June. I don't even know where you live nowadays; I hope this letter will be forwarded to you, should you have changed your place of residence. Naturally, we all were greatly worried about you and your family and none of us really know what is happening with you. I hope that you got through the whole mess without harm. I am impatiently awaiting your news, even if it's only about the weather, like I probably write to you.

> We also had a stormy summer; the last torrential rain hit our district and several surrounding ones. Coincidentally, I had some work in Peking then, for which I left on August 16; four days later it was already impossible to return due to the red floods, which still persist here. And so I again live in Peking and I don't think I will return to the Brethren hospital. Here in Peking I work at the Peking Union Medical College, where I already spent the spring. It is one of the most modern

institutions in the world. I am still salaried by the mission but I will most likely be taken on by the PUMC and that would even be better financially for me. Besides that, they wanted to send me to Shantung [Shandong] to the University in Tsinan for some time, as a second surgeon, but it has still not been sorted out and so I am waiting.

From home I have not had any news for six weeks, since all my correspondence sent to Shansi is hung up somewhere along the road. Naturally, because of the flood I can't get it back in Peking and I hope to receive it in about three months, if I do at all. I don't really have any special news; my parents moved. They have a room and a kitchen somewhere on Slezská Street, which somewhat contradicts their "prosperously-doing" news, but it makes little sense to worry about them. I tried to get them a landing permit and I would have surely succeeded, but they kept writing they did not need it, so I quit...[As the number of Jewish European refugees surged after the war began, local authorities grew uneasy. They enacted a "Landing Permit" regulation which required the resident applicant to guarantee work and accommodation for the new arrival.]

Dad had some problems with the house in Benešov but that's about all they wrote to me in that extensive correspondence. As soon as I get any news, I will write to you right away. I simply ask you to write to me soon, if possible. As for myself, I am concluding this, as I really don't know how I should write without getting caught on some nail. Please, temporarily write to me at the old address in Shanghai (P.O. Box 1591) until I am able to provide you with a new, definitive address.

The letter was sent from Peking just two weeks before he proposed to my mother, on September 28, 1940.

There was no more saved correspondence from Rudla or Erny Fischer from 1940, but there were two more letters from 1941. The first was a handwritten note, dated August 15, from Erny in New York City to my father in Long Beach, California, where my parents settled in May 1941 upon arrival in America.

> ...I will try to write you in English but don't smile as it is difficult for me. Czech I can't write, German I don't like, so I will try in English. I am very glad that you and your wife arrived in this wonderful country and that you are satisfied and happy.
>
> I arrived with Tommy the 25th of April. Since a month, I have been working in a glove factory and for the beginning I am satisfied. After our arrival Tommy was ill; he had German measles, chicken pox, and after it he was operated on for his tonsils. I had much trouble but now it is over.
>
> From my husband I have letters. He is in the Czechoslovak Army in England, a soldier, and he had to stay in England over the war. You can imagine that we are very unhappy to be separated but there is nothing to be done. The child is in a children's home and I hope in a short time I will make our living. I thank you very much, I do not need any help from you but I was really touched when I read your dear letter.
>
> We had to suffer very much in France and so I am glad to be here in this country...
>
> If you have some photos of you and your wife, I would be very glad to see them.

The final saved letter was from Rudla in London on August 23, 1941.

> ...I just got a letter from Erny, in which she divulged your address. I do not wish to write much about myself. You heard about our fate from Erny. I wrote to you twice from England to China. I did not know then that you would be in the U.S.A., but that was two months ago when Erny told me and then I heard it from Mr. Dubský, who is here with me.

> First of all I would like to congratulate you belatedly on your marriage and I hope that you selected the right one. I am sorry but I haven't got the possibility to give you and my new cousin a wedding gift now but the present is held by me until I get out of this hole. I would be very grateful if you would write to me something about your wife and I would also hope that you would send me some photographs so that I could see what my new cousin looks like.

> I am sure that you can speak good English; the same is not the case for me because I am moving in Czech circles all the time. I have progressed a bit but after one year here it is not enough; it is truly little.

> I have one big request of you and that is for you to be kindly inclined toward Erny who needs kindness and love around her, which she is missing after I left. I wish to assure you that she does not need financial but needs moral support. You have probably heard from her by now that she is working in a glove factory, apart from that she has been receiving $20 monthly from the consulate and

probably very soon this will go up to $50, which is enough for living. I am telling you this in case you should think that she needs something from you. No, but you can imagine what it is like for a woman with a child in a foreign country, after all she went through, and that is why I am pleading with you if you could write to her from time to time and if you could possibly ask her if she needs anything at all, so that she could feel that someone cares [for her], that she is not alone.

I don't have a clue how far you are from New York. I don't know if you are working in your profession of medicine. I am not acquainted with how you are situated; because Erny must have received [your] letter as she was writing to me, and noted only the address and added that you are doing well. I am sure that you are maintaining your contact with your parents and I hope that they are well, which I heard from Karlička [Rudla's mother, Karolína]. I am hoping that I shall receive a detailed letter from you in return about what is happening to you now and that we shall continue with our correspondence which would please me at the present time. I wish to finish now because I don't seem to have much time, but I shall write to you more next time in a longer letter. It is important to me that you receive this very soon. I am wishing you and your wife much luck and I am heartily greeting you.

That was the last news my father heard of Rudla and Erny until April 1997, when he got a startling telephone call from a man in Boston who identified himself as Thomas Fischer Weiss.

The little boy who'd left his mark at the bottom of his father's letters to China had grown up to earn a PhD and become a respected scientist and author. At 62, Tom continued to lead a busy and productive life as a professor at the Massachusetts Institute of Technology and had recently completed the two-volume textbook, *Cellular Biophysics*.

With encouragement from his wife, Aurice, Tom took on a more personal challenge: filling in the details of his own murky family history. His research revealed that his father had a brother, who in turn had a child. He found his newly discovered first cousin, Alena Fischer Morgan, living in far-off Wales in the United Kingdom. In their first telephone conversation, Tom heard the name Oswald "Valdik" Holzer. Tom called him soon after—and my father, then eighty-six, was stunned but excited. He had not laid eyes on "the boy" since Tom was four years old in prewar Prague. My father especially relished the renewed connection because his interest in sharing the past was growing as he accepted that his own future was diminishing.

For me, their reconnection was also a great gift, as it helped me solve the riddle of one of the central letter writers, a decade after Tom's connection with my father. In 1999, two years after Tom's first phone call, Tom and Aurice met my parents in Indialantic. The gathering provided meaningful information for Tom to add to his growing family history book. Thanks to his remarkable photographic memory, Dad was able to provide information Tom couldn't have learned anywhere else. There was great excitement, for instance, when Tom found out for the first time that his paternal grandmother had two brothers and three sisters.

Tom not only bonded with Dad; he also bonded with me. We sensed that we shared even more than the common blood that flowed from our great-grandparents, Teresia Vodička and Jacob Orlík, parents of my paternal grandmother, Olga, and Tom's grandmother, Karolína. My father died less than a year after meeting

Tom. Soon after, Tom mailed me a large, two-and-a-half by six-foot chart showing the Vodička/Wodicka family tree, dating back to 1710. The branches eventually led to our fathers' names and then to ours, using the Bohemian spelling of Vodička with a "V" (from the diminutive of *voda*, the Czech word for water).

In the conversations between Tom and my father, there had been no mention of four hundred hidden letters written by seventy-eight writers during the war—including Rudla Fischer. I don't think my dad could bear to speak about them. It was not until 2008, when I was organizing the letters, placing them in protective plastic covers, that I noticed the name Rudla and realized I held an exchange of eleven letters between our fathers from 1939 to 1941.

With great delight at the find, Tom asked his cousin, Alena (Fischer) Morgan, to help with translations, which would reintroduce Tom to his father and Alena to her uncle. And unbeknownst to me, I was about to join an emotional and introspective journey my father took in his mid-twenties in a very foreign land. Tom was also great about commiserating when I fell into the many frustrating rabbit holes one ends up encountering when conducting genealogical research.

When the translations of our fathers' letters arrived, it was evident that they shared a very warm relationship, similar to what Tom and I developed long-distance as we both nurtured our growing obsession with mapping our family histories. Tom had gotten so far in extensive research that he had compiled the names of over one hundred relatives who lost their lives in the Holocaust. A few of those names came from information I provided him from the list of forty-four relatives who perished that my father wrote down for me in 1993, at the time of the premiere of *Schindler's List,* the movie my father never went to see. This is the same list on which I recognized Hana Winternitz's parents.

refugees in France were classified as enemy aliens. To get further from the Nazis, Erny and Tom moved south in August to Marseille. Two months later, the Vichy government passed anti-Semitic laws and it became even clearer they needed to leave France altogether. Through great efforts, Erny was able to obtain an "Affidavit in lieu of Passport" for each of them through the US Consulate in Marseille with attached entry visas to the US. They made it to Spain for ship transport out. The affidavit was signed by Myles Standish, a colleague of Hiram Bingham—both vice consuls were sympathetic to the plight of the many Jewish refugees seeking to leave Europe for America.

By then, Erny and Tom had spent some twenty hair-raising months as refugees in war-torn Europe, including an internment in a French prison at the time of Tom's sixth birthday. Finally they were poised to leave for the land of the free. "We sailed from Lisbon on April 15, 1941, aboard the *Nyassa*, a Portuguese ship bound for the US. Music was playing as the ship left harbor and the people were waving farewell. Within an hour out to sea, a large storm appeared. I can recall the captain throwing up from an upper deck. Everyone on board was sick but I was relatively well. However, my mother and I were in a lower deck area that was stuffy and uncomfortable."

Fortunately, a man named Eugene Weiss, whose American cousins had somewhat better accommodations, befriended them. He invited Tom to share his quarters. Tom remembers the kindness of his benefactor, who spent much of the trip studying a book called *1,000 Words of English*. More disturbing than the storm was a rumor that a German submarine was nearby. The captain gathered all eight hundred passengers to try on life preservers and assigned them to lifeboats. "Everyone knew the German U-boats were attacking Allied shipping in the Atlantic," Tom said. "However, we saw no German submarine and were not attacked. Another escape!"

They arrived safely in New York. Tom never saw Rudla again, but there were letters. "After we arrived in the US, there was a steady stream of correspondence from my father in England. He often requested photographs and sent photographs of himself. The writing on the back of the photographs expressed great affection, e.g., '3000 miles away and 4 years of separation have not and will never change my deep and sincere love to you. All the very best and tons of kisses, your Daddy.'"

Often, Rudla's letters had an air of mystery, and said that they were from "somewhere in England," as if he was on some secret assignment. "In truth he had a desk job and apparently had lots of time for writing long letters to my mother," Tom said. "When I inquired about my father, my mother always said that he had been a good father and a good husband but had made a bad mistake in abandoning us in France. She did intimate that he had some selfish qualities. Apparently, his soccer matches and card games were quite important to him and few things got in his way to attend them. This was a mild complaint. Most of her descriptions of him were quite positive..."

Erny finally asked Rudla for a divorce in May 1944. He refused at first but eventually consented. Erny married Eugene Weiss in April 1947. After the divorce, Tom's contact with Rudla diminished. "I heard from him on rare occasions, usually through intermediaries. A family friend who stayed in touch with both Rudla and Erny brought me a fountain pen as a gift from my father and another time a lead soldier. Somehow my father felt that these occasional gifts satisfied his paternal obligations. When he was later asked to contribute funds for my education, he refused..."

Because Rudla had become a British subject, Tom wasn't naturalized automatically when his mother became an American citizen. When he became a citizen in 1951, he changed his legal name from Tomáš Hanuš Fischer to Thomas Fischer Weiss to acknowledge the fact that Eugene Weiss had become his father. "The timing was to allow me to start college with my new name," Tom said. In February 1952, Tom entered City College of New York (CCNY). Two years later, his mother died of a heart attack. Tom was nineteen when the door closed on his opportunity to learn more about his family from her.

Erny had kept meticulous photo albums—from her courtship days with Rudla to their arrival in America—but much of what they contained were mysteries to Tom. His genealogical discovery journey did not begin for another forty years. If his reluctance stemmed from his fractured relationship with his father, the feeling was reinforced by an unexpected letter that arrived in January 1972, after decades of silence:

> Dear Tommy, that's what I called you when I left you in May 1940, forced to join the Czechoslovak Army in France. Now you will be surprised to suddenly hear from me after all these years as we became strangers to such an extent that I am not sure whether I should call you Professor Weiss instead. You may not even feel inclined to read this letter, BUT PLEASE DO, as now that I am getting on in years I decided to reveal to you what actually led to the divorce of your late mother and myself. I held it inwardly all these years not to destroy the image of your mother, as I imagine that you were brought up believing that I was to blame. As you are mature now I do not like the idea of taking this blame with me into my grave. I am positive you were misled as there were no more letters from your mother or you after the divorce. THIS IS THE ONLY REASON WHY I AM WRITING TO YOU."

Rudla went on to say that in May 1944, he made preparations to come to the United States to join Erny and Tom, and that he asked her to arrange for a visa. In her reply, she revealed the new man in her life and said she wanted a separation. Rudla also wrote: "As a cover up she used an excuse against me that I stayed in the Army instead of joining my family which was in my unit an impossibility."

Rudla held Erny responsible for the breakup. He dismissed her claim that he abandoned them. "But historical records suggest that it was a policy of the Czechoslovak Army to give those soldiers with families in France a choice of whether to go to England or stay in France," Tom said. "According to my mother, many of the men in Néris-les-Bains chose to return to their families." Why Rudla didn't return is beyond Tom's ability to understand, "but it appears that his act was essentially cowardly and selfish. The result of his action was clear: Rudla was safely in England; my mother and I remained in a life-threatening situation in France. I suppose Rudla could not live with the thought that he abandoned his family so he gradually concocted the story that in his unit it was not possible to stay in France. After a while, perhaps he began to believe this story as the truth, not an uncommon human defense mechanism. Even three decades later, Rudla was still not able to admit the truth and still not able to face the consequences of his decision. It was sad."

There was a further exchange of letters in February 1972, but nothing had changed in Rudla's tone or attitude. Tom had no enthusiasm for continued contact. In his last letter to Tom, Rudla revealed a little of his life in England. He met a woman and planned to marry but didn't have enough money to support her. He borrowed enough from friends to buy a run-down café. He sold it for a profit and tried to repeat his good fortune with nine other shops. After two severe heart attacks in 1961, he retired to a quiet life with his wife, Hilda Marion Terry, whom he married in July 1947.

On August 23, 1972, Tom received a letter from Rudla's wife. Rudla had been ill since March, entered the hospital in May, and died of lung cancer on July 12, 1972, at the age of 71. Four years later, Tom's stepfather Eugene Weiss died of the same disease. Tom was an adult orphan still dealing with the effects of the war he'd lived through as a very young, innocent child.

In 1998, Tom visited his cousin Alena and her husband Alan in Wales. She told him of her flight from Prague in April 1951 to escape the repressive Communist regime and her London reunion with her only relative outside Czechoslovakia, Uncle Rudla. Although she was penniless and owned only the clothes she wore, Rudla did not offer Alena much support. She borrowed money from him but he asked that she repay it promptly and sometimes with interest. Unable to return to the banking business, Rudla by then operated a snack bar near Wembley Stadium. On days of soccer matches, Alena worked for him making sandwiches, for which she was paid one pound. When she fell in love with Alan, she asked Rudla to give her away at her wedding but he didn't attend because the date conflicted with a sporting event. Alena's descriptions did not help heal the wounds that Tom suffered from his father's behavior, but he also learned that Alena and Alan grew to admire Rudla when the relationship was somehow repaired after the wedding.

In the end, Tom learned much from Rudla's letters to my father. They provided him with a clearer picture of the man he had glimpsed only through a few childhood memories. With this new look through the lens of time, it was clear that Rudla was under great pressure to support his extended family while he waited in limbo with no certainties for their future.

Tom and I talked at length. On occasion I felt a little like Tom's therapist, as I helped him discuss unresolved feelings about the painful abandonment by his father. When asked about his religious belief, Tom told me he was an atheist. What I saw in this nonbeliever was a very bright, curious, and tolerant man of great heart and kindness who was very lucky to have made it out from under the impending catastrophe of the Holocaust to have a chance to create a meaningful life. After much discussion, we agreed fully on one belief: neither of us could fathom the emotional and physical toll of being ruthlessly displaced from your homeland, separated from loved ones who would later perish in such a heinous way—a powerless survivor.

In the book of Deuteronomy, Moses speaks to the Israelites with prophetic words: "I have set before you life and good or death and evil." When I think of Rudla and my father, I realize how —by their quick actions immediately after the Nazi occupation—they chose life, without even knowing it. For their parents and millions of other innocent people, evil prevailed, leaving a trail of death. Rudla and my father understood the totality of the horror that overtook their relatives and recognized the impact their actions or inactions had on what happened. Even though they were blameless in this atrocity, they felt survivor guilt. The way they endured the pain was to internalize it, keeping silent so as not to encounter guilt's reemergence in their everyday "good" life.

The testimony the letters provided was unambiguous as to what Rudla and my father's chosen actions were. Tom's and my contemporary observation coupled with hindsight history added to childhood memories of fathers we could not fully know because they didn't share their painful truths. I so wish that I had been given the chance to tell my dad I believed he did the best he could with the information that was on hand. His guilt was unearned.

As we worked together, Tom and I became hooked on the written documents that brought heart and soul to people who had been dropped on foreign soil with no parachutes—and no way of knowing that they were the lucky ones—and I realized it was time to return to Vláďa Wagner's writings.

LEFT COLUMN DOWN: ERNA "ERNY" FRENKEL, 1932; RUDLA FISCHER WITH ERNY, 1933; RUDOLF "RUDLA" FISCHER, 1929

RIGHT COLUMN: TOP: RUDLA WITH SON TOM, 1937; ERNY, RUDLA AND TOM, 1938

LEFT: Rudla Fischer; Erny with second husband Eugene Weiss, 1947; Tom with mother Erny, 1938; bottom: Rudla (4th from rt.) & soccer teammates; Karolina (née Orlik) Fischer

TOP: WALTER FRENKEL AND BROTHER-IN-LAW RUDLA FISCHER WITH SONS GEORGE "JOJO" FRENKEL AND TOM FISCHER; BELOW: RUDLA AND HIS CZECHOSLOVAK ARMY UNIT (CIRCA 1922);
RIGHT: ERNY AND RUDLA, 1932

TOP LEFT: AURICE AND TOM WEISS, 2012   BELOW: TOM FISCHER WEISS, 1956

RIGHT TOP: DR. OSWALD "VALDIK" HOLZER & TOM WEISS, 1999

BOTTOM: TOM FISCHER WEISS FAMILY, 2012 (PHOTOS COURTESY OF FAMILY)

praktik. Naší povinnosí bylo pro studenty nařezat na mikrotomu 10 um tenké řezy tkání zalitých v celoidinu. Ty tkáně jsme brali z obrovských labv umístěných v podzemí. Tam byly uloženy ve formolu celé orgány z popraveného vraha Valšíka. Myslím, že mohlo trvat celá léta, než se dopotřebovaly poslední zbytky. Nedovedu si představit, jak by bylo možné ho dát při posledním soudu dohromady. Raději ten problém nechám theologům.

K naší práci jsme s Valdou sdíleli jednu z mnoha desítek místností ústavu. Zakladatel Srdínko nešetřil místem a tak na každého zaměstnance připadalo několik místností. Člověk se tam cítil poněkud opuštěně. Povinná práce nám mnoho času neubrala a tak jsme projevili zájem o pokročilejší činnost, chtěli jsme pracovat na nějakém třeba malém problému. Na to Nešp reagoval poněkud neurčitě. On sám měl totiž doktorát přírodních věd a svoje místo asistenta užival k tomu, aby studoval lékařství tak jako my, jenže on už byl ve finiši. Proto jeho zájem na nějaké vědecké práci byl minimální. Takže naše snaha vyšla naprázdno. Byli bychom potřebovali teoretické i praktické vedení a toho se nám nedostalo. Tak jsme se s Valdou bavili o všem možném, jak už to studenti umí. Ukázalo se, že jeho rod pochází ze Sedlčanska *Vlašimska* a tak se mi trochu otevřel svět venkovské židovské rodiny, protloukající se obchodem a občas i vysokoškolským vzděláním. Vyprávěl mi o rodinné tradici , v které jedna větev rodu měla pocházet z renezanční šlechty protenstantského vyznání. Když měli na vybranou po bělohorské bitvě přestoupit na katolickou víru, nebo se vystěhovat, volil třetí variantu. Tou byl přestup na židovskou víru.

Valdovi to dobře myslelo; to mi vyhovovalo a brzy se z nás stali dobří přátelé. A tehdy došlo k důležitému kroku. Na počátku třicátých let přichézela do módy kavárna Mánes a Valda mně tam zavedl. Chodili tam někteří členové spolku Mánes, kterému budova patřila, i když měli o patro výše svoje klubovní místnosti. Většinou tu však bylo vidět samé mladé tváře, ještě se nemohla vytvořit vrstva starých štamgastů s vyhraněnými zájmy, tak typická pro ostatní už zavedené kavárny. Tím se stalo, že se

Chapter 9:

Vladimír "Vláďa" Wagner, MD

Dramatis Personae

Vladimír "Vláďa" Wagner, MD

(Valdik's friend and classmate)

No family names available.

After the last events I am greatly pessimistic and even though I still

believe in England's victory, it will all take tremendously long and the

mayhem following the war will be enormous, nothing will be spared.

—Oswald "Valdik" Holzer, August 2, 1940

Although I knew very little about Vláďa, the co-author of "How I Met Jews"—the document that served to unlock what I discovered in the Chinese boxes—I had the good fortune of shaking his hand in July 1995 during the only trip I made to the Czech Lands with my father.

The trip was filled with great emotion. At eighty-four, my aging-yet-spry father was finally introducing me, the youngest of his three children, to the place he adored. The visit, six years after the 1989 Velvet Revolution, when his homeland finally regained freedom after forty-one years of oppressive Communist control, showcased centuries-old buildings in mid-renovation, like roses blooming after a long winter. By the time we met, Vláďa was an Emeritus Professor of the First Medical School of Charles University. My memory of this moment is quite clear. We were standing in the heart of Prague near a sausage (*párky*) stand in Old Town (*Staré Město*), waiting at the stroke of the hour for the famous Old Town City Hall's Gothic astronomical clock to parade animated depictions of the twelve Apostles. My husband Roger, our ten-year-old son Derick, and I had just returned with my father from viewing the second-largest library of ancient books in the world at the Strahov Monastery.

Before that, we had visited the Pinkas Synagogue, site of Jewish worship for some four hundred years. After World War II, it began to serve as a memorial to the over 77,297 Bohemian and Moravian Jews who perished in the war. Their names, arranged according to the towns they were living in prior to deportation or arrest, cover the walls. My father led us to the list for Prague and showed us the red letters of his parents' last name, *Holzer*, followed by black letters spelling their first names, *Arnošt* and *Olga*, and listing their birth dates. Next to these words was painted 1942—the year they were taken away by the Germans on a transport, ultimately to the gas chamber at Sobibor death camp. As we stood staring, tears streamed down my cheeks. My father and I held hands in silence.

After a quiet walk, we arrived at the twenty-seven crosses that commemorate the twenty-seven Bohemian Protestant nobles beheaded in 1621 after rebelling against the Catholic Austrian Habsburgs who ruled the Holy Roman Empire. This event and the wars that followed postponed Bohemian independence for over three hundred years and would figure prominently in the Czech national historical consciousness. For a moment, as thousands of tourists lingered around us, the warm peacefulness of the summer sun contradicted the city's violent history, which seemed so evident wherever we went. I remember my father's anxious mood as he waited to meet his old friend.

Vláďa arrived with a smile that overtook his elderly yet youthful face. The men kissed each other's cheeks, one side, then the next, and then engaged in a hearty hug in the high spirit of schoolboys. They immediately bid my son, husband, and me farewell and headed off together with an adolescent swagger, walking jauntily arm in arm, no doubt looking for a beer. Their rapid-fire Czech and crisp laughter floated our way as they disappeared across the cobblestones and around the corner. I imagined that each of my father's ten trips to Prague, beginning in 1963, included such a nostalgic jaunt with Vláďa. That assumption was shattered in 2008 when I read the translation of their collaborative essay.-

In it, not only did Vláďa reminisce about their student days and mutual friends in the Mánes coffeehouse before 1938, but he went on to write about what happened afterward. From some of the remarks in the text, it is evident that Vláďa was a Communist sympathizer, who eventually ran afoul of the Communist government after it came to power in Czechoslovakia in 1948 and spent some time in jail. My picture of him and my father joyously revisiting their youth was now replaced by a vision of Vláďa locked in a cell. Vláďa's writing helped me understand that the end of the war did not mean the end of tyranny in my father's homeland.

> Today I am already an old man. Of course other friends entered my life even if there weren't many after the war. For about five years somewhat nostalgically some of us who survived the war kept getting together. Every Wednesday about five aging men tried to relive old times. That of course did not succeed, especially since all of us—except for [one]…were viewed by the State Security agency as an anti-regime group. After we returned from jail there was no more question of any get-together; it was even more dangerous than under Hitler.

> So it seems that dictatorships only change colors but the methods remain basically the same. Anyway, fascism always liked various colors. Mussolini selected black and I never found out why his selection fell on the color of death. Hitler selected brown, maybe because all other heraldic colors were already taken; or, because the Nazi Party had advantageously bought kilometers of brown fabric. The war erased both these colors together with their clumsily organized government.

> Unfortunately, it did not expunge from fascism that which was completely unacceptable: of course

275

I refer to the inhumanity. Today it is called the elimination of human rights. So in fact fascism continues to fester, only under other names; also under different colors.

But there is an important difference. The fascists of our youth with their anti-humanistic approach did not hide anything. Today the administrators of concentration camps are eager to trumpet to the world their self-satisfaction about their humanity and their actions that are all for the benefit of man and his happiness. War becomes the defense of peace and betrayal becomes friendship; in short, everything in reverse.

As I continued to read I discovered that my father's friend Vláďa Wagner's work for the Czech resistance went far beyond conversations at a café. He used his positions as a hematologist in the Bacteriological and Serological Institute of Charles University and at the State Health Institute to further anti-Nazi resistance. As a part of the underground, Vláďa's activities varied from intelligence gathering to preparation of bacteriological materials for use in assassination of several journalists who collaborated with the Nazis: they were served poisoned food at a state dinner.

In the 1960s, Vláďa described his various clandestine efforts to my father, who subsequently told me about them in interviews I taped in 1989. One incident at Bulovka Hospital involved a doctor who had graduated from medical school in 1934, two years before Vláďa. He was a leader in the Czech Fascist Youth and became friendly with the German Nazis who occupied Bohemia and Moravia, renaming those lands the Protectorate. He was apparently carrying news from the hospital to the Germans, so the Czechs wanted to get rid of him. They got a pure TB culture from the lab and put it in his milk one morning. He died of pulmonary tuberculosis about ten days later.

Toward the end of WWII, Vláďa's specialty involved the German blood-transfusion supply chain. His secret laboratory work rendered blood useless for a period of up to three weeks by purging the antibodies necessary for crucial blood-typing diagnostics. The time allowed the blood serum to make it from the hospital through Nazi inspection on its way to the front. For that limited time, the serum was unusable for determination of correct blood groups of Wehrmacht members. When Dad told me this story, he said when he told Vláďa he "thought it was a kind of dirty business," Vláďa responded, "Well, it was a dirty war." That it was.

But of all the wartime stories shared with my father by Vláďa Wagner, one held me spellbound. It was about Reinhard Heydrich—a Nazi whose life was eerily woven into my own family's destiny—as well as that of so many others. In early 2008, Dr. Peter Black, Senior Historian of the United States Holocaust Memorial Museum, brought up Reinhard Heydrich's name as he recounted what may have ultimately happened to my grandparents in the Holocaust. The second most powerful man in the Nazi SS after Heinrich Himmler, the militant anti-Semite Reinhard Heydrich is remembered as the architect of the Final Solution. A major purpose of the Final Solution involved the implementation of human extermination camps. Peter described three Nazi killing camps in eastern Poland placed into action in early 1942 to murder millions of European Jews. One camp was named Sobibor.

Although impossible to say for sure, Peter suggested after review of my grandparents' Az transport and train records that it was very possible they perished in Sobibor. Until that moment, I had known nothing about Heydrich or Sobibor. When I grew up, the time spent on the Holocaust in public high school history classes was almost nonexistent. Of Hitler's senior staff, the familiar names were Heinrich Himmler, Hermann Göring, and Adolf Eichmann. Soon I

Vláďa told my father a far more dramatic tale, one that rewrites an important page of history: as Heydrich lay bleeding, the Czech medical team at work in the hospital secretly switched the blood for his transfusions to the wrong type, knowing the mismatched blood would kill the patient. Vláďa did not say whether he played a direct part in this, and he did not elaborate with further details.

I have no reason to doubt Vláďa's story. He is certainly a credible source, one intimately familiar with the inner workings of the Czech resistance as well as with the use of blood and other biological materials for covert operations. His credentials speak for themselves: from 1941-1945, he served as Health Commissioner of the National Health Department; was an assistant at Charles University in the bacteriological, serological, and pathological anatomy departments during the war; and in the 1990s, he was an active member of the New York Academy of Science.

I spent several weeks studying the issue of Heydrich's assassination, his time in the hospital, blood transfusions (there were no blood banks as there are today), and what I could learn from people familiar with the autopsy (much different from today's thorough process). I reviewed books about Heydrich, spoke to blood experts (like Morey Blinder, MD, of Washington University School of Medicine, Hematology Division), and medical journalists (like Amos J. Wright, MLS, co-author of "The Puzzling Death of Reinhard Heydrich," published in the 2009 *Bulletin of Anesthesia History*). To help me, Leo Greenbaum at YIVO Institute for Jewish Research Archives in New York enlisted a volunteer to read a German version of Heydrich's autopsy.

Beyond the most prevalent speculation about horsehair-induced infection and the poison grenade, conjecture also landed on a massive pulmonary embolism. Finally, I realized that the answer to Heydrich's cause of death could never be known for sure. The definitive sources are now gone—physicians are deceased and records from the hospital were lost in a 2002 flood. The Germans removed sixty tons of documents as they left Prague in May 1945, and Allied bombers destroyed Berlin Gestapo files in 1943, which may have held important facts.

What was repeatedly reported in the documents I read was that the protective squad of SS guards, not immediately present upon Heydrich's arrival at the hospital, later barred any Czechs from approaching him. But just perhaps, some very brave staffers ensured that the man known as "the Butcher of Prague" was finished off by early intervention, either through a laboratory or pharmacy technician tampering with blood, or by infusing a bacteria through an injection performed by a nurse. Heydrich died seven days after my grandparents, Arnošt and Olga Holzer, were executed at his Sobibor mass extermination camp.

My father never knew what I later learned through my research— the eerie link between the Butcher of Prague and his parents' demise. If he had known, the tone of his voice as he repeated Vláďa's tale would have revealed how he felt about this man. The story he heard from Vláďa was one Dad repeated on audiotape at different times for me and my cousin, Tom Weiss—an uncorroborated account that offered for my father some justice in a world full of injustices that he had witnessed firsthand. And I'm sure he appreciated how Vláďa summed it up in his narrative:

> But all is not over. Every once in a while I meet Valda H. in Prague, of course visibly aged but still cheery *and still eager to see everything that is beautiful in the world*...Today I look at it with the eyes of the biologist who sees that the most capable survive. From that point of view, anti-Semitism is really anti-biological stupidity. Other opinions

exist in the world, or rather other approaches. One of them is an approach based on emotions. Hit someone and he will hit back. Befriend them and they will be your friends. Maybe that is why Jews always liked me and I liked them.

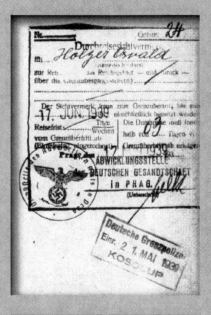

CARICATURES BY DR. OSWALD "VALDIK" HOLZER; VALDIK'S STAMPS & PASSPORT (COURTESY OF HOLZER COLLECTION)

LEFT TOP: RUTH ALICE (NÉE LEQUEAR) AND OSWALD "VALDIK" HOLZER (CALIFORNIA 1941); RIGHT TOP: OSWALD AND RUTH ALICE (INDIALANTIC, FLORIDA) 1964

PELICAN DRAWN BY OSWALD A. HOLZER; HOLZER FAMILY, 1955: LEFT TO RIGHT: JOANIE, TOM, RUTH ALICE, OSWALD, PAT

Chapter 10:

For Truth

The letters can never be plainly seen,
or the words be clearly heard.
For Truth does travel with grace and speed
as the soundless flight of a bird.

—Ruth Alice Holzer, 1976

Many of the secrets kept in those Chinese boxes were ghastly: lives shattered and lost; friends abandoned; lovers betrayed. The paths I followed beyond the letters made clear that guilt and grief continued to wound and sometimes cripple long after the war was over.

Yet my journey of discovery was ultimately uplifting, even inspiring. I wrote *Adventurers Against Their Will* to celebrate the triumph of Valdik, Karel, Franta, Bála, Hana, Pavel, Rudla, Vláďa, and the rest who made it through.

I know the word "triumph" may seem misplaced in the context of the Holocaust, but surely survival is its own victory and was the alpha and omega of the letters. When I interviewed him in Chicago, Paul Kraus cited "survival" as his greatest accomplishment. Beyond the survival of the individual in the treacherous circumstances so many encountered was the survival of their spirits leading to an ultimate triumph: the gift of resilience passed on to the next generations.

As Vláďa Wagner wrote about my father:

> …Valdo…he met an American girl, the daughter of a former missionary in Hunan. They started to date and eventually they married. After some peripatetic experiences they returned to the US where they eventually settled in Florida. *So no one should say that in our times it wasn't possible, that things happen that way only in fairy tales.*

Chapter 10: For Truth

This book is a celebration of my father and his friends, but also of John Lekner, Tom Weiss, Carole Kraus, Allen Kraus, Nick Bala, Ann Matyas, Carol Hylton, and all the rest who forged a heritage network as we exchanged emails and images. We are forever bound by our common identity as descendants of Prague's adventurers against their will. It is an identity that has become important to all of us, although it may be difficult for others to see in such a diverse group that includes myself (a retired owner and manager of a geotechnical engineering firm), a scientist from New Zealand, a law professor in Canada, an Anglican priest, a retired MIT professor, an art consultant from New York State, and a former Czech Ambassador to the United States, Israel, and now Great Britain.

We are outwardly different in so many ways, including religious affiliations and nationalities. Yet we all feel connected to each other and to the place our parents and grandparents once called home. A unique and wonderful bond emerged as we grappled with questions at the heart of who we are and better understood our families' past and its meaning to us.

My attempts to understand that past and its meaning began from an unusual and challenging perspective. Of the books I've read about the generations that followed the Holocaust, most were written by Jewish men exploring their heritage in middle age. I'm a woman of essentially Christian heritage through my mother's guidance, inching toward my sunset years. I'm also acutely aware that I am a modern-day American struggling to unravel the mysteries of religious and cultural identity in a very different time and place. I am fortunate to have received plenty of help from a variety of viewpoints. My research contacts included religious Jews, secular Jews, and Czechs of many religious or agnostic or even atheist convictions, as well as historians.

All were smart and shared my sense of mission and urgency. Yet none of us could truly explain how so many people like my father put their faith in the ideals of assimilation and tolerance, only to suffer because of an identity imposed on them by others. When you add religion and ethnicity to any discussion, subjectivity enters in and the situation becomes even more confusing.

What I'm certain of is that the legacy and impact of the Holocaust are much broader and more enduring than I had imagined when my journey began. I know this has been said often, but intolerance hasn't been eradicated in my lifetime. My father kept silent to shield his children from the horrors he knew, but I see now why these stories must be told—and told forcefully. It is through them we encounter the challenging vision of man's vulnerability in the face of evil. These stories give us the chance to illuminate a fundamental fact: the need for a moral renaissance to rediscover and commit to our common good.

The writers in *Adventurers Against Their Will* tell a vivid story of their struggles. I felt the weight of those struggles push me to my limits as I reread their words in the comfort of my home overlooking a tranquil lake in Central Florida. We are helpless to correct decisions that were so impaired by emotion. We know when the writers are missing essential facts, or fail to recognize the urgency of circumstances. We see the worst coming when they can't. We understand why all were left with an overwhelming sense of guilt, but we also understand that it was mostly undeserved because they did the best they could when presented with circumstances they could not anticipate, much less prepare for or control.

No one, of course, can be blamed for failing to imagine the unimaginable—the Holocaust. In the letters are mentions of concentration and prisoner camps. After the 1939 Nazi occupation, rumors circulated of men being dragged off and beaten to death for political reasons. Although alarming, this knowledge corresponded to the heinous acts the world already was familiar with from the

Great War that ended twenty years earlier. That "war to end all wars" exhibited man's thirst for more effective and terrible weapons—it introduced the use of gas on humans. One summer while in medical school, my father worked in the medical department for the Bata Shoe Company, measuring face profiles for gas masks for the Czechoslovak Army. The breathing device was one of many products the company manufactured. It was not lost on my father that this was a product meant to equip man for a harrowing situation—when the enemy would use gas to choke, blind, or kill.

Many of the fathers or grandfathers of Prague's displaced youth had fought in the Great War, so they understood the horror that could be inflicted by others, but my father's generation grew up in the relative tranquility of the twenty years between the two great wars, so they didn't understand how quickly and dramatically things can change. They were young during a time of prosperity, political stability, and cultured society. They could not foresee the reality of the sophisticated slaughter that lay ahead—men, women, and children transported en masse to be exploited by forced labor, rape, and medical experimentation, and then gassed or shot.

Clearly when all hell broke out, the letter writers were deeply affected by what they saw, heard, and did. In Shanghai, both my father and Pavel saw beggars dying in the streets, and had no choice but to step over them. In response to the exigencies of the underground resistance, Vláďa made choices in direct conflict with what he would have dreamed possible during his medical training meant to save lives.

The greatest lessons for our time and future generations may lie in the adventurers' sense of betrayal by the nation they loved and that they believed accepted them as equals. The letters reveal the backstory of failed assimilation during the first republic of Czechoslovakia. A country forged from two sibling nations and slivers of borderland from other countries, it contained a number of ethnic minorities that were extended special political rights, including those regarding language use and education. It allowed Jews to choose if they wanted to be nationally Jewish or belong to the Czech, Slovak, Hungarian, or German nations.

Idealistic Czechs expected that all citizens would assimilate and learn Czech or Slovak, depending upon where they lived. They expected that Jews who decided to be Czech would live as Czechs. Theoretically there was room for Jews to live as Jews and Germans. But as time passed, nationalists expressed frustration with Jews, whom they accused of spreading German language and culture.

The position my father's young friends had assumed was an overtly political and progressive one aimed at being recognized as Czech. It was at the core of successful assimilation expressed by President Tomáš Masaryk in his progressive and perhaps idealized Czechoslovak society. What broke my father's heart was that, in reality, many others viewed Judaism, beyond a religious designation, as a blood inheritance by which a person would be defined or identified. In his view he was Czech and his religion could never define him.

Despite this viewpoint, Dad came to realize that he had experienced life as a second-class citizen, and he saw this as unjust. He sought a peaceful world where human beings could survive with dignity. Coupled with the facts of how and why his parents and other relatives were murdered, the letters clearly revealed to me the basis for his choice to live in America.

From my father's April 18, 1940, letter to Rudla Fischer, then in France:

> I don't want to recall all the old wrongs I felt from the moment when I began to meet children at school, even though I was raised in the spirit of the

nation in which I lived and of which I felt a part—there was not an occasion when it wasn't made clear to me that I was an unwanted stranger...

There was rampant anti-Semitism in America in the 1940s, and he foresaw a hardship that might overtake his new family. The feeling of disrespect and persecution for being Jewish became more than my father wanted to take with him to his new life. During the remainder of his life he chose to practice no particular religion, but if he had, as I wrote earlier, it would have been Bahá'í. It was a religion I knew little about until his nurse mentioned their conversation to me. When I read about it, his interest made perfect sense. It is a monotheistic faith that advocates the unity of the human race and worldwide peace. And as my father did, it puts a high value on universal education.

Marginalized from the time of his earliest memories, all that my father wished for was respect and equal footing. I believe my father's core values never changed. He supported my mother's spiritual pursuits and her desire to have each of her children baptized as a Presbyterian.

My mother was one in a long line of devout Christians. When she died, I inherited her white leather Bible and I can attest to her diligence in reading the scriptures from the Old and New Testaments. Just as my mom highlighted important words in red in the September 1940 letter she wrote her parents announcing "this time next month I will be Mrs. Holzer," she underlined important Bible verses in red ink.

She saw Jesus Christ as her Lord and believed that He is the final judge. She told me that for both Testaments, all writers, but perhaps one, were Jewish. She reminded me that Jesus was Jewish. He taught the Beatitudes—teachings about mercy, spirituality, and compassion. She told me that faith always expresses itself not merely in words but in the deeds of everyday life. There are good and bad people that comprise any faith just as there are good people and bad that hold no faith. "In the end," my mom said, "God will judge all men and women by their actions, not their words." And that is how, since I was very young, I have reconciled that my parents would be together in heaven—God's eternal place, I believe made for those who act with compassion toward humanity.

Some may view my dad's personal proclamation as an agnostic as gentler than if he had been an atheist. In no way do I apologize for what may have been my father's path to or away from religion; we should all be free to make our own choices about faith. The God I envision as that ultimate judge my mom described won't be so hard on atheists or others who have their own point of view. That higher being will have a view point beyond our understanding today. If there is a grand afterlife, or even a return life, God will show the way.

As to my father's view, I believe he thought there was more to life and death than any of us understood. Some people may view his proclamation as an agnostic as a reasonable response to what happened during World War II to forty-four of his relatives and an action to protect his new family. Through my journey of understanding, I have retained my belief that there is something greater in the Universe than us. Eventually, we will understand all these mysteries of life and death. What I know is that my father never taught me hate. He taught me to take action when I witnessed injustice and intolerance or saw someone in need.

As a teenager, I complained one Sunday morning to Dad that I didn't want to go to church, saying, "After all, *you* don't go." My father didn't miss a beat, telling me that the name of the church's denomination came from the Greek word *presbuteros*, meaning "elder." With an accompanying stern look, he proclaimed, "Respect your elders, especially your mother." Then he smiled, never explaining why he didn't go.

From the stories of the other adventurers against their will, I realize my father was not unique in distancing himself from organized religion. It was when I delved deeply with the descendants into the subject of religion that I realized we had the most in common. To varying degrees, the members of that generation kept critical information from their children, each building a new facade with some element of deception. A few even felt compelled to live the second half of their lives with a protective new identity, taking on a different surname because their name was "too German" or "too Jewish."

In fact, these uncertainties about religion are in sync with contemporary Czech people. It is a topic that goes much deeper than just the effect of the Nazi era. Their opinions about religion are indicative of deep emotional impacts from their long history of brutal religious coercion and suppression, including forty recent years under Communism.

In a 2005 Eurobarometer Poll, when Czech citizens were asked about religious beliefs, 50 percent responded that "they believe there is some sort of spirit or life force" (as my father would have). Another 30 percent responded that "they do not believe there is any sort of spirit, god, or life force." Only 19 percent responded that "they believe there is a god." It was the lowest rate among European Union countries after Estonia with 16 percent. In comparison, in the United States in 2008, 92 percent of the respondents to a survey by the Pew Forum on Religion and Public Life stated they "believe in God or a universal spirit," and nearly 80 percent believed miracles can occur.

Knowing that the descendants of the adventurers against their will were raised mostly in a variety of Protestant religions (Unitarian, Methodist, Presbyterian) or without any designation, I can only surmise parents went through their own thoughtful decision-making about what they deemed would be the most secure status for their children. I believe none did this with malice in any way toward their Jewish heritage. At least for my father, he was not particularly religious before the war. In fact, his indifference toward religion may have been a natural course for him.

I assume that each adventurer dealt thoughtfully with the issue of which organized religion they would engage in, or not, when they rebuilt their lives. It seems most religions explain that you earn your way to an afterlife, or the next life, by being a good and loving human being while here on earth. The God I choose to believe in accepts all people, no matter what their faith, skin color, or nationality. God only looks to us to love one another and act accordingly.

No sane person could have anticipated the Nazis' atrocities, so how can we blame Karel "Bála" Ballenberger for not confronting his father-in-law and insisting his wife Milena and their two children escape with him to England in 1939? Or Pavel Kraus, for not demanding his mother, father, and brother go to China with him? Or my father, for accepting his parents' "No, without jobs we don't want to be a burden," when he repeatedly asked them to join him?

Who, after all, would imagine anyone who would find reason to murder them all? Regardless of what the adventurers came to know after the war's end, I am sure a part of the silence in their recreated lives came from their own harsh judgment of themselves as to whether they had done everything possible to save loved ones. Haunting sorrow, feeding on deserved or undeserved guilt, found solace through silence. I doubt any amount of intellectual discourse could have healed those wounds.

On February 1, 1942, after the United States had entered the war, Hana Winternitz was already second-guessing herself about her attempts to save her parents: "It is my fault...as after the fall of France, I should have been more energetic to get them to leave; anywhere would have been fine...now they can't. Talking about it is easy, doing it is harder. What happened, it's done and now I will not have any news from them until the end of the war. I am not the only one, unfortunately."

It was evident that all felt they could have done more, and thus after the war they stayed silent as best they could. They knew the reality of it all and could not change it. The underpinning of their apparently successfully rebuilt lives rested on pretense, requiring them to hide their pain from those around them. I do not recall a moment growing up that my father shared his feelings about the loss of his parents or his own survival in the face of almost insurmountable odds. It was not until the last hours before his death that he may have divulged this pain to my brother.

Two days after our mother passed away at eighty-three years of age from the ravages of Parkinson's disease, our father, eighty-eight, lay dying from what I believe was a combination of heartbreak from losing the love of his life and congestive heart failure. My brother Tom was sitting at my father's bedside, making small talk about his genealogical research many years earlier when he was a student at Princeton University. Tom brought up my father's family, noting that even though most of Arnošt and Olga's generation had been murdered, miraculously my father and other first cousins had "won—made it through the Holocaust and sprouted new branches on the family tree."

Suddenly my father, without opening his eyes, shook his head very violently back and forth, signaling my brother to stop talking. When Tom and I spoke about it later, we agreed it was apparent that our father felt no "victory" from his situation and didn't want to discuss it at all. Breaking the silence was too painful.

I wondered about the choices each of the adventurers against their will made and the lives they managed to live because of them. My father chose wisely. In the imperfect world he found himself, after all the darkness he passed through, he chose to go toward the light. He chose the pursuit of happiness, not just for himself, but for his family. I'm sure that my mother was a big part of that choice, but I also suspect his attitude was already an integral part of his nature when he departed from Prague in 1939. I learned that from the letters and photographs he left behind. A photograph taken aboard the ship he sailed on to China in 1939—after escaping the Nazi stranglehold—shows a relaxed young man, dressed in a blue double-vested jacket and sailor-like white hat, smiling from ear to ear, looking as if he didn't have a care in the world.

Just as his father Arnošt did, my dad saw life as a great adventure and humankind as collectively good. After the war, he served humanity in meaningful ways as a doctor. I watched him provide thousands of pro bono hours to those in need of health care, like the low-income fishing families of Grant and Micco and the African Americans who walked to my father's office from what was then known as "colored town." He treated them all with equal respect, and often at no cost. Nurse Sue Barge told me "Every pastor in Melbourne came to him, probably because he never charged them." After retirement from his medical practice, he continued this charitable path, contributing ten years of his expertise to the Florida Institute of Technology (Florida Tech) as Student Health Services Director, the campus doctor. He donated his entire salary to the school to use in building a permanent student health center, which the school administration decided to name after him. He and my mother also created the Holzer-Lequear Endowed Chair for Genetics Research. For the remainder of his life, he served on several nonprofit boards, helping the mentally ill and elderly.

A friend, whose mother was a registered nurse at a Melbourne nursing home where my father served, told me what her mom said about my dad. "My mom, who was very vocal about her view that medical professionals, including doctors, should comfort and serve, talked about your dad all the time during the several years in which they worked together. In her view, your dad represented everything a doctor should be. He came to see the patients, many of whom had no family and were no longer coherent, and he treated them as individual, full human people, something that was not common."

My father became a model American citizen—loyal and engaged. Exhibiting a fierce gratitude and a Norman Rockwell view of patriotism, he cherished his freedom of speech and his right to participate directly in governance. I have a collection of political bumper stickers showing his diverse involvements.

Sadly, as Czechoslovaks were denied that right by the ruling Communists for forty years, he could do little but contribute to anti-Communist causes. Never forgetting his homeland, he proudly took each of his children to see the people and places that forever held a piece of his heart.

In the hot summer of 1995, my husband, Roger, son Derick, and I accompanied my eighty-four-year-old father on what turned out to be his last trip to his native soil. We mostly visited happy sites from his childhood and medical school days. On one of the nine days we spent in Prague, my white-haired, slightly stooped father took us on a long walk down many cobbled lanes lined with medieval buildings, baroque churches, and lively outdoor cafés, to a place nestled next to the Vltava River. As we passed through the still-modern building known as the Mánes Café, my father only commented briefly that in his youth he used to go there with his friends—nothing more.

He never mentioned that he planned to leave a magnificent legacy in two Chinese lacquer boxes. Or that in that treasure trove I would come across the very souls of his many cousins and friends, some of whom, in a time long ago—after the Austro-Hungarian Empire collapsed and before the Nazis marched in—called Mánes Café their home away from home.

As I observed how each personality developed over time, I thought of their lives like good books. The further I got into them, the more sense they made. From this experience I learned the heart can hold far more than we imagine. It can survive a serious emotional fissure but it will not be unaffected. What is important is what happens next. My father knew he had to adjust to his losses or he would sentence himself to a life of grief.

In the massive puzzle my father left for me to solve lay the answer to his most important choice: a heart that never hardened. He focused on the immediate, on the people around him. My dad had a warm, generous spirit that touched the lives of those people, including the legion of patients he served as a skilled and compassionate physician.

I look back on my childhood as ideal; I was lovingly pampered from the very beginning. My father provided his children a sense of security by choosing to keep secret the details of the excruciating pain and guilt he endured. For the hardest parts of his life he sketched a caricature-like illusion, a new canvas filled with intriguing stories about the people he had met during his adventurous life. That became the image on which we children based our view of life.

And along with his caricature, he provided the model for the highest form of virtue we all can achieve: human compassion. I grew up understanding that the foundation of one's moral being requires action—making a difference.

That tremendous legacy is truly my greatest inheritance. His values and outlook live on because they are woven into my fabric. And with my benevolent mother at his side, he opened up the gates of happiness, allowing Tom, Pat, and me to grow up with fond memories.

Bedřich Smetana, remembered today as the father of Czech music, honored his homeland with the debut of his opera *Libuše* at the 1883 opening dedication of Prague's magnificent National

Theatre. The libretto is based on an old Czech myth of a heroine who prophesied the founding of Prague as she sings:

> ...Mist shrouds my eyes and much is hidden from my troubled sight—terrible secrets, curses...My beloved Czech people shall not perish, but shall triumph over the horrors of hell. Glory!

Those prescient words washed over my heart as I listened to them while sitting in that same theater in 1995 with my father, husband Roger, and son Derick. As I've learned the truth about the ordeals of my father's generation, they've echoed with new meaning many times since then.

I'm embarrassed that until I read the four hundred translated letters, I knew so little about the horrors that consumed my father's young life—how the Nazis ruthlessly murdered his family and friends and stole his homeland. I have no excuse except the naiveté of youth.

Now that I know the truth, I feel his pain, but it is too late. I should have tried harder while my father was still alive to understand what he went through and break down his wall of silence. As my missionary mother would have said, I should have offered my own "fellowship in suffering."

Maybe I could have helped my father find peace in a way the letters he left behind have helped me to do. I realize now that no one can own a sunset like the one I saw nightly over the Indian River from my bedroom window growing up. It belongs to everyone. The letters that my father hid away offered the same lesson, and he knew this. Their messages belong to the ages; a piece of history that will live forever. They will eternally remind us of the millions of people needlessly taken away from us in the Holocaust and of the brave soldiers throughout the world who gave their lives so that peace could return to our world.

The letters teach us the truth that even in the darkest of circumstances, life offers the lucky ones a chance to transform themselves. When I was a teenager, my father used to say, "You can be happy or sad. You get to choose." I understand now what he meant. No matter what weight falls upon us, we can turn about and choose to find the treasure in life. He celebrated life. Czech life. American life. He knew what it meant to be free.

Roger and I returned to the Czech Republic in 2009 and again in 2011 to visit relatives and see important places from my young father's life. Cousin Tomáš Mařík served as our tour guide as we traveled in his Peugeot over hilly roads throughout the Czech Lands, Slovakia, and Poland. As I wrote copious notes about what we encountered, I could imagine my father's broad smile and remember his colorful stories—beautiful evidence that each life is worth remembering.

With the renaissance of the coffeehouse tradition following the return of a vibrant free market economy, many of the old cafés in Prague have taken on a new life, once again providing a place for people to meet and discuss the topics of the day. In 2011, the gleaming white Mánes building still featured an art exhibition hall, a gallery café, and an upstairs restaurant and bar that provide catering and an avant-garde venue for weddings. Mánes still promotes all forms of art and strives to keep alive the spirit that my father and his friends loved and lost.

Mánes Café is now being restored and renovated to its 1930s splendor. The magic of the place still beckons; the fresh coffee simmers in the pot. What do you think? At the legendary Mánes in enchanting Prague, shall we meet for a *turek* with a thick layer of grounds on the bottom of our cups? I recommend we get seats on the terrace overlooking the magnificent Vltava River. I think it would make the patrons-of-old very happy to know that their stories have become our legacy.

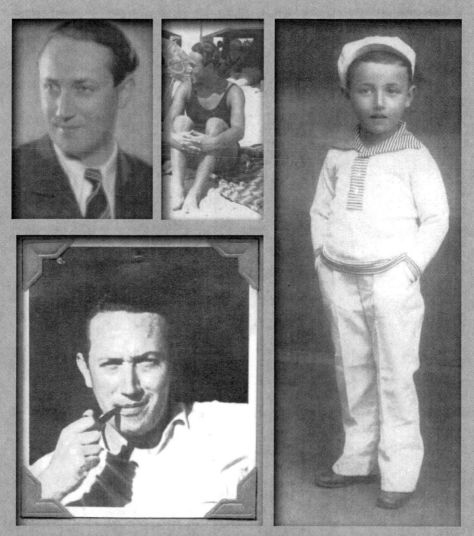

TOP RIGHT: OSWALD HOLZER 1939 PASSPORT PHOTO; "VALDIK" CHILD PHOTO 1914; OSWALD WITH PIPE FROM WEDDING ALBUM 1940

TOP LEFT: ARNOST HOLZER, RIGHT TOP: OSWALD WITH MOTHER OLGA (NÉE ORLIK) HOLZER;
BOTTOM: VALDIK WITH FATHER ARNOST; ARNOST AND OLGA HOLZER 1942

萬壽山

Top: Oswald "Valdik" Holzer in Czechoslovak Army 1938; right: Ruth Alice Lequear 1940 passport photo to China; Oswald and Ruth Alice, Peking (Beijing), 1940

> I SHALL PASS THROUGH THIS WORLD
> BUT ONCE, ANY GOOD THEREFORE I CAN
> DO OR ANY KINDNESS THAT I CAN SHOW TO
> ANY HUMAN BEING, LET ME DO IT NOW.
> LET ME NOT DEFER IT, FOR I SHALL NOT
> PASS THIS WAY AGAIN.

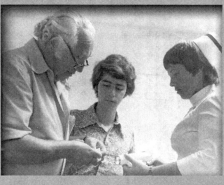

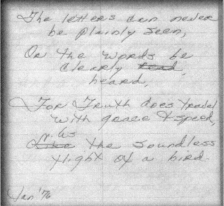

QUOTE: STEPHEN GRELLET, QUAKER MISSIONARY, QUOTE FOUND IN RUTH ALICE (NÉE LEQUEAR) HOLZER JEWELRY BOX AFTER HER DEATH; LEFT COLUMN, TOP: RUTH ALICE HOLZER 1942; BELOW: OSWALD AND RUTH ALICE HOLZER; RIGHT COLUMN, TOP: DR. O.A. HOLZER WITH FIT STUDENT PATIENT AND NURSE SUE BARGE; BOTTOM: POEM BY RUTH ALICE HOLZER, 1976

TOP LEFT, CENTER LEFT AND CENTER RIGHT: TOM HOLZER, PAT (NÉE HOLZER) HOLM, JOANIE (NÉE HOLZER) SCHIRM;

BOTTOM LEFT: RUTH ALICE "CHICKIE" HOLZER WITH GRANDDAUGHTER KELLY (NÉE SCHIRM) LAFFERMAN; RIGHT BOTTOM: "CHICKIE" WITH GRANDSON DERICK SCHIRM

TOP LEFT: JOANIE HOLZER WITH FATHER VALDIK (A/K/A "BUBBIE), 1967; MIDDLE: KELLY SCHIRM LAFFERMAN WITH DAUGHTER AVA AND SON TY, 2012; MIDDLE BOTTOM: DERICK & WIFE CAROL (NÉE INCARNACAO) SCHIRM; RIGHT COLUMN: JOANIE WITH HUSBAND ROGER NEISWENDER, PRAGUE 2009; BOTTOM: KELLY SCHIRM LAFFERMAN AND DERICK SCHIRM, 2013 (PHOTOS COURTESY OF FAMILY)

Biographies and

Postscripts

Do you remember how we used to go to Mánes Café?

...Today I would give much just to relive our outings together! How the

world changes.

—Kary Lasch, Valdik's Prague friend, May 23, 1939

Holzer, Oswald, known as Valdik (1911-2000). My father, correspondent and adventurer against his will, who preserved the hundreds of letters that form the basis for this book and the companion volume, *My Dear Boy: The Discovery of a Lifetime.* Studied medicine at Prague's Charles University and was serving as a doctor in the Czechoslovak Army when Germany invaded his country in 1939. Escaped to China, where he married Ruth Alice Lequear, daughter of American missionaries. The couple moved to the United States in 1941. They eventually settled in 1952 in Melbourne, Florida, where he served as a family physician, and raised three children: Tom, Pat, and Joanie.

Ballenberger, Karel, known as Bála (1908-1996). One of the Mánes Café circle. A politically active lawyer, he encouraged Valdik Holzer to contribute anti-Hitler cartoons to the left-leaning Social Democratic Party's newspaper. Was evacuated from Prague with help from the party as the German Army approached in 1939. Wife Milena (Langer) stayed behind with their two children; all three later died in Auschwitz. Changed family surname to Bala; remarried to Vera Judith "Mima" Lowenbach; raised two children in Canada: Ann and Nicholas; their half-brother Hugh Thompson lives in Great Britain.

Postscript: Soon after Carol Provisor contacted me about the letter from Bála that she had discovered, she and Ann Matyas, aided by genealogy researcher Gary Silverstein, found they were related. She shared the news with me in an email: "After studying the Ballenberger chart, I believe Ann and Nicholas, together with my brothers and I, are sixth-generation descendants of Jakob Ballenberger. We are probably third or fourth cousins."

Fischer, Rudolf, known as Rudla (1901-1972). Valdik's first cousin. Successful banker who fled from Prague to Italy; then to France, along with wife, Erna (Frenkel), and son, Tom. Left family to serve with Czechoslovak Army-in-Exile in England. Remained there for the rest of his life. Erna divorced him, arranged passage to the United States, and remarried.

Postscript: Out of all the people I encountered on my discovery voyage, there is no doubt that Tom Weiss, the son of Rudla and Erna Fischer, has gone the farthest in family history research. And it wasn't until his sixth decade of life that Tom began his quest. In fact, it was his wife Aurice who started the family roots obsession through her own interest, beginning in the 1970s.

Busy at work as a faculty member at MIT, Tom supported Aurice's efforts, including research going back to her American Revolutionary War descendants, but at the time he thought it was unlikely he would ever be able to uncover his own European family history. That changed in 1998 when he and Aurice spent a ten-month sabbatical leave in England, where he met his first cousin Alena Fischer Morgan and her husband, Alan. During that same year, Tom visited Prague with Aurice and his son Eric, as well as Alena and Alan, returning to his roots for the first time in six decades. Tom also visited Vienna, on the first of four trips, where he found extensive family records on his mother's side. He realized the pieces of his puzzle were actually there for him to find. In Prague, he located a researcher who traced his paternal side back to the early 1700s with four great-grandparents' lines. Beyond family records, the researcher, Eugen Stein, and his wife, Iva, provided colorful old maps and charts, creating a picture of the old Bohemian villages and homesteads of the past.

Tom retired from MIT in 2000, in part to be able to pursue his family history to his heart's desire. The results are stunning. As of August 2011, Tom had 1,500 pages of material, including written memoirs, maps, photos, and documents. He shared two bound volumes with the United States Holocaust Memorial Museum Archives Department at the request of Michlean Amir, who became a good friend of mine during my own quest. The large Samuel Vodicka descendent wall chart that he shared with me ten years ago has now grown to 632 names, of which two reflect our closest blood connection—our grandmothers, sisters Karolína and Olga (née Orlík). All included, Tom's genealogical database consists of 3,670 people, only a few of whom are from Aurice's family lineage, as she maintains her own massive list.

Tom's research has included several roots trips with his wife and children, Max, Lisa and Eric. Aurice and Tom have attended International Association of Jewish Genealogical Society meetings in Jerusalem and New York City. Most of his grandchildren are now old enough to grasp what his work means in the context of who they are. Sadie, 12, can identify in photographs her grandparents and even her great-grandparents. When visiting her grandparents' kitchen, Olivia regularly pauses at the wall chart and asks when her name will appear. Tom created it before she was born; she is now nine. Prompted by a visit to the Holocaust Museum, grandson Madison, fifteen, is now able to ask his grandfather meaningful questions. As a result of all his related research, Tom is able to teach his grandchildren European and United States history through the lens of their family history.

When I first engaged Lukáš Přibyl for translation, I had no idea that Tom Weiss already knew him. Referred to me by Michlean Amir, Lukáš had extensive knowledge about Terezín from development of his documentary series, *Forgotten Transports*. When Lukáš gave me the first of his four films to watch, I was shocked to see the name Tom Weiss in the credits. It turned out that Tom played an important part, as he introduced Lukáš to one of his first financial backers for what became the 2010 Czech Lion Best Documentary Film, the highest award in film achievement in the Czech Republic.

Still going strong with their research, Tom and Aurice visited Roger and me in 2010 at our Orlando lakeside home. Tom visited his second cousin (me) along with third and fourth cousins that he had uncovered—all hanging out in sunny Florida.

Holzer, Arnošt (1885-1942) and Olga (née Orlík) Holzer (1888-1942). Valdik's parents. Both born in Czech Lands of the Austria-Hungarian Empire, they were representative of the region's historically assimilated Jewish population. Moved from Benešov to Prague to be with Valdik when he enrolled at Charles University. Killed by Nazis in 1942, likely at Sobibor death camp in Poland.

Schoenbaum, Franta (1910-2001). Valdik's best friend and frequent correspondent, whose letters showed consistent good humor, even in the darkest times. Remained in occupied territory, shielded through the efforts of his non-Jewish wife Andula (Nejedlá) until the final months of the war, when he was imprisoned at Terezín concentration camp. Andula also arranged for their son Honza (later John) to be hidden from the authorities at a home in the country. Second son Martin born

6th Century		Slavic tribes arrive in the Slovak and Moravian lowlands and the Bohemian basin, driving out Germanic tribes and settling in what will later be known as the Czech Lands.
	1050	First settlers believed to arrive in Benešov (Valdik Holzer's hometown in Bohemia, Czech Lands).
12th Century		The Kingdom of Bohemia established in a confederation of states inhabited by two nations, Bohemia and Moravian Margraviate.
	1346	Charles IV, King of Bohemia, crowned Holy Roman Emperor, ushering in the Golden Age of Bohemia.
	1348	King Charles IV establishes the University of Prague (later known as Charles University), the first university north of the Alps and east of Paris.
	1415	Religious reformer Jan Hus burned at the stake in Constance. Supporters become known as Hussites.
	1583–1601	The Habsburg Monarchy moves its capital from Vienna to Prague.
	1618	Hussite Bohemian nobles throw Catholic councilors from Prague Castle windows. The "Defenestration" (the act of throwing something from window) starts a prolonged conflict known as the Bohemian Revolt.

Nov. 8	1620	Battle of White Mountain near Prague. Bohemia's Protestants defeated by Catholic Austrian Habsburgs. Czech Lands become occupied for 300 years.
	1848	Habsburgs suppress an uprising of Czech nationalists.
Sept. 9	1885	Arnošt Holzer born in Benešov, Bohemia, Czech Lands of Austria-Hungary.
April 8	1888	Olga Orlík born in Tabor, Bohemia, Czech Lands of Austria-Hungary.
June 25	1901	Rudolf Fischer born in Prague, Czech Lands of Austria-Hungary.
April 22	1906	Karel Schoenbaum born in Benešov, Czech Lands of Austria-Hungary
June 4	1908	Karel Ballenberger born in Prague, Czech Lands of Austria-Hungary.
June 27	1909	Arnošt Holzer marries Olga Orlík at the Hotel Bristol in Prague.
Dec. 21	1910	Franta Schoenbaum born in Benešov, Czech Lands of Austria-Hungary.
July 23	1911	Oswald A. "Valdik" Holzer born in Benešov, Czech Lands of Austria-Hungary.
July 18	1914	World War I begins.
	1914	Czechs forced to fight for the Austrian Habsburgs in World War I, but thousands desert to the Russians.

Oct. 1–10	1938	Germany annexes the Sudetenland.
Oct. 5	1938	Edvard Beneš resigns as President of the Czechoslovak Republic and creates a Czechoslovak government-in-exile in London.
Nov. 9-10	1938	Kristallnacht, a violent anti-Semitic pogrom, is launched throughout Germany and Austria. Synagogues, Jewish shops, and homes are set ablaze; around ninety people were killed.
Feb. 21	1939	Nazis require German Jews to relinquish all their gold and silver.
March 14	1939	Slovakia cedes territory to Hungary and the new First Slovak Republic is established. It passes anti-Jewish measures.
March 15	1939	Nazi Germany invades and occupies the Czech provinces of Bohemia and Moravia in the rump Czecho-Slovak state.
March 15	1939	Karel Schoenbaum and his wife Katka escape to London.
March 16	1939	Hitler decrees the Protectorate of Bohemia and Moravia, annexed directly to the Reich but under the authority of a Reich Protector.
March	1939	Karel Ballenberger escapes to London and joins the Free Czechoslovak Army. Milena and their two children remain in Prague.

March 31	1939	Valdik Holzer escapes from the Nazi-controlled Czechoslovak Army to Prague.
May 21	1939	Valdik Holzer leaves Czechoslovakia and sails from Marseille, France, to China on the ship *Chenonceaux*.
June	1939	Anti-Jewish laws, based on the Nuremberg Laws, are proclaimed in the Protectorate. More measures will follow.
July	1939	The Czech Refugee Trust Fund (CRTF) forms in Britain.
Aug. 19	1939	Rudla Fischer, wife Erna, and son Tom escape to France.
August	1939	Hana Winternitz escapes to Holland, then to Great Britain.
Sept. 1	1939	Germany attacks Poland.
Sept. 3	1939	Britain and France declare war on Germany. WWII begins in Europe.
Oct. 12	1939	First Nazi deportations of Austrian and Moravian Jews to Poland.
Jan. 24	1940	The Czechoslovak Army in France established.
April	1940	Pavel Kraus travels from Prague to Shanghai.
April 9	1940	Germany occupies Denmark and Norway.
May 10	1940	Germany occupies Belgium, Luxembourg, and the Netherlands.

May 29	1940	Rudla Fischer leaves his family to join the Czechoslovak Army-in-Exile in Paris.
June 14	1940	The Nazis occupy Paris, France.
July 14	1940	Rudla Fischer sails to England to join the Czechoslovak Army-in-Exile.
Sept. 11	1940	As a soldier, Karel Ballenberger petitions the Czechoslovak Ministry of National Defense-in-Exile and receives approval to use the surname "Bala."
Sept. 18	1940	Ruth Alice Lequear returns to China as a teacher.
Sept. 20	1940	Valdik Holzer meets Ruth Alice Lequear in Peking, China.
Sept. 28	1940	Valdik Holzer proposes marriage and Ruth Alice Lequear accepts.
Oct. 19	1940	Valdik Holzer and Ruth Alice Lequear marry at the Peking Union Church.
Nov.		US Embassy in Peking recommends all foreigners evacuate due to the escalating war between Japan and China.
Feb. 28	1941	Valdik Holzer and Ruth Alice Holzer leave on US evacuation ship from Shanghai for America; settle in Long Beach, California.
April 15	1941	Rudla Fischer's wife, Erna, and son, Tom, leave Portugal for New York City.
June 12	1941	Karel & Katka Schoenbaum leave Guayaquil, Ecuador on Chilean ship *Aconcagua* for New York City

June 28	1941	Karel and Katka Schoenbaum leave England for South America, then New York City.
June	1941	Karel and Katka Schoenbaum apply for surname change to Sheldon in New York City.
June 28	1941	Pavel Kraus arrives in San Francisco.
September	1941	Hitler appoints Reinhard Heydrich as Acting Reich Protector for the German Protectorate of Bohemia and Moravia. Protectorate Jews are made to wear a yellow Star of David.
Oct. 21	1941	Karel Bála's wife, Milena, and two children are deported from Prague to Łódź, a Jewish ghetto about 75 miles southwest of Warsaw, Poland.
Nov. 24	1941	Terezín (Theresienstadt) ghetto established 37.5 miles (60 km) north of Prague.
Dec. 7	1941	Japan attacks Pearl Harbor.
Dec. 8	1941	US enters WWII.
Jan. 20	1942	At the Wannsee Conference in Berlin, SS General Reinhard Heydrich, chief of the Reich Security Main Office, meets with fourteen other Nazi leaders to solidify plans for deportation and extermination of European Jewry (the "Final Solution"). Eight of the fifteen have PhDs. Agreement to proceed with human extermination camps at Belzec, Sobibor, and Treblinka.

	1947	Karel Bala (Ballenberger) marries Vera Judith "Mima" Lowenbach and is posted as the Commercial Attaché to the Czechoslovak Legation in Ottawa, Canada.
	1948	The Communist Party seizes power over Czechoslovakia and Eastern Europe.
July 4	1948	Valdik Holzer and family move to Chattahoochee, Florida, where he works as a staff physician for the Florida State Mental Hospital.
Dec. 15	1948	Valdik and Ruth Alice Holzer's daughter Barbara Joan Holzer is born.
Oct. 1	1949	Chinese Communist People's Liberation Army leader Mao Zedong proclaims establishment of the People's Republic of China.
	1951	Valdik Holzer works as a doctor in Chipley, Florida.
	1952	Valdik Holzer establishes a private medical practice in Melbourne, Florida. Known by nickname "Bubbie" in social circles and at home.
April 1	1958	Karel Sheldon (Schoenbaum) dies in Washington, DC.
July 12	1972	Rudla Fischer dies in England.
	1974	Valdik Holzer retires from private medical practice; begins ten years of volunteer service as Student Health Director at Florida Tech (Florida Institute of Technology) in Melbourne.

	1989	The Velvet Revolution overthrows the Communist regime in Czechoslovakia. Václav Havel elected president of Czechoslovakia.
	1993	Czechoslovakia separates peacefully into the Czech Republic and Slovakia.
	1995	Valdik Holzer visits Prague with youngest daughter Joanie and her family.
Jan. 1	1996	Karel Bala (formerly Ballenberger) dies in Kingston, Ontario Canada.
Jan. 1	2000	Ruth Alice Holzer dies in Florida.
Jan. 3	2000	Valdik Holzer dies in Florida.
July 25	2001	Franta Šeba (formerly Schoenbaum) dies in the Czech Republic.
	2004	The Czech Republic joins the European Union.
March 25	2004	Hana (Winternitz) Bell dies in North London.
March 2	2008	Vladimír "Vláďa" Wagner dies.
November	2008	Joanie Holzer Schirm visits Karel (Schoenbaum) Sheldon's wife, Katka, age 91, in Washington, DC.
June	2010	Joanie Holzer Schirm visits Paul (Pavel) Kraus, age 91, at his home in Chicago.
	2009, 2011 & 2014	Joanie Holzer Schirm and husband Roger Neiswender travel to Czech Lands
Sept. 22	2014	Pavel/Paul Krauss dies in Chicago, IL

Glossary

American Brethren Hospital : Hospital founded by the American Brethren Mission in 1914 in Ping Ting Hsien, Shansi (Shanxi) Province, northwest of Shanghai, China; 209 miles (337 kilometers) southwest of Beijing. Dr. Valdik Holzer served as physician in 1940.

Auschwitz-Birkenau (Oswiecim-Brzezinka): Nazi concentration and extermination camp in southern Poland where an estimated 1.1 million people died from 1940–1945. Largest of Germany's World War II concentration camps.

Anschluss: The occupation and annexation of Austria into Nazi Germany in 1938.

Baha'u'llah: Founder of the Bahá'í faith.

Bata: An eighth-generation shoe-making company started in 1894 in Zlín, Czechoslovakia. By 1939, Bata sold sixty million shoes in thirty countries, including in the Far East. After 1932, Bata diversified into production of tires, aircraft, gas masks, and other machinery. Their documentation helped save my father's life.

Benešov: Town in the Central Bohemian Region, Czech Republic, about 25 miles southeast of Prague. Birthplace of Oswald "Valdik" Holzer.

Bohemia: Historic region in Central Europe, occupying the western two-thirds of the traditional Czech Lands, including Prague and Benešov. Part of the current Czech Republic. Birthplace of Oswald "Valdik" Holzer.

Brandenburg Gate: Former city gate considered one of the major symbols of Berlin. It was commissioned by King Frederick William II of Prussia as a sign of peace and built by Carl Gotthard Langhans in 1791.

Bubeneč: Northwest district of Prague, Czech Republic.

Charles University: Founded in 1348, the second-oldest university in Europe and largest university in the Czech Republic.

Concentration camp: Originally called re-education centers. The SS began calling them concentration camps as they concentrated enemies in confined areas, including a wide array of people deemed undesirable (Jews, political prisoners, criminals, homosexuals, Gypsies, the mentally ill, and others). Prisoners were used as slave labor, and often starved, tortured, and killed.

Czechoslovak Government-in-Exile: Name used by World War II Allies for the Czechoslovak National Liberation Committee established in Great Britain. Initially set up in Paris after the Nazis occupied Czechoslovakia but relocated to Britain in 1940.

Czechoslovak Military of National Defense in Exile: Army that fought to free Czechoslovakia; originated in France during early World War II, then relocated to Great Britain. Often referred to as the Czechoslovak Army-in-Exile.

Day of Atonement: Yom Kippur, one of the most important holidays of the Jewish year, a day set aside to atone for the sins of the past year.

Gestapo: Secret state police, *Geheime Staatspolizei,* of Nazi Germany under the administration of SS leader Heinrich Himmler.

Ghetto: Designated section of a city or town occupied by a specific social, economic, ethnic, or racial population. During WWII, Jews were confined in crowded ghettos prior to transportation to concentration or death camps.

Havel, Václav: 1936–2011. Playwright, essayist, poet, and dissident. Leader of the Velvet Revolution and the first democratic President of Czechoslovakia after the fall of Communism, later the first president of the present-day Czech Republic.

first thirty-nine years of his life under the Communist regime; now he freely and happily travels the world with his wife, Lida. Although modest in nature, he exhibits a certain determination and intelligence that for me marks the soul of his enduring Czech nation. His free-spirited character, curiosity, and humor are much like what the correspondents exhibited during the twenty-year interwar period when they lived in an outpost of democracy. There are no words adequate to describe what Tomáš's friendship means to me.

Intertwined in all I have accomplished are the inspiring friends who paved my way. Bill and Barbara Kercher win the prize for having spent the most evenings talking about the emerging books and the unique process of modern publishing. Ellen Titen often found herself on the other end of a plaintive phone call when I felt overwhelmed. She and my friend Joan Matthews always encouraged me to put one finger in front of the other on the keyboard of life. I'll never forget the kind yet dogged efforts on my behalf by Andrea Eliscu and Roman Inochovsky (Orlando's Honorary Consulate for the Czech Republic). To my soulful girlfriend Sibille Pritchard who early one morning while reading one of my earliest manuscript drafts, gazed outside upon our inland lake, spotted a pelican, knew it meant something special, and then didn't keep quiet about it as she prodded me to continue my meant-to-be journey.

When I needed quick feedback on something I wrote, I could always count on Charley Williams for his honest, yet gentle, review. I thank my sister-in-law, Linda Neiswender, an award-winning poet, for constant helpful emails about writing and modern publishing. With their loving memories of my parents, my loyal lifelong friends, the "Beach Babes"—Amy Sewell Rickman and twin sister Ann Sewell Butz, Stephanie Sawyer Rubin, Nina Rothschild Sonnier, and Kathe Glass Parker—provided a constant, collective wind beneath my wobbly wings.

Other groups of friends, of which I won't name every individual, have pet names—GEC, Jan Stratton's assembled girlfriends, College Park Neighborhood, WOW, Rita Bornstein's Discussion Group, Mary Johnson's book club, and more. I'm sure I've forgotten to highlight an important group but appreciate all greatly for their hands and hearts along the way.

And then, of course, there is Pavel Kraus, also known as Paul, and the many descendants of the correspondence who gave freely of their family history to make each chapter complete. This book could not have been written without the memories of many others. In addition to his memory, Paul opened both his door and his files of old photographs and documents, displaying an outstanding generosity with his time and spirit. Most important, believing that the stories needed to be written down, he shared his trust in me, a person he never knew until late in his life.

The tale told in this book owes as much to Paul and the other descendants as it does to my dad and me. They each greeted me with enthusiasm and put their most personal recollections out in public, so that our understanding of these lives could be fully realized. A big thank you goes to each for being so open with their personal and family stories.

Lastly, there is the assembled team for book publication. From organization to translation, research, writing and reading and editing—these are the core people who helped me actually produce the book that some doubted I had the stamina to complete in my sixties. I have newly gained immense respect for authors of any genre. This is the hardest job I have ever undertaken, except for the pains of labor when I gave birth to my two children.

It should be clear to anyone who reads this book that I had a colossal task before me upon discovery of the letters. Before that, I thought that the seven hours of interviews with my dad were going to yield what I needed to write a nice WWII adventure tale. Little did I know that I was about to meet three hundred other people through these old letters. I was well into engaging translators and sending scanned letters through the airwaves when it became obvious I needed organizational help. That came to me in the form of a "she"—Kathy Bowman, a thirty-something Czech-American who was brought to this country along with her brother Robert in 1989 by their mother, Zorka Pinkas.

Kathy arrived in my life in 2008 through pure serendipity from a chance meeting she had with my former company assistant, Anabel Schwartz. Kathy had recently relocated to Orlando with her husband, John. Working on her master's degree in business, she joined me as a part-time assistant, sometimes working forty hours a week. Kathy stayed on for over a year and continued to drop back on the scene whenever I asked for her help.

Among many contributions to the cause, Kathy ensured all the letter-writer voices were properly catalogued. She spot-checked translations and introduced me to the nuances of Czech personality and humor. While deciphering emerging stories from various letters, like me, Kathy fell in love with the friends and relatives of my father. She brought her own humanity to the story I was trying to tell and became my sounding board on which stories and photos were the most important to include. Over time, she became a great friend and even birthed a son, Adam, in the middle of our work together.

I owe an intellectual debt to Alice Peck, Doug Kalajian, and Jacob Labendz. A talented New York City editor and writer, Alice Peck worked early on as editor and advisor as I attempted to gel the stories that became my two simultaneous books-in-the-making. She returned at the end of the process to ensure that *Adventurers Against Their Will* was ready to go—with improvements galore and better organized chapters with stronger threads. With every conversation, Alice provided inspiration.

Doug Kalajian served not only as another *Adventurers Against Their Will* editor, perfecting my words, but also as an important developmental editor. He went about his business of polishing and trimming with great courtesy. An accomplished writer in his own right, Doug was there to commiserate and celebrate the difficulties and periodic euphoria of the writer's life with me. He set a fine example for how experienced writers can help those of us who are just starting out.

Jacob Labendz, a doctoral candidate with a focus on modern Czech-Jewish history, ensured that I didn't make a fool of myself as I synthesized volumes of important history into a key sentence or two. He offered his studied wisdom and own philosophy as I worked to accurately describe what my father and his Jewish cohort went through during the interwar period of Jewish assimilation in Czechoslovakia. History is complicated and often gets reported through the filter of a historian's opinion. The beauty of the letters is they allow us to live through WWII while the letter writers report their own history— with no filter. They connect yesterday with today and tomorrow as we share their extraordinary experiences and think about the future. But there is still a need to understand historical context and Jacob provided that important aspect.

Primary translators Lukáš Přibyl and Mirek Katzl brought the sleeping voices alive for all of us to hear. Each an accomplished professional in other fields, they took on the task after being drawn in by just a few of the letters. Bright and cultured Czech men, not too much older than the letter writers were at the time, Lukáš and Mirek added much to the process. They pointed out prominent names in the correspondents' cultural circle as well as other relevant historical context, which I might have otherwise missed. Both became lasting friends who visited with Roger and me in both Prague and Orlando.

An award-winning documentary filmmaker for his series, *Forgotten Transports*, Lukáš used his skill to prepare a three-minute book trailer, utilizing old 1939-1947 films from my parents' collection. His creative talent is evident in all his work.

At the earliest stage of my research, I visited the United States Holocaust Memorial Museum. There, I gathered advice from Reference Archivist Michlean "Miki" Amir on how to be most productive in my research. Her own Czech background meant she had deep feelings for the information. She served as Reference Coordinator for the Holocaust Victims and Survivors Resource Center. Subsequently, Miki became my stalwart friend in so many ways. To free the voices, she led me to Lukáš Přibyl and USHMM volunteer Margit Meissner, who had herself escaped the Nazis and created a happy life. When in need of a specific subject expert, Miki provided names. Miki reviewed my manuscript and encouraged me to keep going because she knew firsthand how important the story was to tell.

In addition to the terrific resources available at the USHMM, I want to thank other organizations who assisted my research— the Jewish Museum in Prague, archives at Charles University and Benešov, memorials at Terezín and Sobibor, the YIVO Institute of Jewish Research in New York City, and Yad Vashem in Jerusalem. Associations that played a critical part in research as well as moral support include the American Friends of the Czech Republic (AFoCR), the Czechoslovak Genealogical Society International (CGSI), the National Czech & Slovak Museum & Library, and the Jewish Genealogical Society of Greater Orlando (JGSGO). Search engines like Google and the website Ancestry.com brought forward helpful information to peruse.

There are many more resources which I am unable to list due to space considerations. They provided me with information to enrich my knowledge of the time period, culture, and people that live in my books. I remain very thankful to organizations that dedicate their efforts to ensure accurate information is available to us all.

When the manuscript reached its final draft stage, readers included Michlean Amir, Caroline Munro, Mayor Bill Frederick, Alice Peck, Mary Johnson's Book Club, Bill Younglove, daughter Kelly Lafferman and of course more than once, Roger Neiswender. Without this group's sage advice, the final book would not have been sent out into the universe.

Lastly, I want to thank those who helped me get the word out about this important discovery—the Holzer letter collection. I believe a higher being gave me the responsibility to be the letter writers' modern storyteller. But stories can't be shared widely unless someone helps you spread the word. I sincerely thank my local newspapers—the *Orlando Sentinel* and *Orlando Business Journal*—for early reporting of the find. And a huge thank-you goes to the good folks at Growing Bolder Media—Marc and Jill Middleton and Bill Shafer—who aired multiple stories about the discovery and my efforts to uncover what it meant, broadcast throughout America on Growing Bolder television and radio shows (www.growingbolder.com). I gained great benefit from this exposure and my gratitude to them is boundless.

Now I ask that you, the reader, please pass along the word about this story so a larger audience has the chance to learn important lessons from the past. If you want to learn the complete adventure and love story of Valdik Holzer, please read the companion book: *My Dear Boy: The Discovery of a Lifetime.* Godspeed to all stories that carry the truth about our lives. May we always remember that we are one as humankind. We should treat each other with the utmost dignity and respect.

Peace.

Jannie Holger Schism

October 2012
Orlando, Florida

Adventurers Against Their Will

Book Club Discussion Questions

Adventurers Against Their Will

For Teachers: Visit www.joanieschirm.com for Teacher's Guide that includes Lesson Plans with State Standards to accompany Adventurers Against Their Will; Listed on the Florida Department of Education (FDOE) Recommended Reading List, 2015, Grades 9-12

1. After getting to know each adventurer, what enduring themes strike you as universal for today? Share two or three phrases or lines of dialogue from the letters to emphasize your points.

2. What background trait exerted the most influence upon each particular adventurer? What lasting images, lessons or messages did *Adventurers* leave will you?

3. In a 1940 letter, Oswald "Valdik" Holzer described what he and his peers who had left their homeland experienced as "emigrant psychosis." Discuss what this term means to you should you be forced to abandon all that is dear to you.

4. Within their occupied territory, the Nazi regime implemented a multitude of restrictions on persons they defined as "Jews" under the Nuremberg Laws. Discuss the rights lost in the 1930s and 1940s and any similarities you observe in today's world.

5. *Adventurers* offers the reader a chance to experience a world different from our own. Did this story expose you to new cultures, world history and geography, or points of view? What did you learn? What topics would you like to learn more about?

6. Who was your favorite "character"? Share a favorite scene or phrase from *Adventurers*. What makes it powerful, shocking, funny, or otherwise memorable?

7. What does the term "survivor guilt" mean to you? Use examples from the Holocaust or other events with which you are familiar. What are possible ramifications for subsequent generations from those who suffer with survivor guilt?

8. The final chapter of the book, "For Truth," expresses the personal revelations and feelings of author Joanie Schirm. Share your own thoughts as they relate to what you learned and believe.

9. Joanie Schirm's initial objective in *Adventurers* was to explore the early adult lives of her father and his friends. Through the letters, she discovered so much more. Have you ever thought about writing your own family history? Have you spoken with your grandparents, parents, or other relatives to learn the stories that can bring that history to life? Choose a small portion of your own life, reflect and write about it, and share it with the group. Leave a legacy for your own family.

Author Joanie Schirm

J oanie Schirm is a writer, photographer, community activist, and retired Orlando, Florida award-winning businesswoman. The daughter of Dr. and Mrs. Oswald Holzer, she grew up on a sandy barrier island on the Space Coast of Florida, a place where extraordinary memories are made and pelicans soar. Joanie never dreamed fifty years later she would be awarded the 2013 Global EBook Award for Best Biography, have book placed on the Florida Department of Education 2015 recommended reading list for Grades 9-12, and be published in Czech language; proving big dreams do come true. She is internationally known for her leadership role in Orlando's hosting of FIFA's 1994 World Cup USA 1994. After raising two children, Kelly and Derick, she lives in Orlando with her husband, Roger Neiswender. Look for Joanie's companion book to *Adventurers Against Their Will*:

My Dear Boy: The Discovery of a Lifetime.

www.joanieschirm.com

CPSIA information can be obtained at www.ICGtesting.com
Printed in the USA
LVOW08s0834230316

480388LV00002B/5/P